D0855960

PREVENTION FIRST

PREVENTION FIRST

Policymaking for a Healthier America

ANAND K. PAREKH, MD, MPH

Foreword by Senators Tom Daschle and Bill Frist, MD

JOHNS HOPKINS UNIVERSITY PRESS | *Baltimore*

© 2019 Johns Hopkins University Press
All rights reserved. Published 2019
Printed in the United States of America on acid-free paper
9 8 7 6 5 4 3 2 1

Johns Hopkins University Press
2715 North Charles Street
Baltimore, Maryland 21218-4363
www.press.jhu.edu

Library of Congress Cataloging-in-Publication Data

Names: Parekh, Anand, author.
Title: Prevention first : policymaking for a healthier America / Anand K. Parekh,
    MD, MPH; Foreword by Senators Tom Daschle and Bill Frist, MD.
Description: Baltimore : Johns Hopkins University Press, [2019] | Includes
    bibliographical references and index.
Identifiers: LCCN 2019010080 | ISBN 9781421433653 (hardcover : alk. paper) |
    ISBN 1421433656 (hardcover : alk. paper) | ISBN 9781421433660 (electronic) |
    ISBN 1421433664 (electronic)
Subjects: | MESH: Preventive Health Services—organization & administration |
    Health Policy | Primary Health Care | United States
Classification: LCC RA445 | NLM WA 108 | DDC 362.10973—dc23
LC record available at https://lccn.loc.gov/2019010080

A catalog record for this book is available from the British Library.

*Special discounts are available for bulk purchases of this book. For more information,
please contact Special Sales at 410-516-6936 or specialsales@press.jhu.edu.*

Johns Hopkins University Press uses environmentally friendly book materials,
including recycled text paper that is composed of at least 30 percent post-consumer
waste, whenever possible.

For Eesha, Aanika, and Krish
Always focus and you'll reach your dreams
&
For Rinky
Thanks for being my better half

Senators Tom Daschle and Bill Frist, MD

To many, the American healthcare system is an enigma. We have among the best-trained health professionals, the finest hospitals equipped with advanced technology, and the most cutting-edge treatments for a multitude of conditions. Patients travel from around the world to receive care in the United States. On the other hand, for our own citizens, access to these services is not guaranteed. Unaffordable services, uneven quality of care, and health disparities are a reality for many Americans. We spend twice as much on healthcare compared to other similarly developed nations, and yet we lag behind on many outcomes of care and population-level indicators of health.

What might be the missing piece of the puzzle? A hint comes from a twentieth-century Italian American physician named Louis Lasagna. In addition to playing a prominent role in influencing US federal drug regulation, Dr. Lasagna was deeply committed to medical education. In 1964, he modernized the Hippocratic Oath, long considered the sacred oath for physicians. His revision, which is now used by many medical schools across the country, added the sentence: *I will prevent disease whenever I can, for prevention is preferable to cure.*

Dr. Lasagna's addition to the Hippocratic Oath was prescient. Six in ten Americans now live with chronic diseases and account for 90% of total healthcare expenditures. And most chronic diseases, such as type II diabetes, chronic obstructive pulmonary disease—as well as some cancers—are entirely preventable. These conditions are taking a substantial toll on the nation's economy and our military readiness.

The urgency of addressing preventable health conditions is now more acute as the United States is experiencing its first consecutive three-year decline in life expectancy since the end of World War I and the 1918 Spanish flu. The opioid epidemic, obesity crisis, and the plateauing of the decline in cardiovascular disease deaths are all contributing to this phenomenon. How can it be that in the twenty-first century, in one of the most developed and technologically advanced countries in the world, life expectancy is falling? This is not something we should accept for our children and the next generation of Americans.

In this book, Dr. Parekh argues that policymakers must prioritize prevention first. Dr. Parekh served in the US Department of Health and Human Services as a deputy assistant secretary of health under several US assistant secretaries of health, the secretary's primary advisor on matters involving the nation's public health. Further, for many years Dr. Parekh cared for patients at a health system's health center, strengthening his belief that primary care must be the frontline source of care for all Americans. As such, he is intimately familiar with federal policy issues related to prevention, public health, preparedness, and population health.

Relying on his background as a clinician, public servant, and policy advisor, Dr. Parekh makes the case that this country has not invested nearly enough in prevention and that policymakers have a role to play in correcting our nation's course. The problem is twofold. First, our health policies start from the point when one first becomes sick, as if all illness is inevitable and disease prevention is impossible. Second, policymakers are reactive, at times only intervening during crisis, whereas prevention requires proactive, forward-thinking action.

For our nation to optimally deal with its pressing health challenges, Dr. Parekh argues that policymakers must look to elevate prevention both within and outside the healthcare sector. He draws upon his experiences and offers many examples of prevention in action from across the country to conclude that we must leverage health insurance programs to promote disease prevention, expand primary care, attend to the social determinants of health, support making the healthier choice the easy choice for individuals, and increase public health investments.

For the past four years, we have had the pleasure of working with Dr. Parekh at the Bipartisan Policy Center to develop innovative, actionable policies in support of better health. Building a culture of prevention in this country requires everyone's participation—individuals, families, faith-based and community organizations, businesses, media, and, as discussed in this book, policymakers.

We, too, have long been champions of prevention. A decade ago, during congressional testimony touting the need for health reform and the benefits of preventative care, one of us declared to lawmakers: "We've got to make prevention hot and wellness cool." The other realized that while his hometown of Nashville was a healthcare mecca, its citizens fared poorly when it came to health outcomes, and formed NashvilleHealth, a collaborative health movement to prevent chronic disease and improve child well-being.

We also know sustainable policies require bipartisanship. Over the years, while representing different political parties, we have come together on many issues to improve the health of the nation. While serving as the Senate Majority and Minority Leaders, we passed the Project BioShield Act to increase preparedness against chemical, biological, nuclear, and radiological threats. We also came together to pass the United States Leadership Against HIV/AIDS, Tuberculosis, and Malaria Act of 2003, which created the PEPFAR program to support prevention, care, and treatment of HIV/AIDS.

Prevention must not be a partisan issue. Dr. Parekh's book is a reminder that we have a shared responsibility to improve the health status of all Americans. Generations from now, people will look back upon this time and ask why we didn't do more to cover the uninsured, control healthcare costs, improve healthcare quality, and reduce disparities. Those will be valid questions. But the question that we should be most concerned with is why we allowed hundreds of thousands of potentially preventable deaths in America each year. *Prevention First* is an apt title for a critical and timely message that resonates with all of us in search of better health.

I have always believed that health provides the foundation and education provides the acceleration for individuals in pursuit of their life goals. This philosophy in large part stems from my upbringing. My parents came to this country as immigrants from India seeking higher education. Both ultimately went into healthcare, my mother as a solo family physician and my father as a hospital administrator. My extended family is full of physicians; there are too many to count, in fact.

In following this family tradition, I found my medical school training, residency in internal medicine, and experience over a number of years as a volunteer primary care physician at an underserved health center fulfilling, in that it allowed me to care for the sick, vulnerable, and frail and guide them back to health. But in so many cases, I discovered that the underlying cause of illness in my patients was in fact preventable. It occurred to me that to a certain extent, we had been failing our patients. The time for healing should not start when our patients are sick; it should start before they get sick to prevent illness.

It's this realization that inspired me to join federal public service and look for ways to improve our nation's health through health promotion and disease prevention. Over the course of a decade, I was privileged to lead a number of efforts focused on improving public health and supporting clinical and community-based prevention programs; many of these examples are captured in this book. But I also found that prevention as a priority frequently took a backstage to more downstream healthcare priorities. Similar to my clinical experience, I recognized that as policymakers we too frequently took the health status of the population as a given, only to concentrate on the consequences of poor health. But the health status of our nation is not a given; we can change the trajectory by refocusing on prevention. That's what this book is about.

If Americans are to achieve their individual life goals and if America is to achieve its future goals as a world leader, there is little doubt that we need to be in better health. Poor health reduces worker productivity, economic output, and military readiness, while preventable healthcare costs take away from vital areas such as education, public safety, and infrastructure improvements. Sadly, in America today, life expectancy is falling, maternal mortality is increasing, and infant mortality is no longer declining. Never before in our nation's history has Benjamin Franklin's adage "An ounce of prevention is worth a pound of cure" been more important than at the present moment.

Only a resolute commitment to preventing disease both by individuals and by society will allow America to maximize health and quality of life for its citizens. We are increasingly used to our governmental leaders waiting for a crisis to emerge prior to acting. Similarly, Americans, reinforced by a healthcare system that is really a "sick care" system, often find themselves waiting until symptoms of an illness set in before attending to their health. Indeed, the vast proportion of our healthcare resources go to treating illness instead of preventing illness in the first place. The consequences of this is millions of Americans with preventable conditions, many others with conditions not detected at an early, treatable stage, and millions of others experiencing preventable complications from their chronic conditions. To realize a vision of this volume will require a healthcare system built on primary care and incentivized to keep Americans healthy; community supports, programs, and policies that reinforce healthy behaviors and the care plan; a robust and well-funded public health system; and Americans inspired to seek better health even in the absence of disease.

Everyone has a role to play in creating a culture of prevention in this country. Prevention starts at home with individuals and families having a crucial role in subscribing to healthy living practices and refraining from risky behaviors. Americans also need an environment that supports and incentivizes healthy choices and, conversely, disincentivizes unhealthy choices. Schools and workplaces have enormous opportunities to impact the health of children and adults given the sheer time spent in these settings daily. Faith-based organizations can provide powerful motivation and support to Americans with respect to disease prevention and health promotion. The media have an influential role in setting cultural norms and communicating evidence-based health information. And of course, the healthcare community has enormous potential, so long as the incentives can be aligned to focus not only on treating sick people but also on keeping people healthy.

This book focuses on an additional key stakeholder that has tremendous leverage in creating a culture of prevention—that of policymakers on both sides of the aisle. Unfortunately, prevention has been undervalued and underfunded by governmental leaders for far too long, partially a reflection of "reactive" policymaking as opposed to being forward looking. The publication of this book comes at an important time in our nation's history. We are at a crossroads in health policy. Partisan battle lines have hardened on issues ranging from access to health insurance to controlling healthcare costs to the responsibilities of federal versus state governments to the roles of the public sector versus private sector. By fostering a healthier population, prevention can positively influence many of these debates and be the glue that brings policymakers together. I hope this book inspires us to act.

In the summer of 2017, I told Jason Grumet, the president of the Bipartisan Policy Center, that I wanted to write a book on health policy. I thought my rationale was sound. I wanted to share my experiences as a public servant, elevate prevention in the health policy debate, and consolidate my thinking on a wide variety of topics in one place with a cohesive message. There was one problem. Not only had I never written a book, but my wife and I were expecting our third child. This was clearly not the time to be starting a book project. And yet, as a father of three and an author of a widely acclaimed book himself, Jason was supportive. He said the only hurdle I needed to clear was with my wife—somehow, I would need to convince her that this was her idea and repeat it over and over for a year or two until the book was done. Well, that worked . . . sort of.

There are far too many people to acknowledge for their contributions to this book, but I will start professionally and end personally.

First, thank you to the Bipartisan Policy Center for its unique and critical mission as well as to the superb staff that everyday share the premise that the best ideas are those shaped by all sides. In particular, thank you to Bill Hoagland for his stewardship of BPC's Health Program and to Lisel Loy and Hannah Martin for leading BPC's Prevention Initiative. Thanks also to Dan Glickman, former secretary of agriculture, whose words of wisdom and collegiality I have treasured throughout this process. Of course, thank you to former senators Tom Daschle and Bill Frist for their more than a decade of bipartisan leadership on so many BPC projects. They are true visionaries, and I'm appreciative that they have lent their voice to this book in support of building a culture of prevention.

I have been fortunate to have had several mentors along the way who shaped me in significant ways, many of which are mentioned in this book. My time as a public servant at the Department of Health and Human Services was both meaningful and productive, and for that I am immensely thankful to Bill Raub, John Agwunobi, Joxel Garcia, Howard Koh, and Karen DeSalvo. They have been exemplary role models for me. My time in academia, both at the University of Michigan and then at Johns Hopkins University, also afforded me the chance to be shaped by leading minds in clinical medicine and public health. Gerard Anderson, Charlie Wiener, Myron Weisfeldt, Jack Billi, and Ken Warner have all played instrumental roles in helping me bridge the medicine and public health divide and forge my own unique path.

There were many people I turned to while writing this book who deserve recognition. First off, thank you to Mike McGinnis, Chris Jennings, and Sheila Burke for providing constructive feedback and input on the key themes and structure of the book. In addition, several colleagues reviewed individual chapters of the book and for that I am very thankful to Jack Billi, Catherine Gordon, Marianne Udow-Phillips, Rosie Henson, Paul Jarris, Bobby Pestronk, Bill Raub, Loyce Payce, Greg Downing, and Regina LaBelle. Thanks to them for making sure that I was never too far off the "right track."

Writing a book is a team sport, and I realize now that your publisher can be your best friend. When I pitched this book to Robin Coleman at Johns Hopkins University Press, neither of us knew each other. But it was quickly apparent that this was the right fit. Thank you to the entire team at the Press for their support throughout the production process.

And now for the personal. Most people think their parents are the best in the world, and I'm no different. My father was a hospital administrator, and my mother still is a solo family practitioner in the city of Detroit. I ended up taking a bit of both of their career paths and making my own. I will always be grateful for their blessings and guidance. Equally, thank you to my mother-in-law and father-in-law for their constant support and encouragement through this process. And finally, thanks to my cousin, Bhavesh, who asked me tough questions as I started writing to make sure I had a sense of clarity in my thoughts.

My daughters, Eesha and Aanika, represented my fan club throughout the process. They were each hoping that I would finish writing the book during their respective birthday months. Toward the end of the writing process, Eesha started to ask me if I was famous. I said, yes, only because I was her daddy. Krish, my son, will not remember this period in his life but toward the second half of his second year, he knew when I was working and didn't need interruptions. Of course, he still interrupted—a good reminder for me that however demanding writing this book was, it was never the first priority.

And finally, coming back full circle to my wife, Rinky. I am incredibly fortunate that she gave me the space and time while managing her busy cardiology practice and taking care of the children (and me) to complete this book. I am grateful for her love. Though I never could convince her that this was all her idea, I think she realized how important it was for me to find my voice and share it with others. Well, I found my voice, and here it is.

PREVENTION FIRST

The State of Disease Prevention

E ACH DAY, thousands of people die in America prematurely. Many of their deaths are preventable, and yet our efforts to intervene are too late. These Americans are our family members, our neighbors, and our coworkers. They include the factory worker whose uncontrolled high blood pressure leads to a catastrophic stroke; the veteran who doesn't obtain a flu shot only to succumb to a virulent strain of influenza; and the teenager who overdoses on a combination of sedative medications found in the family medicine cabinet.

These are also Americans whose deaths are preventable partly because of the circumstances where they live, work, and play. They include the bar owner who after years of being exposed to secondhand smoke is diagnosed with late-stage lung cancer; the retired school teacher living in decrepit housing with mold and rodents who perishes from one too many asthma exacerbations; and the elderly grandmother who lives in a food desert and whose obesity and diabetes eventually lead to irreversible heart failure.

Preventable deaths tear families apart. They also hurt this country economically through lost productivity. Many of the risk factors driving preventable deaths are also negatively impacting our nation's military readiness. This book is meant to sound the alarm that we can and must do better in this country to reduce preventable deaths. It is divided into two parts—

the first part focuses on enhancing prevention efforts within the existing healthcare sector and the second half focuses on supporting activities outside the sector.

Specifically, the first half focuses on better integrating prevention into our current "sick care" system to truly create a healthcare system. This will require integrating prevention into healthcare's value equation, strengthening the primary care infrastructure, constructing clinical-community linkages, and partnering with social and human services providers. The second half focuses on the need for communities and systems to better support individuals in optimizing health. This will require an emphasis on policies, systems, and environmental changes to make the healthy choice the "easy," or default, choice and a recognition that public health and even global health have essential roles in disease prevention and health promotion. A final chapter discusses additional challenges and opportunities for prevention today and looks into the future. The epilogue summarizes five overarching recommendations for federal policymakers.

Prior to engaging in these discussions, it's important to understand the state of prevention in this country today and to answer a few basic questions. The following sections seek to review definitions of disease prevention, the drivers of preventable death, evidence-based prevention interventions, spending on disease prevention, and investments in prevention research. The chapter concludes with a discussion about why it has been so difficult to prioritize prevention as a leading health policy goal.

Definitions

So, what is disease prevention? Prevention encompasses a set of evidence-based activities that either avert, detect, or control illness and disease.[1] Public health experts characterize these activities as primary, secondary, or tertiary prevention.

According to the Institute for Work and Health, primary prevention forestalls disease or injury before it occurs. Examples include legislation to mandate safe and healthy practices (use of seatbelts and bike helmets), education about healthy and safe habits (eating well, exercising regularly, not smoking), and immunization against infectious diseases.[2]

Secondary prevention reduces the impact of a disease that has already occurred. Examples include screening tests to detect disease in its earliest stages (mammograms to detect breast cancer) and medications like low-dose aspirin to prevent further heart attacks or strokes.[3]

Tertiary prevention aims to manage the impact of ongoing diseases. Examples include chronic disease management programs (for diabetes, arthritis, depression) and cardiac or stroke rehabilitation programs.[4]

Does Prevention Matter?

But does disease prevention really matter in influencing our overall health compared to genetics, for example? One person who has thought quite a bit about this question is Dr. Michael McGinnis. Dr. McGinnis has been one of the nation's foremost prevention experts over the last four decades, having held leadership positions in government, philanthropy, and academia. He has provided leadership in disease prevention and health promotion across four presidential administrations (Carter, Reagan, Bush, and Clinton). He also coincidentally helped facilitate my transition into public service more than a decade ago.

In 2002, Dr. McGinnis and colleagues published a seminal paper entitled "The Case for More Active Policy Attention to Health Promotion." Using the best available estimates of the impacts of various factors on early deaths in the United States, Dr. McGinnis found that roughly 30% of health is influenced by genetics, 15% by social circumstances such as income and education, 5% by environmental exposures, 10% by medical care, and importantly 40% by behavioral patterns. These behavioral choices include decisions about diet, physical activity, and substance abuse, to name a few.[5] Subsequent analyses of the relative contribution of behavioral patterns have found similar contributions.[6] More recently, experts have sought to focus on determinants that can be directly impacted by individuals and society. The University of Wisconsin Population Health

Institute excludes genetics from its analysis and estimates that 40% of health is influenced by social circumstances, 30% by behaviors, 20% by medical care, and 10% by the environment.[7] This reflects a growing sentiment and body of literature that social factors such as employment, education, housing, food insecurity, public safety and violence, and transportation options affect health outcomes directly and also indirectly by influencing behavioral patterns. In short, individual decisions and societal policies have a profound influence on health and wellness.

Researchers at the Centers for Disease Control and Prevention (CDC), the nation's foremost public health authority, assessed the impact of prevention in another way. They developed a model to analyze the five leading causes of death in the United States—heart disease, cancer, stroke, chronic lower respiratory diseases, and unintentional injuries—to estimate how many are potentially preventable. These causes accounted for 63% of deaths from all causes in that year. By comparing the number of expected deaths for each condition based on the states with the lowest death rates with the number of actual observed deaths, researchers estimated nearly 250,000 preventable deaths occur annually in the United States. Specifically, 30% of deaths from heart disease, 15% cancer, 43% from unintentional injuries, 36% from chronic lung respiratory diseases, and 28% from stroke were considered potentially preventable.[8]

What Are the Drivers of Preventable Deaths?

Well then, which modifiable, or preventable, risk factors are contributing to the leading causes of death? There are a number of behaviors and conditions in this category, including tobacco use, high blood pressure, type II diabetes, poor diet, being overweight, lack of physical activity, and drug and alcohol use (including prescription drug misuse).

Unfortunately, as a nation we don't fare very well with respect to these risk factors. Here are a couple of examples.

The *Physical Activity Guidelines for Americans* issued by the US Department of Health and Human Services (HHS) provides recommendations on the types and amounts of physical activity that should be performed by various population groups. Unfortunately, only 26% of men, 19% of women, and 20% of adolescents report meeting these recommendations.[9] With respect to the *Dietary Guidelines for Americans*, issued by the US Department of Agriculture and HHS jointly, only 12% of adults and 9% of high school students meet the daily fruit intake recommendation, and only 9% of adults and 2% of high school students meet the daily vegetable intake recommendation.[10] These statistics have contributed to the fact that nearly 40% of adults are obese[11] and nearly one of five youths aged 2–19 years are obese.[12]

In terms of tobacco use, 14% of all adults aged 18 years or older (34 million people) were cigarette smokers in 2017.[13] Cigarette smoking is responsible for more than 480,000 deaths per year in the United States, including more than 41,000 deaths resulting from secondhand smoke exposure. This is about one in five deaths annually, or 1,300 deaths every day. In addition, each day, more than 3,200 people younger than 18 years of age smoke their first cigarette, and an estimated 2,100 youth and young adults who have been occasional smokers become daily cigarette smokers.[14]

These risk factors pose extraordinary challenges and lead to chronic diseases such as diabetes, cancer, and heart disease. According to the World Health Organization, if these risk factors were eliminated, at least 80% of all heart disease, stroke, and type II diabetes would be prevented and over 40% of cancer would be prevented.[15] Instead, the reality is that chronic diseases impact nearly half of the American population and account for approximately 75% of US healthcare spending.

Recently, researchers at the Harvard University School of Public Health followed over 123,000 men and women for more than three decades to examine the impact that healthy behaviors could have on life expectancy. They found that if study participants at age 50 adhered to five health habits—eating a healthy diet, exercising daily, keeping a healthy body weight, drinking alcohol only in moderation, and not smoking—women and men would be expected to gain an additional 14 and 12 years of life, respectively.[16] While the conclusion may not be shocking, the magnitude of benefit is remarkable.

In addition to these risk factors contributing to the leading causes of death, a new group of "deaths of despair,"[17] related to drug overdoses, alcohol abuse, and suicide, are rising in America. A recent report by the Trust for America's Health and the Well Being Trust revealed that more than 1 million Americans have died in the past decade from drug overdoses, alcohol, and suicides (2006 to 2015).[18] Specifically, it is estimated that excessive alcohol consumption is responsible for 88,000 deaths each year, more than half of which are due to binge drinking.[19] Drug abuse, being driven by the opioid epidemic, is now the leading cause of unintentional injury death, with approximately 72,000 Americans dying each year.[20] Suicide rates have risen across the United States by 25% between 1999 and 2016.[21]

In fact, preventable deaths in the United States have increased to such an extent that the nation has been experiencing a decline in life expectancy for three years straight for the first time in one hundred years, going back to World War I and the 1918 Spanish flu, the last great worldwide influenza pandemic.[22] The combination of the opioid overdose epidemic, obesity, and the leveling off of decreases in mortality from heart disease and cancer are all contributing to this trend. The significant prevalence of lifestyle risk factors driving preventable death should not be construed as blaming individuals. Whereas personal responsibility has a role, broader policy, systems, and environmental factors are crucial to optimizing health and well-being and are discussed in depth in chapter 6.

Are There Evidence-Based Prevention Interventions?

Fortunately, there are evidence-based interventions to reduce these diseases as well as chronic diseases and their risk factors. Many of these interventions are provided in the healthcare setting and are called clinical preventive services. These include cancer screenings and behavioral counseling interventions. Others are community preventive services, which include policies and programs that aim to improve the health of populations. Examples include policies that increase the price of harmful products, such as tobacco, and programs that increase the amount of time students spend in physical education class.[23]

The gold-standard sources for clinical and community preventive services are the US Preventive Services Task Force (USPSTF) and the Guide to Community Preventive Services (Community Guide). Created in 1984, the USPSTF is an independent, volunteer panel of national experts in prevention and evidence-based medicine that works to improve the health of all Americans by making evidence-based recommendations about clinical preventive services.[24] It's perhaps best known for recommending biennial screening mammography for women aged 50–74 years in 2009, placing it at odds with the recommendations of other scientific organizations. The passage of the Patient Protection and Affordable Care Act (ACA) in 2010 led to a requirement that private insurance plans cover recommended USPSTF preventive services without any patient cost-sharing. In spite of this, many Americans still do not receive preventive services. The CDC estimates that only 25% of adults aged 50–64 years are up to date on services and less than 50% of adults aged 65 years or older are up to date.[25] Using cardiovascular health as a specific example, data from the federal Million Hearts campaign, a national initiative to prevent one million acute cardiovascular events, showed that appropriate aspirin use decreased between 2011 and 2012 and again between 2013 and 2014; in addition, there was no significant improvement observed for hypertension control or statin use among eligible persons.[26]

One study published by the Partnership for Prevention concluded that increasing the use of only five preventive services to 90% of adults could save the lives of more than 100,000 Americans per year. Specifically, increasing the use of daily aspirin for eligible adults could save 45,000 lives per year; increasing the percentage of smokers who receive professional services that help them to quit their habit could save another 42,000 lives; timely colorectal cancer screening of adults aged 50 and older could save an estimated 14,000 American lives; increasing the utilization of breast cancer screening could save 3,700 lives; and increasing the percentage of adults age 50 and up who were vaccinated for influenza could save 12,000 lives per year.[27]

It's important to note that there are also clinical preventive services that are not recommended by the USPSTF. For example, prostate specific antigen-based screening for prostate cancer in men 70 years and older and cervical cancer screening in women 65 years and older who have had adequate prior screening and are not otherwise at high risk for cervical cancer are not recommended, because the overall harms outweigh the benefits.[28] This speaks to the notion that not all preventive services have a sufficient evidence base, nor are they all recommended, however noble their intent.

So why are Americans not receiving recommended evidence-based clinical preventive services? The answer to that question is multifactorial and includes factors related to missed opportunities by healthcare professionals as well as lack of patient knowledge and demand for these services. Also important are systems issues, such as millions who remain uninsured and millions more who lack a usual source of care such as a well-established relationship with a primary care provider.

Similar to the USPSTF, the Community Guide is a collection of evidence-based findings to improve health and prevent disease. The Guide includes areas such as asthma, diabetes, mental health, obesity, oral health, tobacco, and workplace wellness.[29] Highlighted interventions take place outside the four walls of the clinical setting and in communities. Over the years, the CDC has collected numerous examples of health departments, companies, and nonprofit organizations utilizing the Community Guide to implement evidence-based programs. These programs have helped communities across the country reach immunization targets, increase breast and cervical cancer screenings, reduce tobacco use, increase child safety seat use, and expand access to places for physical activity, among other things.[30]

Unfortunately, as with clinical services, full nationwide implementation of evidence-based community services is lagging. For example, community-based interventions for curbing tobacco use include mass media and communication interventions, smoke-free policies, and increases in the unit price of tobacco. Currently, only two states (Alaska and California) fund comprehensive tobacco control programs, supporting these interventions at 70% of the "recommended" levels set by the CDC. Twenty-eight states and the District of Columbia fund programs at less than 20%

of the recommended levels set by the CDC. This is in spite of the fact that states have billions of dollars from tobacco taxes and tobacco industry legal settlements to prevent and control tobacco use. However, states currently use a very small amount of these funds for tobacco control programs. Specifically, in fiscal year 2019, states will collect $27.3 billion from tobacco taxes and legal settlements but will only spend $655 million—2.4%—on prevention and cessation programs. The Campaign for Tobacco-Free Kids, a leading advocacy organization, estimates that this amount is less than 20% of the $3.3 billion required to fund every state tobacco control program at CDC-recommended levels.[31]

How Much Money Is Spent on and Saved with Prevention?

An important factor in gauging prevention's impact in this country is understanding our level of investment in prevention. Does the United States invest enough resources in prevention? Dr. George Miller and his colleagues at the Altarum Institute looked at the National Health Expenditure Accounts (NHEA)—the US government's official source of national healthcare expenditures—to help shed light on this question. In their approach, the group included medical preventive services (including primary prevention and secondary prevention but excluding tertiary prevention), dental preventive services, public health, and prevention research all as components of prevention.

They estimated that 8.6% of 2008 NHEA expenditures goes to prevention overall, but only 5.3% when consideration is limited to clinical preventive services such as counseling, immunizations, and screenings, and only 3.1% if one were to count public health expenditures that include many community preventive services.[32] Where does the rest of our roughly $3.5 trillion in healthcare expenditures go in this country? It goes to treatment—to hospital care, physician and dental services, nursing home and home health services, pharmaceutical drugs, devices, and durable medical equipment—for conditions many of which are largely preventable in the first place.

This begs the question of what should the right ratio be, then, of spending on prevention versus treatment to optimize health outcomes in this country? Fortunately, Dr. Miller and colleagues performed another analysis that might give us a rough idea. They focused on cardiovascular diseases and modeled shifting spending between treatment interventions and prevention interventions to improve health. At baseline, they found that 28.1% of cardiovascular spending was on prevention services. To maximize a health metric called QALYs (quality-adjusted life years), their modeling demonstrated that increased annual spending on prevention to 37.7% of total spending would optimize health outcomes—an increase of roughly 30% compared to greater levels.[33] Ideally, increased spending on prevention interventions would reduce the need of future spending on treatment interventions. This is just one study but a striking example of how an increased investment in prevention may lead to improved health.

While prevention can reduce disease burden and may yield even better health outcomes with an increased investment, could it also lower healthcare costs? Theoretically it should, and that was the hypothesis of a group of researchers several years ago at the Urban Institute. They were able to model potential national and state medical care savings from primary disease prevention. Specifically, they modeled a reduction in cases of diabetes and high blood pressure, which was assumed to be accomplished through diet, exercise, and reduced smoking. They found that reducing these two conditions by 5% in the population would save $9 billion annually in one to two years. They also found that when taking into account reductions in complications of these two conditions—such as heart disease, stroke, and kidney disease—the savings could rise to approximately $24.7 billion over five years or more.[34]

A separate modeling exercise by researchers at the RAND Corporation looked at the effect of an array of medical innovations on health and medical care spending of the future elderly. Their analysis showed that, while eliminating any disease would not dramatically affect future healthcare costs, obesity might be an exception to that rule. The reason, they contend, is that obesity is a "double whammy" for Medicare, in that it raises annual healthcare expenditures but does not affect longevity and thus the number of years spent on Medicare. Specifically, the research team found no difference in overall life expectancy between an obese 70-year-old and one of normal weight. At the same time, they found that obesity is correlated with disability, and greater disability translates into higher healthcare spending.[35]

Other researchers have tried to look at the impact of clinical and community preventive services separately. With respect to clinical preventive services, researchers at Tufts University and the Harvard University School of Public Health found that potential cost savings essentially depend on the particular service and specific population in question. In roughly 20% of cases, preventive services do in fact save money.[36] For example, childhood immunization, tobacco screening and prevention, counseling adults on use of low-dose aspirin, and alcohol screening and counseling have all been found to be cost-saving.[37]

In other cases, preventive services have been found to be cost-effective. Cost-effective interventions have favorable impacts on health benefits per their relative costs. Factors that influence the cost-effectiveness of a service include the population targeted, technology used, screening frequency, what the service is compared with, and the proportion of the population already receiving the service.[38] So, in general, the most cost-effective services are those targeted to a population that otherwise has not received the intervention or any comparable intervention and those delivered infrequently using inexpensive technology. Examples of cost-effective preventive services include screenings for high blood pressure, cholesterol, and diabetes along with several common cancer screenings (e.g., breast, cervical, colon).[39] Beyond this, preventive services are largely like treatments, in that both types of interventions span the full range of cost-effectiveness. Efforts to encourage the provision of preventive services that have significant benefits relative to their costs would seem to be worthy endeavors.

Fortunately, there have been several attempts to identify high-priority preventive services to help decision makers focus on services that might lead to the greatest quality of care and health improvement in a cost-effective manner. First in 2001, then in 2006, and most recently in 2017, a number of committees and commissions published rankings of clinical preventive services based on their ability to reduce illness (clinical preventable burden) and based on their cost-effectiveness. Both categories were weighted equally. Which services were ranked the highest? Three services tied for the highest score—immunizing children, counseling to prevent tobacco initiation among youth, and tobacco-use screening and brief intervention to encourage cessation among adults.[40]

Other experts have looked at whether community preventive services can save money. The Community Guide performs economic reviews of many of its interventions and has found several interventions to be cost-effective. These include combined diet and physical activity programs to prevent type II diabetes in individuals at increased risk, as well as quitline services. Other interventions such as motor vehicle–related injury prevention and community water fluoridation have been found to be cost-saving.[41]

In its 2015 report entitled *A Prevention Prescription for Improving Health and Health Care in America*, the Bipartisan Policy Center (BPC) recommended a greater focus on the need for more and better data concerning the cost and cost-effectiveness of prevention interventions. Specifically, the BPC recommended that federal agencies and private funders should encourage and fund studies of the health and economic effects of proven and emerging population-level interventions and prevention strategies.[42]

Cures Are Great, but What about Preventing Disease in the First Place?

Another way to assess prevention's influence on the nation's health sector is by evaluating the nation's medical research enterprise. The National Institutes of Health (NIH) is its most important component and has an annual budget of $37 billion across its 26 institutes and centers. Traditionally, the work of the NIH has been to focus on the basic sciences (knowledge of the mechanisms of biology and behavior) and the search for medical treatments and cures. However, the NIH claims that it has also supported most of the research that provides the evidence underlying the prevention services provided to Americans.

Between 2008 and 2012, the portion of dollars awarded and the portion of total awards for prevention research focused on the leading causes of death increased. Specifically, NIH support for prevention research in 2012 was estimated to be 19% of the total NIH budget—almost $6 billion.[43] Whether that's the right percentage of the budget devoted to prevention is hard to gauge, but the very fact that this data point has been estimated demonstrates that prevention is not being ignored.

This is further supported by the fact that the NIH regularly convenes a Prevention Research Coordinating Committee, which includes representatives from each NIH institute and provides a forum for planning and implementing collaborative prevention research efforts. The NIH's Office of Disease Prevention has also developed a five-year strategic plan to support prevention research focused on the leading causes of death. Part of this plan includes working closely with the USPSTF and the Community Guide to ensure appropriate NIH input and involvement at every step in their review of clinical preventive services and community preventive programs, respectively.[44]

Beyond the NIH, the CDC also invests in prevention research, most notably through Prevention Research Centers, a network of 26 academic research centers that study how people and their communities can avoid or counter the risks for chronic illnesses, such as heart disease, obesity, and cancer. The centers work with communities to develop, test, and evaluate major community changes that can prevent and control chronic diseases.[45]

While these efforts are promising, the visibility of prevention research overall across the biomedical research enterprise is quite low. Research is usually advocated as a means to search for cures. The best example of this is the oft-cited statistic used to garner funding for biomedical research—that there are 10,000 diseases and we only have treatments for 500.[46] I was sensitized to this while serving as the executive secretary of the Chronic Fatigue Syndrome Advisory Committee during part of my tenure at HHS. For years, we heard from researchers struggling to identify the cause of this illness and possible treatment modalities. It was once a diagnosis of exclusion, but there has recently been significant progress in defining the illness (now called myalgic encephalitis / chronic fatigue syndrome, or ME/CFS) and expanding funding for new NIH research centers.

While there are many such complex, and even rare, diseases that have not been fully characterized, it is also true that we in fact do already have treatments for many diseases, especially the ones that cause the greatest morbidity and mortality from a population health perspective. Not only that, but many of these diseases can be prevented in the first place and would benefit from additional investments to identify optimal prevention strategies.

The most high-profile recent example of this is the Cancer Moonshot initiative launched in 2016. A noteworthy $1 billion initiative, it has focused on finding cures for cancer. However, soon after its launch many public health experts expressed concern that the initiative ignored the impact and promise of public health and prevention measures, including screening, on reducing cancer mortality and incidence.[47] In addition, an unprecedented editorial in the premier biomedical research journal, *Nature*, implored that the Cancer Moonshot initiative must strike a balance between research and prevention.[48] Indeed, a recent study by American Cancer Society researchers concluded that about 42% of cancer cases and over 45% of cancer deaths were linked to modifiable risk factors such as smoking, excessive weight, and alcohol use. In addition, many of these cases could have been prevented by effective strategies, such as excise taxes on cigarettes to reduce smoking and vaccinations against human papillomavirus (HPV) and hepatitis B infections.[49]

The final Cancer Moonshot Blue Ribbon Panel report did acknowledge redoubling a focus on prevention strategies such as colorectal cancer screening, HPV vaccination to reduce cervical and other cancers, and tobacco control. However, its specific recommendation for funding focused on hereditary cancer testing for cancer prevention in a small subset of the population.[50] This is a worthy research endeavor but as a stand-alone will not realize the promise of broader cancer prevention in our population.

Other high-profile disease-focused initiatives have been slightly more cognizant to include prevention from the outset. While at HHS, I worked on the first *National Plan to Address Alzheimer's Disease*, which was released in 2012. Under its first strategic goal was to expand research aimed at preventing and treating Alzheimer's disease, a key action item included continuing clinical trials on the most promising lifestyle interventions and on risk factor reduction in the prevention of the disease. Annual updates of the National Plan through 2017 have included this action item.[51] An expert committee of the National Academies of Sciences, Engineering, and Medicine recently concluded that, although there is no strong evidence that anything prevents Alzheimer's disease, a few common-sense practices such as controlling high blood pressure, regular exercise, and specific memory training exercise may help delay memory loss.[52] Ongoing clinical trials will help shed more light on the promise of lifestyle interventions.

Prevention: Where Do We Go from Here?

The opportunities to reduce preventable deaths in this country are numerous. In most cases, we know what needs to be done, and yet we fail in the implementation of evidence-based interventions. One thing is for certain, a nation focused on prevention needs measurable goals and objectives. Fortunately, for four decades such a framework has existed under the auspices of Healthy People. Created in 1979, Healthy People provides science-based, ten-year national objectives for improving the health of all Americans. Through these objectives, the initiative strives to encourage collaborations across communities and sectors, empower individuals toward making informed health decisions, and measure the impact of prevention activities.[53]

In its current iteration, Healthy People 2020 contains 42 topic areas with more than 1,200 objectives. A smaller set of Healthy People 2020 objectives, called Leading Health Indicators (LHIs), have been selected as high-priority health issues that require action. The LHIs include topics such as nutrition, physical activity, and obesity; tobacco; substance abuse; and clinical preventive services.[54]

A progress update conducted in March 2014 demonstrated positive progress toward achieving the Healthy People 2020 targets for more than half of the LHIs. The report showed fewer adults smoking cigarettes, fewer children exposed to secondhand smoke, more adults meeting physical activity targets, and fewer adolescents using alcohol or illicit drugs.[55]

While Healthy People offers a framework for tracking the progress of prevention in this country, provides evidence-based resources and tools, and shares community best practices, it doesn't come with funding or accountability to ensure that goals are reached. Thus, its impact as a catalyst to dramatically improve health in the United States has been limited.

Why Has Prevention Not Been Prioritized?

If disease prevention is so important, it's fair to ask why policy leaders have not placed this goal at the top of their priority list. The best paper to answer this question again comes from Dr. McGinnis, who in a 2001 *American Journal of Health Promotion* article, enumerated a dozen reasons why strong evidence for prevention and public health has not translated into action. These included factors such as politics, vested interests, a technophilic culture, blunted time horizons, and stealth results, just to name a few.[56]

From my experiences, there are six reasons why prevention has not been prioritized by policymakers as it should. First, executive branch leaders seem to be facing constant crises, whether it's a public health emergency or a political controversy, and the default mode in government is reactive. Disease prevention demands being proactive and is thus often cast aside to deal with more "urgent" policy issues. In addition, measurable results in the prevention area often require time (as opposed to "quick wins") and even then, are often invisible in the sense that they're averting disease or outbreaks.

Second, many members of Congress and their staff are not always up to speed with the evidence base behind prevention interventions (perhaps due to a limited number of stakeholder and advocacy groups disseminating this information). If they're not sure something will work, they'll naturally hesitate in supporting it. Policy proposals that change policies, systems, and the environment to create healthier conditions, though evidence-based, might be seen as "slush funds."

Third, and related, is the characterization by some members of Congress that government support for prevention amounts to a "nanny state." They may feel that individuals should take sole responsibility for their behaviors and government should not go beyond disseminating health education to Americans. The irony is that many of these same members are also fiscal hawks and may not fully appreciate the significant healthcare costs of preventable chronic conditions to the federal budget.

Fourth, most prevention initiatives are funded through discretionary appropriations, and it's difficult in this fiscal climate to significantly increase annual appropriations. With respect to mandatory spending, one additional reason prevention has not been prioritized relates to the history of Medicare (since Medicare and private payers influence each other, when it comes to issues related to coverage and benefits, Medicare's impact on the availability of preventive services cannot be understated). In 1965, when Medicare was established, the program was created to provide hospital and medical coverage for the treatment of disease. The notion of covering preventive services did not come to fruition until decades later, starting with the 1997 Balanced Budget Act, when individual clinical preventive services began to be added into statute by Congress.[57] This has continued to date in piecemeal, sporadic fashion, given that Congress faces requirements under budget neutrality to ensure that any new benefit is paired with a cost reduction elsewhere.[58] Further, the Congressional Budget Office utilizes a ten-year budget scoring window, which doesn't allow the full long-term benefit of many prevention initiatives to be taken into account.

Fifth, our $3.5 trillion "sick care" system makes it rather difficult to make money from the prevention of disease. Value-based healthcare transformation, with its emphasis on health outcomes and keeping people healthy, should change this over time; however, presently, treatment, not prevention, is what is emphasized from health professional training programs all the way to payment for professional services.

Sixth, prevention has not mobilized the public nearly enough. There's an unspoken cultural barrier to embracing prevention, perhaps tied to our nation's origins of rugged individualism or rather a manifestation of a stressful and competitive quality of life in this country. Many Americans would rather wait to get sick and then take a pill rather than engage in the crucial health promotion activities necessary to avoid preventable illness. In addition, broader public health efforts keep Americans safe each and every day without their direct knowledge; thus, it's easy to take these prevention efforts for granted. Finally, there are few interest groups or lobbying firms pressuring our nation's policymakers to substantially devote more attention and resources to disease prevention.

While all of these reasons explain why a Prevention First orientation to health in America may be challenging, none of these reasons are insurmountable. As I'll discuss in this book, prioritizing disease prevention by our nation's leaders is both necessary and possible. Governmental leadership can go a long way to complementing the role of individuals, families, communities, and the private sector in creating a healthier nation. Ultimately, achieving a culture of prevention will require both individuals and society to step up and take decisive action to change our country's health prognosis. This book explores how to prioritize disease prevention both inside and outside the healthcare sector. We begin our discussion focused on the former and on how to transform our sick care system into a true healthcare system.

PREVENTION *WITHIN* THE HEALTHCARE SETTING

[1]

How Do You Insert Prevention into Healthcare's Value Equation?

I N THE SUMMER of 2015, New Yorkers reading local newspapers or using social media were exposed to an ad campaign sponsored by Mount Sinai Medical Center. While there's nothing new about healthcare entities running ads to promote their unique and unparalleled services, there was something different about this campaign. A large spread in the *New York Times* that July showed a New York City skyline, presumably with Medical Center buildings and at the top, the header declared, "If our beds are filled, it means we've failed."[1]

This was one of those moments when I knew that prevention, in the form of what's called "population health," had made it into healthcare's mainstream. A major medical center, part of our country's $1 trillion hospital sector that has been built for decades to fill, or at least make available, beds to treat the sick, had just stated that the opposite notion was also its goal. In doing so, Mount Sinai was not saying that it no longer wanted to care for complex patients or provide state-of-the-art, specialized care; rather, it was saying that for those patients hospitalized because of preventable conditions or circumstances, there was a better way. Mount Sinai had bought into the notion of keeping people healthy and well, even if that meant less revenue from filling beds. Financially, as we'll explore in this chapter, this is now increasingly possible because of the steps being taken in this country to change the way healthcare is paid for.

While healthcare's proportional contribution to premature death is roughly only 10%, it may seem counterintuitive to first focus on the healthcare sector to maximize prevention's impact. However, with 18% of the US gross domestic product going to this sector, there are enormous opportunities to leverage healthcare dollars to maximize prevention. Most healthcare dollars go toward treatment of disease. Indeed, healthcare providers have long been paid largely based on the volume of services they provide, with fees paid for each service. Over time, this incentivized excessive volume, and coupled with higher-than-inflation prices in healthcare, helped drive healthcare spending to its high level in this country today.

Over the past decade, policymakers in the public and private sectors have urged a shift from volume-based healthcare provider reimbursement to value-based provider reimbursement. Inherent in this push is the idea that providers should get paid for, and consumers should pay for, the quality of care they provide as opposed to the amount of services they provide. This is a notion that has had bipartisan interest at the federal level. In 2006, US Department of Health and Human Services (HHS) secretary Michael Leavitt issued a broad challenge to healthcare purchasers to implement four cornerstones of "value-driven health care": utilize health information technology, measure and publish quality information, measure and publish price information, and create positive incentives for high-quality, efficient healthcare.[2] Secretary Leavitt once recited a story about his experience obtaining a screening colonoscopy. After a number of inquiries, he quickly learned that different providers charged different amounts for the preventive test without any relation to the quality of service.[3] Secretary Leavitt lamented that healthcare, as opposed to sectors such as banking, telecommunications, and airlines, lacked a competitive environment based on value where everyone has a motivation to have higher quality at lower costs.

The passage of the Patient Protection and Affordable Care Act (ACA) in 2010 by a Democratic Congress further accelerated value-based healthcare transformation through the introduction of a variety of Medicare payment programs based on performance on quality metrics. As an example, the ACA created a star rating system for Medicare Advantage plans (private insurance plans that provide comprehensive benefits for Medicare beneficiaries) to help guide seniors to plans that provide cost-effective and higher-quality benefits. Having increased in popularity over the last decade, Medicare Advantage plans now cover one-third of Medicare beneficiaries, or roughly 20 million Americans.[4] The star rating system, which includes several measures of prevention, has been successful in driving nearly three-quarters of seniors to plans with a rating of four or more stars on a five-notch scale.[5]

The ACA also created the Innovation Center at the Centers for Medicare and Medicaid Services (CMS) to test payment and delivery models to reduce Medicare and Medicaid program expenditures while enhancing beneficiary quality of care. One of the most high-profile models being tested by the CMS's Innovation Center is the accountable care organizations (ACOs) model, which serves approximately 10.5 million seniors.[6] In this model, doctors, hospitals, and other care providers collaborate to improve health outcomes while keeping costs down. One would think this is the norm; however, the largely fragmented nature of our healthcare sector hasn't always facilitated this type of care coordination.

Among the most promising ACO ventures have been those that require financial risk if groups of providers don't reduce enough preventable costs. The Next Generation ACOs launched in 2016 saved Medicare $62 million in their first year by preventing unnecessary hospitalizations and postacute care.[7] Other promising ACO models include the ACO Investment Model created to help rural providers by giving them upfront capital in the form of loans to build the infrastructure necessary for optimal population health management. After just the first year of operations, these ACOs saved Medicare $82 million.[8]

In addition to ACOs, the law accelerated testing of bundled payments, which reimburse healthcare providers for a discrete episode of care such as a surgery and its postoperative care. By aligning incentives for different providers such as hospitals, postacute care providers, and physicians, bundled payments allow them to work closely together across all specialties and settings. As of July 2018, the CMS, through its Bundled Payments for Care Improvement initiative is working with 1,025 entities to test this model with Medicare beneficiaries.[9] Preliminary evidence demonstrates that bundled payments for knee and joint replacement surgeries can reduce costs without sacrificing quality of care.[10]

Likely the most exciting test to date to prevent unnecessary healthcare costs might be the CMS's experiments with global healthcare budgets. The highest-profile effort has been with the state of Maryland, given its unique independent hospital rate-setting system where all healthcare payers reimburse hospitals at the same rate. In 2010, the state launched a pilot program for 10 rural hospitals in which each was guaranteed a set amount of revenue for the coming years, regardless of the number of hospital admissions or emergency department visits. Hospitals began focusing on prevention by launching outpatient clinics to care for individuals with chronic conditions and behavioral health diagnoses. They saw admissions go down while profits went up.[11] When visiting one of the hospitals in western Maryland, Dr. Joshua Sharfstein, then secretary of the Maryland Department of Health and Mental Hygiene, called it the "antigravity zone," given that the hospital was quiet, only 60% full, and seemingly hard-wired to get people back home.[12] In 2014, the Maryland pilot was expanded to all 46 acute care hospitals in the state. After 30 months, Maryland saw a 48% reduction in potentially preventable complications, like hospital-acquired infections, and saw hospital readmission rates fall compared to the national average. The model has also saved $319 million for the Medicare program as of 2017.[13] The next phase of Maryland's experiment will include extending global payments to the rest of the healthcare system. The initial success of this payment model has now spurred Pennsylvania to partner with the CMS to test global hospital budgeting for some of its rural hospitals.

Oregon has done something similar with its Medicaid program. Back in 2011, in order to convince the federal government to help patch a budget hole, the state agreed to grow its Medicaid budget at a rate that is 2% slower than the rest of the country. State officials designed a plan that divided the state into 15 regions and gave each one a set amount to care for each patient. Like Maryland's global budget model, these regions, known as coordinated care organizations, must meet quality metrics, but otherwise they have the freedom and flexibility to decide how to best prevent illness and keep their patients healthy.[14] Preliminary estimates over the first few years of the model suggest that the state is meeting spending targets while improving on a number of quality metrics.[15]

While still in its early stages, the shift to payments for keeping people healthy and outside the healthcare system is encouraging. These developments are leading to an array of opportunities for prevention to increase value in healthcare. But how is value being defined? I tackled this subject in an article for the *Milbank Quarterly* several years ago.[16] Most healthcare leaders view value in two dimensions, with quality of care as the numerator and costs of care as the denominator. Looking at the value equation in this way, it's worth exploring both dimensions to identify specifically how to better integrate prevention into healthcare.

Prevention as a Quality Measure: The Numerator

Over the last decade in healthcare, there has been a proliferation of metrics to measure the quality and performance of healthcare professionals. Most of these measures have focused on the processes of care and are thus called process measures. Included in these measures are metrics to help track the delivery of preventive services. For example, Medicare Advantage's Star Ratings include measures such as breast cancer screening, colorectal cancer screening, annual flu vaccine, and adult body-mass index (BMI) assessment.[17] As another example, of the 31 quality measures for ACOs, 9 focus on preventive health services including influenza and pneumococcal vaccination, adult weight screening and follow-up, tobacco use assessment and cessation intervention, depression screening, breast and colorectal cancer screening, screening for falls risk, and statin therapy for the prevention of cardiovascular disease.[18]

Process measures of quality focused on preventive services are important. They encourage and incentivize healthcare professionals to keep patients healthy. One recent initiative led by the Bipartisan Policy Center in conjunction with the Alliance for a Healthier Generation inspired 11 public and private payers and employers to offer a minimum number of obesity counseling visits consistent with evidence-based guidelines. As part of the "My Healthy Weight" pledge taken by these organizations, beginning in 2019, 10.5 million individuals have access to this benefit. It is expected that payers will track utilization of this benefit to assess how many of their members are receiving this preventive service.[19]

But even more important than process measures of quality focused on preventive services are outcome measures of quality. For example, there has been considerable interest and substantial progress since passage of the ACA to reduce preventable hospital readmissions and hospital-acquired conditions. However, these measures are still largely focused on healthcare as opposed to health status. Ultimately, it's outcomes such as the presence of disease and unhealthy behaviors that most profoundly affect health and functional status.

Imagine if healthcare professionals were accountable for measures such as the prevalence of chronic disease risk factors within their patient population; alternatively, what if they were accountable for the incidence, or new cases, of chronic conditions? In 2015, the BPC's Prevention Task Force recommended that the CMS integrate population healthcare quality measures, such as the prevalence of risk factors and the incidence of disease, into the next iteration of ACOs to drive system change that supports health.[20]

I have previously argued that healthcare entities should be held accountable for a limited set of health status measures for their patient population. These measures should not supplant critical process or outcome measures of quality but rather supplement them. For example, these measures might include the prevalence of tobacco use and obesity measured at appropriate intervals and the incidence of chronic diseases such as diabetes, ischemic heart disease, and chronic obstructive pulmonary disease (chronic conditions with substantial burden of disease and largely preventable) over appropriate periods of time. To address measurement challenges such as adverse selection, risk-adjustment strategies could be used in addition to assessing the healthcare entities' relative improvements over time.[21]

I have also noted that the healthcare community may be reluctant to be held accountable for measures that are not traditionally under their purview or areas in which it may not have immediate expertise. This is a valid concern that should be debated. However, I have argued that the reason many call the sector a healthcare system as opposed to a sick care system is that we expect healthcare entities to be in the business of keeping patients healthy, not just treating sickness. In addition, given that most national health expenditures are spent on the provision of clinical care, at some point, society should consider holding the entities receiving the bulk of healthcare's dollars accountable for the health of the population.[22]

There is progress on this front. In the winter of 2016, I was invited to the Danish embassy for a meeting organized by Novo Nordisk on quality metrics and the obesity epidemic in the United States. Novo Nordisk is a Danish multinational pharmaceutical company that has been a leader in diabetes management for over 90 years. Though most of its products focus on the treatment of diabetes, I was mildly surprised at the company's interest in curbing type II diabetes, the critical driver of obesity in this country. I was even further surprised when the Danish ambassador himself stopped by to provide opening remarks. Incidentally, though obesity is a worldwide epidemic, rates of adult obesity in Denmark are roughly half the rates in the United States.

At this meeting, a diverse group of healthcare stakeholders reviewed the current set of obesity measures used by public and private payers and other purchasers of healthcare. There was also a discussion about measurement gaps, which included the lack of measures of obesity prevalence and weight loss. The meeting catalyzed activities over the next several months led by organizations such as the National Quality Forum (NQF) and the STOP Obesity Alliance to identify new approaches to obesity measure development. Since then, one measure being piloted by the American Medical Group Association and Discern Health would track the percent of patients with a meaningful decline (5% loss) in BMI by age and risk cohorts at the systems level.[23] This could encourage healthcare entities to go beyond simply focusing on process measures, such as screening for obesity, to actually tracking outcomes, such as weight loss. Once a measure is developed and validated, the NQF plays an important role in its endorsement, which then leads to its widespread use by payers such as the CMS. Thus, this is a promising development to create health status measures related to prevention that should be watched in the future.

Prevention as a Reducer of Waste: The Denominator

The second dimension to look at focuses on the denominator of healthcare's value equation. In 2012, the Institute of Medicine (IOM) released a landmark report entitled *Best Care at Lower Cost: The Path to Continuously Learning Health Care in America*.[24] Over the years, the IOM, now called the National Academy of Medicine, has issued outstanding reports. But, I think this one might be one of the most important.

The report concluded that roughly 30% (at the time, $765 billion) of healthcare spending was wasted on unnecessary treatments and spending that did not produce better health outcomes.[25] These estimates were developed by experts participating in a 2009 IOM workshop entitled the Healthcare Imperative: Lowering Costs and Improving Outcomes. (For full disclosure, I also participated in the workshop, but my contributions were focused on the care of medically complex patients and those with multiple chronic conditions.) Categories of healthcare spending characterized as waste included unnecessary services, excessive administrative costs, inefficiently delivered services, prices that are too high, fraud, and importantly, missed prevention opportunities. Specifically, these missed prevention opportunities accounted for $55 billion of the $765 billion in waste.[26]

Experts found missed opportunities in primary and secondary prevention such as tobacco screening, alcohol screening, and discussing daily aspirin use. They estimated that if the current delivery rates of these three services were increased to 90%, nearly $10 billion could be saved.[27] (Coupling this cost savings estimate with the health benefit that accrues from these services, one could argue that public and private payers should assign a higher weight to the associated quality metrics for these services in value-based payment models.) Another approximately $45 billion of savings has been estimated from enhanced tertiary prevention through better care coordination of patients, though experts admit that these estimates have limitations and are uncertain.[28]

Are these cost savings from prevention actually possible with an increased emphasis in the healthcare system on prevention? While this is a difficult question to answer, I went in search of a few illustrative examples.

In 2006, four years prior to what would be called Obamacare, Massachusetts passed what became known as RomneyCare requiring all individuals in the state to have health insurance. Buried in the law was a new benefit for smokers in the Medicaid population. The law mandated coverage for two types of smoking cessation treatments: behavioral counseling and all Food and Drug Administration (FDA)–approved medications. The implementers of the new benefit tried their best to incentivize beneficiaries to utilize these services. For example, they made sure that prior authorization was not required and that copayments were minimal. Most importantly, they launched a broad promotional campaign to get the word out to smokers in the Medicaid program.

These efforts paid off. In the first 30 months of the new benefit, approximately 37%, or more than 70,000, Medicaid smokers used the benefit. Researchers then studied whether smoking rates declined compared to what they were before the benefit period. They found that the crude smoking rate decreased from 38% to 28%, representing a decline of 26%.[29] Researchers also examined hospital utilization of Medicaid enrollees who used the benefit. They found that participation in the program reduced hospitalizations for heart attacks by 46% and for other heart disease by 49%.[30] How do these significant health impacts translate into Medicaid savings? Another group of researchers looked at this question and found that for every $1 in program costs, there was an associated $3.12 in medical savings, for a $2.12 return on investment to the Medicaid program for every dollar spent.[31] Not bad, considering that smoking-related medical costs are responsible for 11% of Medicaid expenditures, representing an estimated $22 billion annually.[32] Imagine if every state in the country replicated the Massachusetts model.

While reducing risk factors for chronic diseases is one thing, what about tertiary prevention? Can preventing complications from chronic diseases save money? In 2007, the National Asthma Education and Prevention Program (NAEPP), initiated by the National Institutes of Health almost three decades ago, brought experts together from all over the country to update guidelines for the diagnosis and management of asthma.[33] The guidelines counseled clinicians on how to assess asthma severity, dispense medications appropriate to patients' asthma severity and control, and follow up with patients to monitor progress and reduce preventable healthcare utilization.[34] In subsequent years, studies of healthcare providers who followed the NAEPP guidelines have shown that their patients had up to a 45% decrease in asthma-related emergency department visits and up to a 56% decrease in asthma-related hospitalizations. Many of these studies focused on poor, minority, urban children, which is important considering the significant health disparities that exist by socioeconomic class and by race and ethnicity.[35] Return on investment has been reported as $2.40 to $4.00 per $1.00 spent due to fewer asthma-related emergency department visits and hospitalizations.[36]

Not all disease management and care coordination programs have been shown to save money. In fact, with respect to the Medicare program, the first decade of this century saw many more failures than successes. Why? Well, when I was at HHS, we launched a department-wide initiative focused on individuals with multiple chronic conditions.[37] The goal of the initiative was to identify ways that federal agencies, in conjunction with the private sector, could improve the quality of life and health status of this vulnerable population. What we found with respect to Medicare's past care coordination efforts was essentially a failure to match the intensity of an intervention to the acuity of the patient. Specifically, in order to improve health outcomes and realize cost savings, medically complex patients should be matched to "high-touch" interventions, whereas healthier patients should be paired with less intensive interventions. For example, a case manager calling a patient with ten chronic conditions and on fifty medications once a month may not be effective. That individual likely needs closer follow-up with a team of healthcare professionals that might include a nurse and pharmacist.

This is exactly what Massachusetts General Hospital started to do in 2006. The hospital created an integrated care management program that matched high-risk patients with a nurse care manager. Together, along with the patient's family, a customized care plan was created to address the patient's specific healthcare needs. The care managers attended office appointments, made home visits, and coordinated clinical and social services. Data from program participants demonstrated reductions in acute care hospitalizations, emergency room visits, and mortality rates. For every dollar spent the program saved $2.65 in healthcare costs.[38] The care management program was subsequently incorporated into the hospital's accountable care organization and led to substantial reductions in emergency department visits, hospitalization, and Medicare spending. Just because this program worked at one hospital, does that mean it will work everywhere? Probably not, but there is nothing inherently unique about this program that couldn't be replicated elsewhere.

One of the best examples from the ACA of matching intensive interventions with high acuity patients involves the Independence at Home Demonstration. Patients with multiple chronic conditions and limitations in activities of daily living who had been previously hospitalized and received rehabilitation services in the last year were offered home-based primary care services. Preliminary analyses have shown high quality of care with a potential savings of $1,300 per beneficiary per year over the first three years.[39] Congress has twice enacted legislation extending the program and recently increased the number of beneficiaries who could participate to 15,000.

Yet another example of focusing more intensive services to medically complex patients involves Medicare's chronic care management payment. In alignment with HHS's multiple chronic conditions initiative, since 2015, the CMS has been paying providers for non-face-to-face visits with beneficiaries having two or more chronic conditions that carry a significant risk of mortality or functional decline. In exchange for around-the-clock access to a care team, development of a care plan, enhanced care coordination, care transitions, patient communication, and medication management, healthcare providers receive a monthly fee per beneficiary.[40] A preliminary study of the payment demonstrated a $74 reduction per beneficiary per month for the first 18 months of the program, largely due to reduced costs from hospitalization, emergency department use, and nursing home stays.[41] While this program builds on the old fee-for-service chassis, it does offer a bridge for healthcare professionals to provide optimal tertiary prevention to a vulnerable population until a time when they'll be able to provide more comprehensive care through robust value-based payment arrangements.

More broadly, with the gradual shift away from fee-for-service to value-based payment models, all healthcare entities are looking for ways to reduce costs through better tertiary prevention. An attractive place to start, following the Willie Sutton rule, is looking at the highest-cost patients, usually defined as the top 1% or top 5% of patients. In 2015, the top 1% of the population, ranked by their healthcare expenses, accounted for a whopping 23% of total healthcare costs, and the top 5% accounted for 51% of total costs.[42] Another common strategy is to focus on individuals who frequently use healthcare services, or superutilizers. There are hundreds of initiatives, small and large, currently underway to see how best to wring preventable healthcare costs from the highest-cost patients. Simultaneously, we are learning that focusing on the highest-cost patients is not the only approach to reducing costs. There are preventable healthcare costs associated with both complex and high-cost patients along with more healthy patients. The key, as previously stated, is to match the right interventions to the right patient population to attain better outcomes at lower costs.

Aligning Provider and Consumer Incentives

Thus far I have focused exclusively on changing the way providers are measured and paid to increase value through prevention. While provider incentives are important, an equally important but less talked about strategy focuses on consumer incentives to engage in high-value care. This idea, initially called benefit-based copay was first described by Dr. Mark Fendrick and colleagues at the University of Michigan in 2001.[43] In fact, its first broad application occurred earlier as a tertiary prevention strategy in Asheville, North Carolina, in 1997. The city reduced copayments for employees with diabetes who agreed to participate in a pharmacist-directed program that promoted self-management. At five years, overall cost reductions were 58% lower than expected.[44] This concept, ultimately named value-based insurance design (VBID), is intended to increase consumer adherence with recommended care guidelines by aligning consumer out-of-pocket costs with the potential clinical benefit of certain health services and medications.[45] Thus, high-value clinical services and providers are encouraged through lower consumer out-of-pocket costs, whereas low-value services are discouraged through higher consumer out-of-pocket costs.[46] Over the last two decades, many large employers such as Pitney Bowes, Marriott, and the Mayo Clinic started implementing VBID as either a secondary or tertiary prevention strategy. For example, some reduced copays for screening tests, others reduced copays for generic drugs. In most cases, these initiatives resulted in increased preventive services and medication adherence, leading to better health outcomes. Data on healthcare cost savings have been more mixed, with some studies showing net costs versus others showing savings.[47]

The most impactful execution of value-based insurance design with respect to prevention occurred through the Affordable Care Act, which mandated private insurance plans to eliminate patient cost-sharing for clinical preventive services graded by the US Preventive Services Task Force as A or B. The ACA also eliminated cost-sharing for grade A and B services covered by the Medicare program. All of a sudden, millions of Americans were now able to access evidence-based clinical preventive services for free. There is now some data to suggest that in the years following enactment of the ACA, receipt of blood pressure and cholesterol checks in addition to flu vaccination all increased significantly in the privately insured population.[48] Within the Medicare program, mammography rates among older women in Medicare Advantage plans for whom screening is recommended also increased.[49]

Barriers do still exist for some high-value preventive services, such as colonoscopy, for Medicare beneficiaries. Many Americans who undergo screening colonoscopy are found to have a polyp, an abnormal growth of tissue that could become cancerous, which is subsequently removed during the procedure. Polyp removal led insurance companies to demand patient cost-sharing, although many patients went into the exam thinking that this preventive service would be free because of the ACA. Given that polyp removal is an integral part of a colonoscopy, in 2013, we drafted guidance for the Obama administration stipulating that private plans could no longer require patient cost-sharing in this scenario.[50] Unfortunately, Medicare beneficiaries, due to an eccentricity in the ACA, are still liable for cost-sharing.[51] It's not clear to what extent this disincentivizes beneficiaries from undergoing a screening colonoscopy, but it certainly increases out-of-pocket expenses for them for a service that is of high value. For the last two sessions in Congress, bipartisan legislation has been sponsored in both chambers to fix this loophole and has garnered the support of nearly 360 members of Congress.[52] However, the issue remains unresolved.

Most recently, the CMS's Innovation Center launched a VBID model for Medicare Advantage plans in several states. Plans can select beneficiaries with certain chronic conditions and reduce their cost-sharing for high-value services (usually secondary or tertiary prevention). The model will be expanded to include plans from 25 states in 2019.[53] The Defense Department's health insurance program, TRICARE, is also implementing a VBID program.[54] What is exciting about these developments is that healthcare professionals and consumers will increasingly have aligned incentives to provide and obtain, respectively, specific preventive services. This will further accelerate the integration of prevention into value-based healthcare.

Inserting prevention into the healthcare system will reduce illness, without a doubt. In certain cases, prevention may in fact reduce healthcare costs by, for example, reducing preventable hospitalizations for ambulatory care–sensitive conditions. Even without significant cost savings, prevention's impact on health promotion is more than enough reason to enhance its influence. An environment that shifts away from fee-for-service medicine to one where payments are based on outcomes and keeping a patient population healthy will be most conducive to applying prevention practices. As alternative payment models, including global budgets, are tested, more and more entities will be able to take steps like Mount Sinai Medical Center. In addition, a prevention-oriented healthcare system will also look different from the current sick care sector. The shift in usual site of care from the inpatient setting to the ambulatory setting will only accelerate, while the home, connected through technology, will be seen as an ideal site of care to manage chronic diseases and limitations in activities of daily living of elderly and disabled populations.

In a prevention-oriented healthcare system, the healthcare workforce would need to adjust accordingly. Arguably, the best opportunity for the current sector to reap the benefits of prevention may lie in supporting primary care. Prevention is embedded in the very ethos of primary care medicine, and primary care will be key to the success of value-based healthcare transformation. In the next chapter, I expand on why primary care is so important and how to bolster support for it.

Why Is Strengthening Primary Care So Important for Prevention?

F OR 50 YEARS, Holy Cross Hospital in Montgomery County, Maryland, has been a trusted source of healthcare for hundreds of thousands of individuals. One of the largest hospitals in Maryland, it is home to the nation's first and region's only Seniors Emergency Center and is the only four-time winner of the Joint Commission's highest quality award in the region. However, its most meaningful impact on the health of its community may have been the establishment of the Holy Cross Health Network, which operates primary care medical centers across central Maryland.[1] After years of caring for patients in the emergency department who lacked any usual source of care, hospital leadership made the decision to open three health centers across their catchment area. As patients, mostly uninsured, are discharged from the hospital they are routed to these health centers for follow-up care and to establish primary care.

Dr. Elise Riley, medical director of Holy Cross Hospital health centers, has seen the growth of these centers and their impact on patients firsthand. Under her leadership, the network provides over 30,000 health center visits annually.[2] Services include acute care, preventive health exams, laboratory services, vaccinations, diabetes management, cardiovascular management, behavioral health services, and social service referrals. A small on-site pharmacy exists as well, making these centers one-stop comprehensive sites of care. What was apparent to Dr. Riley from even the first few patients who walked in the doors of these health centers was that they suffered from a wide range of mostly preventable chronic conditions. Obesity, hypertension, and hypercholesterolemia affected most of this patient population, and previously diagnosed diabetes was largely uncontrolled. Substance abuse, both past and current, was highly prevalent. And patients were frequently not up to date with cancer screenings. It took usually a couple visits, mostly focused on tertiary prevention and chronic disease management, before these patients could be engaged in primary and secondary prevention. While no-shows were common, over time more and more patients saw these health centers as places not just to visit when they were sick but rather places to ensure they remain healthy.

As a physician volunteer at Holy Cross Hospital health center for seven years, I treasured the opportunity to provide clinical care to an underserved population. But what has stuck with me has been the opportunity through primary care medicine to build a trusting relationship with patients who otherwise lacked a place to seek medical care and advice. Many of the patients I saw over the years did not speak English, and many others last saw a healthcare professional in their country of origin. I recall many who didn't know what to expect when coming to the health center. My approach to these patients, as I laid out in an article for the *New England Journal of Medicine* in 2011 entitled, "Winning Their Trust," was to demonstrate empathy, respect, and a willingness to learn about and address their perceived barriers to optimal health.[3] Once trust is established, it facilitates discussions about health promotion and disease prevention. Forging these relationships is what motivated me and what motivates primary care providers every day across the country as they try to provide the very best comprehensive care for their patients.

The CDC estimates that of the one billion visits Americans make each year to a physician's office, more than half are made to a primary care physician.[4] If prevention is to be embraced, integrated, and elevated in the healthcare sector, it must start with primary care. Fortunately, disease prevention and health promotion are at the very core of primary care.

Studies demonstrate that greater numbers of primary care physicians per capita have been associated with lower rates of preventable hospitalization.[5] In addition, patients with a regular primary care provider as a usual source of care are more likely to receive high-value preventive services versus patients without primary care.[6, 7]

According to Health is Primary, a collaboration among the nation's leading family medicine organizations, primary care is broadly associated with better health, better care, and lower costs. Specifically, studies suggest that as many as 127,617 deaths (e.g., those caused by cancer, heart disease, stroke) per year in the United States could be averted through an increase in the number of primary care physicians. Communities that have an adequate supply of primary care doctors experience lower infant mortality, higher birth weights, and immunization rates at or above national standards. And US adults who have a primary care physician have 33% lower healthcare costs.[8]

And yet, primary care in this country cannot foster a culture of prevention unless its delivery and financing are adequately supported. A seminal study published nearly 15 years ago by clinicians at Duke University looked at the amount of time required for a primary care physician to provide all services recommended by the US Preventive Services Task Force, at the recommended frequency, to a hypothetical panel of patients. The authors found that to fully satisfy the USPSTF recommendations, physicians would need to spend 7.4 hours per working day just to provide preventive services to their patient panel.[9] More broadly, another study estimated that an average family physician would need to spend 21.7 hours per day to provide recommended preventive, chronic, and acute care services (not to mention the additional time to measure and report quality metrics and utilize electronic medical records). This was clearly not feasible; the analysis pointed to the importance of delivery system reform to incorporate team-based care and payment reform to increase the historically low payment of services for primary care.[10]

The crisis, as many consider it, for primary care has been brewing for several decades. Fifty years ago, half the doctors in America practiced primary care. Today, fewer than one in three do, given an increasing number of US medical graduates avoiding careers in primary care. According to the Association of American Medical Colleges (AAMC), the number of primary care physicians relative to the US population has been virtually flat for nearly the past decade—roughly 90 active primary care physicians per 100,000 population. The crisis is particularly acute in Southern states such as Mississippi, which has just 64.4 primary care physicians per 100,000 Americans.[11] Given a combination of the aging of the population and coverage expansions from the Affordable Care Act, the AAMC estimates a shortage of between 14,800 and 49,300 primary care physicians by 2030.[12] Organizations such as the American College of Physicians have recommended that the number of Medicare-funded graduate medical education positions available be increased by 3,000 additional primary care physicians each year for the next 15 years.[13] Yet, it is hard enough to attract US medical students to fill the current number of first-year residency positions in primary care fields. In the 2018 National Resident Match Program, less than half of primary care positions were filled by US medical school graduates.[14] If it weren't for international medical graduates to fill the void, the country's primary care shortage would be even more dire. While the ranks of nurse practitioners and physician assistants have grown in the last decade, an overall primary care shortage persists. In addition, some of the states with the lowest number of primary care physicians in this country also have the most restricted scope of practice for nurse practitioners.[15] Overall, 84 million Americans reside in federally designated primary care Health Professional Shortage Areas (HPSAs),[16] contributing to a substantial number of emergency room visits for care that could have been provided by a primary care provider.

The lack of adequate primary care not only jeopardizes access to clinical preventive services but also to community preventive services. This is because primary care practices tend to have the greatest knowledge of community prevention services and likelihood of referring their patients to these services. Two developments in the last decade give hope that primary care can be at least sustained and ideally strengthened—the development of a patient-centered medical home (PCMH) and expansion of the network of community health centers nationwide. Both deserve some discussion.

Patient-Centered Medical Home

In response to the challenges of primary care, the PCMH concept developed out of a need to improve patient outcomes and patient experience while reducing healthcare costs. The model aims to optimize primary care so that services are continuous, comprehensive, team-based, coordinated, evidence-based, accessible, and also supported through additional payment. Various principles of PCMH such as seeing the same physician over time, having a higher number of previous visits, and being treated for chronic diseases have been found to be associated with receipt of preventive services such as cancer screening, lipid screening, influenza vaccination, and behavioral counseling.[17]

Some of the best data in support of the PCMH come from Blue Cross Blue Shield of Michigan, which boasts the largest state-level implementation program in the United States. Practices in the program that have fully implemented the PCMH model are associated with higher performance on quality measures and a $26.37 lower per-member, per-month adult medical cost largely from decreases in emergency department visits and preventable hospitalizations.[18] Specifically, the program has resulted in a 15% decrease in adult emergency department visits and a 21% decrease in adult ambulatory care–sensitive inpatient stays. Success has been attributed to a number of lessons learned, including a commitment to long-term support for practice transformation and provision of quality improvement technical assistance to practices, as well as meaningful financial support.[19]

With respect to prevention, implementation of a PCMH has been associated with higher breast, cervical, and colorectal cancer prevention screening rates. In one study, the increase in screening rates over time was greatest for lower socioeconomic groups; for example, the disparity in breast cancer screening was cut in half.[20] Other programs have also demonstrated reductions in disparities with respect to access to preventive services. PCMHs at Hennepin County Medical Center, Minnesota, increased the delivery of multiple preventive care services to adolescents, particularly for Hispanic/Latino and foreign-born patients; specifically, there were increases in rates of meningococcal vaccination, human papillomavirus (HPV) vaccination, STD screening, and contraception prescription.[21]

It should be noted that not all PCMHs have been found uniformly to improve health outcomes and lower costs. Another large multipayer medical home pilot, the Pennsylvania Chronic Care Initiative, found no statistically significant differences in emergency department visits, ambulatory care–sensitive inpatient stays, or overall health costs, or across an array of quality measures, including preventive care.[22] The study demonstrates that the process of implementing a PCMH to ensure that providers have the necessary staffing, patient risk stratification tools, and information technology structures to capture timely patient data is critical to achieving desired outcomes.

Given these important process steps vital to primary care transformation, for the last decade the National Committee on Quality Assurance (NCQA) has developed a PCMH recognition program to identify practices that are providing optimal primary care. The standards include elements of primary, secondary, and tertiary prevention as well as linkages with the community to maximize health outcomes.[23] This recognition is now tied to value-based reimbursement by private and public payers, providing significant further incentive to strengthen primary care infrastructure in this country. It's estimated that more than 13,000 practices (with more than 67,000 clinicians) are now recognized as PCMH practices by the NCQA.[24]

Many of these PCMH practices have also been central to the success of alternative payment models such as accountable care organizations (ACOs), which are predicated upon enhanced care coordination to keep patients healthy and reduce the need for acute care. In 2018, the Patient-Centered Primary Care Collaborative performed a study examining the role of advanced primary care models like the PCMH in the success or failure of ACOs. The Collaborative categorized ACOs by the share of primary care providers with a PCMH certification and found that having a higher share was associated with higher savings in Medicare's ACO program. ACOs with higher shares of PCMHs were also associated with higher rates of preventive services such as pneumococcal vaccination, depression screening, and tobacco screening and cessation interventions.[25]

Community Health Centers

The second development in support of primary care is the investment in a nationwide network of community health centers. One in twelve people across every state and territory receive healthcare services from a community health center supported by the Health Resources and Services Administration (HRSA). Currently, there are nearly 1,400 health centers across the United States providing care through more than 12,000 healthcare delivery sites to approximately 27 million individuals every year. Those served include one in nine children, one in five Americans living in rural areas, and one in three individuals living in poverty.[26] Health centers deliver primary healthcare and preventive services to patients while also integrating a wide range of medical, dental, behavioral, and patient services. The community health center model of care, similar to studies of high-functioning primary care practices, has been shown to reduce the use of costlier providers of care, such as emergency departments and hospitals. Health centers are also known to provide high quality of care and engage in quality improvement programs.[27] As an example, since 2015, more than two hundred community health centers have received recognition from the HRSA for ensuring that over 70% of applicable patients achieved appropriate aspirin use, blood pressure control, and smoking cessation.[28]

A critical feature of community health centers is their delivery of care to patients regardless of their ability to pay. In fact, in 2016, almost one-quarter of health center patients were uninsured and nearly half were covered by Medicaid. Medicaid expansion through the Affordable Care Act has increased the operational capacity of health centers to provide comprehensive primary care. Health centers in Medicaid expansion states compared to nonexpansion states are more likely, for example, to offer substance use disorder and/or mental health services, dental services, and vision care services.[29] With respect to preventive services, one analysis from the Kaiser Family Foundation and George Washington University found that in comparison to 2009, health center patients in 2014 were significantly more likely to receive a flu shot and have a preventive physical exam; uninsured patients were also significantly more likely to have had a physician exam and dental exam in 2014 than in 2009.[30] These findings are likely related to increased insurance coverage and funding for community health centers secondary to the ACA.

It should be noted that support and expansion of community health centers did not start with the Affordable Care Act. In fact, from 2000 to 2016, across the administrations of Presidents George W. Bush and Barack Obama, the number of health centers nearly doubled, and the number of patients served nearly tripled.[31] Access to comprehensive primary care to some of the most vulnerable Americans has been a policy objective shared by both Republican and Democratic administrations. That being said, community health center funding has not been completely immune from politics. The Community Health Center Fund, which provides 70% of all federal grant funding to health centers, expired at the end of September 2017 and was not renewed for over four months, largely because of partisan battles on other healthcare issues.[32] With reauthorization of the Fund only for two years, community health centers will once again be facing a funding cliff in 2019.

With healthcare reform debates raging in 2017, one healthcare expert, Dr. Carolyn McClanahan, offered an intriguing approach: place community health centers at the center of a reformed system and delink primary care from insurance. Dr. McClanahan is a trailblazer. While she started her career as a physician in private practice and emergency medicine, she subsequently made a career change into financial planning after finding fulfillment in helping people plan for their future.[33] She knew that the reason the United States spends more on healthcare than any other country and has little to show for it, from a population health perspective, is that we have a system focused on treating illness late instead of providing early care and prevention. Her expertise in financial planning made it clear to her that primary care shouldn't be considered an "insurable" event. Rather, it's the very care that all Americans need to remain healthy and reduce the likelihood of costly future illness and care.

Her plan would allow for universal primary care to be financed through the government's expansion of community health centers or through direct payment by consumers to primary care providers. Anyone could access care from community health centers, which would receive payments from the government based on patient population and not fee-for-service. Individuals would still purchase health insurance to cover care not provided by community health centers or other primary care providers (e.g., complex specialty care, hospitalization). Dr. McClanahan estimated that community health centers provide primary healthcare at a cost of $516 per patient per year ($763 per patient per year if mental healthcare, vision, dental services, and pharmacy services are provided). Expanding quality, cost-effective care through community health centers to millions more Americans in this country would be much cheaper, in her estimation, than the billions of dollars currently being spent by public and private payers for physician services and for acute care for ambulatory care–sensitive conditions.[34]

While it's clear that her plan would face opposition from certain industry stakeholders as well as face significant implementation challenges (as would any major healthcare restructuring), its premise has face validity. Shouldn't universal primary care be the foundation of our healthcare system? And why shouldn't we build on what is working in thousands of communities across the country for many of the most vulnerable Americans. These are points worthy of consideration when thinking about a prevention first–oriented healthcare system.

The notion of universal primary care may have another ally in the business community. According to the National Business Group on Health, 56% of large employers will have on-site or nearby primary care health centers by 2019.[35] As an example, Fiat Chrysler in Kokomo, Indiana, opened up a free clinic for its employees and their families after learning that 40% of its employees did not have a primary care doctor. By providing convenient primary care, the company hopes that employees will be able to prevent illness and better manage chronic conditions, thereby avoiding unnecessary emergency and inpatient care. The company estimates that it will recoup what it spent in about two years by improving employee health and reducing medical costs.[36]

Moving Primary Care Forward

Short of whole-scale healthcare sector transformation, there are additional ways to incrementally support primary care through both workforce and payment policy. With respect to workforce policy, what is lacking is a national strategy to address workforce needs to improve health in this country. The ACA established a National Health Care Workforce Commission charged with developing recommendations to Congress and the executive branch on national health workforce priorities, goals, and policies, but Congress never allocated the necessary funding for the Commission to be convened. While a National Center for Health Workforce Analysis has been funded and staffed to produce reports related to the healthcare workforce, these issues have not been effectively elevated to demand attention from policymakers.[37] Not being able to align workforce policy with prevention and value-based healthcare hinders our nation's ability to optimize health and reduce preventable healthcare costs.

Given the benefits of an increased supply of primary care physicians to population health, more must also be done to attract medical school students to primary care professions. A culture shift led by medical school administrations to ensure that students understand the importance of primary care to population health is necessary. Too often primary care is treated as a second-class field or discipline that lacks sophistication or rigor. This is in spite of the fact that its intellectual demands are significant due to the breadth of skills required for mastery. Another reason medical students are reluctant to enter primary care fields is the pay differential between primary care and specialty medicine. Taking into consideration the average debt of medical students today (approximately $190,000) and the expected future compensation of primary care physicians, one solution is to expand loan repayment to students agreeing to enter primary care. Other experts have called on the government to cover the cost of medical school for students who remain in primary care for at least ten years.[38] Short of a new national program such as this, medical schools are experimenting with innovative ways to increase exposure to primary care. At Duke University School of Medicine, students who are interested in primary care can enroll in the Primary Care Leadership Track, which provides more intensive coursework and clinical training focused on patient care continuity and clinical-community linkages. Students who enroll in the program sign a letter of intent to pursue primary care and receive a scholarship of $10,000 annually; if students don't proceed into primary care, the scholarship reverts to a loan.[39] At Texas Tech University Health Sciences Center, students with primary care interest can complete medical school in three years through the Family Medicine Accelerated Track. In addition to saving a year of tuition, students receive scholarship support and direct placement into in-state family medicine residency programs.[40] Beyond alleviating the financial burdens of medical school training, it will also be important to enhance training in team-based care to optimize primary care.

Crucial to attracting more medical students is payment reform. Value-based healthcare transformation should in theory elevate the role and importance of primary care; however, while payment bonuses from patient-centered medical homes, shared savings from participation in accountable care organizations, and risk-adjusted monthly payments for caring for complex patients are well intended, overall payment and salaries remain significantly lower than those of specialists. Congress passed the Medicare Access and CHIP Reauthorization Act of 2015 (MACRA), which will offer new opportunities to primary care providers, but it is unclear how much primary care will benefit overall.

In the interim, Congress has also looked at ways to enhance the fee-for-service model, specifically for primary care. The ACA included a 10% increase in Medicare payments to primary care providers for five years, ending in 2015. Researchers at the Center for Studying Health System Change simulated the impact of a permanent 10% increase in payments and estimated that this would result in decreases in inpatient and post-acute care such that overall Medicare costs would drop nearly 2%.[41] The Medicare Payment Advisory Commission (MedPAC) supported continuing the approach, believing that primary care must be better supported by the Medicare program.[42] Similarly, the ACA increased Medicaid's primary care reimbursement in 2013 and 2014 to make up the difference between a state's Medicaid fees and Medicare fees. This was important, as one analysis preceding implementation of the rate increase demonstrated that Medicaid fees averaged just 58% of Medicare fees for primary care services.[43] Other studies prior to implementation of the ACA suggested that high Medicaid physician payment rates are associated with increased rates of breast cancer screening and also possibly cervical cancer screening.[44]

In addition, the most methodologically sound study to date found that increases in Medicaid reimbursement rates were associated with increases in access to care, better self-reported health, and fewer school days missed among beneficiaries.[45] Although the Medicaid "fee bump" ended at the end of 2014, at least 19 states have fully or partially continued the increased payments using state funds.[46] This includes several states that did not expand Medicaid, demonstrating that there is bipartisan recognition of the importance of supporting access to primary care.

While workforce and payment policies may help to increase the numbers of primary care physicians, there is also a need to improve the distribution of practitioners. This is why programs such as the National Health Services Corps and the Teaching Health Center Graduate Medical Education program are so important. The former provides scholarships and loan repayment for healthcare providers to train in underserved areas, whereas the latter exposes trainees to outpatient settings similar to ones where many Americans receive primary care services. These are both important programs that should be strengthened and supported moving forward.

In addition, the growth of nonphysician primary care providers in the form of nurse practitioners as well as physician assistants have been a welcome development over the last two decades. It's estimated that one-third of the roughly 326,000 practicing primary care providers in this country are nurse practitioners or physician assistants.[47] While scope-of-practice issues often place these practitioners at odds with the physician community, the overarching imperative to ensure there are no primary care "deserts" in the nation should compel states to reevaluate scope-of-practice laws. While nonphysician primary care providers will not be able to provide all the care rendered by primary care physicians, studies do show that, on measures such as the delivery of recommended preventive services, they do just as well.

Finally, one of the most promising interventions to increase the role of primary care may be the use of a spending target. No one knows this better than Chris Koller, president of the Milbank Memorial Fund. He previously served as the health insurance commissioner in Rhode Island from 2005 to 2013. During his tenure, he required all commercial plans to increase spending on primary care by 1% of total spending per year over a five-year period (baseline: 5.8% in 2008). Between 2009 and 2014, primary care spending in Rhode Island grew from $47 million to $74 million, and per capita spending by commercial health insurers grew more slowly than in any other New England state. Rhode Island was also the only state in the region to increase its supply of primary care providers per capita over this time period.[48] The state now requires commercial insurers to spend at least 10.5% of their dollars on primary care.[49] For comparison, the national average for primary care spending by an insurance company is between 6% and 8% of its total medical expenditures.[50]

Following Rhode Island's example, Oregon passed a similar law in 2017 requiring insurers in the state to invest a minimum of 12% of their total medical expenditures in primary care by the year 2023 (baseline: 10.2% in 2015). Oregon's law includes not just commercial insurers but also its Medicaid-coordinated care organizations, and health plans serving public employees.[51] Delaware also recently passed a law promoting the use of primary care through provider payment reform, and policymakers have recommended that 12% of total healthcare spending should be directed toward primary care.[52]

While all of these primary care spending targets seem low, the fact that they are lower in the current status quo is even more incredible, given the well-known desirable impacts of primary care. As a first step, all public and private payers should begin to measure their primary care spending. On this point, Koller and his Milbank colleagues have been instrumental in providing recommendations on how to standardize the definition and measurement of primary care spending.[53] More research will be needed to determine what the "ideal" level of primary care spending should be to maximize health outcomes and reduce preventable health costs. Utilized effectively (increased spending should focus on expanding effective models such as PCMHs and community health centers), this policy intervention has the potential to reorient the healthcare system toward primary care.

Though primary care's importance to the delivery of clinical preventive services is significant, its ability to connect patients to community preventive services may be even more important. After all, patients are only patients a small fraction of the time. They otherwise spend the majority of time in their homes and communities. Thus, clinical linkages with community-based organizations and services may help reinforce and support the care plan. Team-based care, specifically utilizing case managers, care coordinators, and social workers, increases the ability of primary care providers to connect patients to community services. A newer discipline includes community health workers, who apply their unique understanding of the communities they serve to carry out a variety of health promotion activities. In the next chapter, we will explore clinical-community linkages and how reinforcing clinical care plans in the community setting can optimize patient health outcomes.

Where Should Healthcare Look outside the Walls of the Clinical Setting?

THE SOUTH SIDE of Chicago has many unhealthy neighborhoods. A 2011 study from the Northwestern University Feinberg School of Medicine in collaboration with the Chicago Department of Public Health tracked citywide healthy resources and assets such as parks, easy access to high-quality medical care, safe places to exercise, and stores that sell affordable healthy food such as fresh fruits and vegetables. It found that the south and southwest sides of Chicago had limited access to these resources. Consequently, they suffered the most in terms of residents' health.[1]

But to Dr. Stacy Lindau, a professor of obstetrics and gynecology at the University of Chicago on the South Side, that didn't sit well. She knew that South Side neighborhoods have a lot to offer, but locating these assets wasn't always easy. So, in 2012, she received an award from the Centers for Medicare and Medicaid Services's Innovation Center to "develop a real-time automated system that links patients with up-to-date information about community-based services and resources that can help them stay healthy and manage their conditions."[2] The program, called CommunityRx, creates a customized referral list, called a HealtheRx, for community services based on an individual's health and needs as documented in their electronic health record. Patients receive a HealtheRx at various clinical sites such as community health centers. They are then connected to a community health information specialist, a type of community health worker, who can help with navigating to community resources. One of the most innovative aspects of this program is the method used to identify community-based health resources. The Urban Health Initiative at the University of Chicago a decade ago created a MAPSCorps (Meaningful, Active, Productive Science in Service to Community), a STEM-education (science, technology, engineering, and math) and youth employment program that trains local high school students to map businesses and organizations on the South Side of Chicago. Studies have shown that the data collected by MAPSCorps are 20% to 40% more accurate than widely used data sources.[3]

In 2013, I had the opportunity to visit the Komed Holman Health Center in Chicago, one site that has implemented CommunityRx. I found it encouraging that a HealtheRx is created within the workflow of the office visit; in fact, the electronic health record automatically combines the clinical summary and CommunityRx resource list into a single document. This was key to gaining provider buy-in and increasing provider compliance.[4] Between 2012 and 2014, the program generated 253,479 personalized HealtheRx prescriptions for more than 113,000 participants. It also generated data in Chicago on more than 16,000 businesses and organizations that impact health. Eighty-three percent of the recipients found the HealtheRx very useful, and 19% went to a place they learned about from the HealtheRx.[5] While the effort did not specifically track improvements in outcomes and reductions in preventable healthcare costs, it has clearly served as a proof of concept.

Clinical-Community Linkages

Why are clinical-community linkages important? Most patients only see a healthcare provider once every few months. If healthy behaviors are not reinforced or social service needs not supported between clinic visits, it's very difficult to change the underlying risk factors that lead to chronic diseases and poor health. CommunityRx isn't the first program to attempt to link the clinical setting with community programs. In fact, the Agency for

Healthcare Research and Quality (AHRQ) for the last decade has tracked innovative clinical-community partnerships and pilot projects. For example, one program tested in 15 practices in three Michigan communities, utilized a community health educator referral liaison (CHERL) to provide health behavior-change counseling and referral to patients needing improvement with unhealthy behaviors (e.g., tobacco use, unhealthy diet, physical inactivity, and risky alcohol use). A randomized controlled study demonstrated that patients supported with a CHERL reported improvements at six months in BMI, dietary patterns, alcohol use, tobacco use, health status, and days of limited activity in the past month.[6] Another program, similar to CommunityRx and led by Virginia Commonwealth University, used an electronic linkage system (eLinkS) to prompt clinicians at the point of care to offer counseling to appropriate patients regarding diet, exercise, smoking, and alcohol consumption. Once a treatment plan is created, the system electronically sends referrals to the appropriate community-based counseling organizations, which then proactively contact patients to arrange services. Through increases in referrals for counseling services, program outcomes have been shown to include both weight loss and enhanced quit rates among smokers.[7]

In spite of these promising examples, clinical-community linked programs have their challenges. They take significant time and effort to integrate the linkage process in the clinical workflow and also to develop relationships with community programs. Beyond this is the question of outcomes. Unfortunately, a major literature review and environmental scan by RTI International researchers in 2012 did not find conclusive evidence that all linked interventions are effective. Specifically, of 49 interventions, many lacked conducting evaluations rigorous enough to measure changes in intermediate or long-term health outcomes. To that end, the authors recommended better research designs and the development of metrics to measure successful linkages.[8] AHRQ has taken a leadership role in this regard by creating a Clinical Community Relationships Measures Atlas and Evaluation Roadmap for researchers. These tools are providing analytic and methodological recommendations for researchers to strengthen the assessment of these relationships.[9]

It is important to note that there are several different models of clinical-community linkages. Some projects such as CommunityRx utilize the clinical setting to provide referrals to community services. Clinicians referring patients to quitline services is another example of this model, which has substantial potential for impact if implemented widely.

Another model involves actually positioning clinical personnel in community settings. For example, a recent study in the *New England Journal of Medicine* focused on uncontrolled hypertension in African American males and leveraged their barbershops to deliver a clinical intervention. Individuals in the intervention group interacted with on-site pharmacists, who prescribed antihypertensive medications, as opposed to the control group, which merely received health education on lifestyle modification from barbers. At six months, mean blood pressure fell significantly more in the intervention group compared to the control group, leading 63.6% of participants in the intervention group to have a blood pressure of 130/80 mm HG or less versus 11.7% of participants in the control group.[10] More broadly, community-based blood pressure screening programs that connect individuals with hypertension to clinical care are urgently needed, given that over 14 million Americans are unaware that they have hypertension.[11]

Diabetes Prevention Program

Yet another clinical-community linkage model attempts to replicate a clinical intervention in the community setting and then encourages clinical providers to refer patients to the program. Perhaps the best example of this with demonstrable improvements in outcomes and reductions in costs, and which exemplifies the importance of clinical-community linkages, is the Diabetes Prevention Program (DPP). The genesis of the program stems from a National Institutes of Health–funded study, which found that lifestyle changes resulting in modest weight loss significantly reduced the development of type II diabetes in people at high risk for the disease, a condition called prediabetes. Specifically, participants in a lifestyle group who received intensive individual counseling on diet, exercise, and behavior modification reduced their risk of developing diabetes by 58%.[12] Importantly, more recent research has found that even after 10 years, people who completed a diabetes prevention lifestyle change program were one-third less likely to develop type II diabetes.[13]

While outcomes improved in the study, many experts questioned the scalability of the intervention. For one, healthcare settings have a limited capacity to offer intensive behavioral interventions. Second, the lifestyle intervention for diabetes prevention costs approximately $1,400 per person in its first year and approximately $700 per person per year thereafter—not exactly inexpensive.[14] So, researchers at Indiana University sought to understand the feasibility of offering such an intervention in a community setting. They found a perfect partner in the YMCA, an organization with 2,700 facilities serving 10,000 communities in every state of the country. In addition, 58% of YMCAs are in communities where household income is below the national average, which is important because of the link between socioeconomic disparities and the prevalence of diabetes.[15] Researchers evaluated the delivery of a group-based DPP lifestyle intervention in two YMCA facilities, and in a randomized trial found that after six months, body weight decreased by 6.0% in intervention participants. (In the original clinical trial, 5% of weight loss was associated with the 58% reduction in diabetes.)[16] Subsequent community studies replicated these findings and laid the groundwork for wide-scale dissemination of the program.[17]

From this, the CDC created the National Diabetes Prevention Program as a public-private partnership to prevent and delay type II diabetes. The National DPP included a recognition program for community-based organizations to ensure quality and adherence to the original evidence-based curriculum. It also aimed to train community organizations that can run the lifestyle change program effectively, increase referrals to and participation in CDC-recognized lifestyle change programs, and increase coverage by employers and public and private insurers.[18] Today, hundreds of CDC-recognized organizations across the country are offering the DPP in their communities.

One of the interesting results in the original NIH study was that the elderly seemed to do even better than the overall population (participants aged 60 and older reduced their risk of diabetes by 71%).[19] This eventually piqued the interest of the CMS; perhaps one reason was that Medicare spends $42 billion more on beneficiaries with diabetes than it would have spent if those beneficiaries did not have diabetes.[20] In 2011, while advising the CMS's Innovation Center (CMMI) on opportunities to further engage in prevention, I identified increasing access to the DPP for Medicare beneficiaries with prediabetes as a top opportunity. In 2012, the CMMI awarded the National Council of YMCAs of the USA (Y-USA) an award to test a model for the primary prevention of type II diabetes in Medicare beneficiaries.

Within two years, an independent evaluation demonstrated an improved quality of care with weight loss among beneficiaries, and the CMS's chief actuary certified that, based on savings projections, expansion of the Diabetes Prevention Program would not result in an increase in Medicare spending. When compared with similar beneficiaries not in the program, Medicare estimated savings of $2,650 for each enrollee in the program over a 15-month period, more than enough to cover the cost of the program. These savings accrued from fewer hospital admissions and emergency department visits.[21] The actuarial certification allowed Medicare to expand the Diabetes Prevention Program to all eligible beneficiaries starting in 2018, with payments going directly to community-based organizations recognized by the CDC's National Diabetes Prevention Program. This is one of the first times that the CMS is paying a nonclinical provider, a recognition that community-based services are important in achieving the public payer's vision of success.

Today, community-based organizations across the country are helping thousands of Americans to reduce their risk for developing type II diabetes. The need is tremendous, as it's estimated that 84.1 million adults have prediabetes, and of this population, unfortunately, nine out of ten people with prediabetes don't know they have it.[22] Thus, building capacity to make community programs available will be critical over the next decade. To this end, digital DPP may play an increasingly larger role, as the CDC has recently officially recognized several on-line programs. Payment from the healthcare sector for in-person and online programs should help build capacity and sustainability. Although clinical referrals are not a require-ment for participating in a community-based DPP program, where there are existing community-based programs, clinicians can play an important role by referring patients to them.

Community-Based Prevention Programs

While DPP has garnered significant attention in recent years in health policy circles, it is hardly the only evidence-based community prevention program. Indeed, there are numerous programs for individuals across the lifespan that clinicians could provide referrals to in order to keep Ameri-cans healthy.

One program with nearly 25 years of evidence and first developed in the 1990s at Stanford University is the Chronic Disease Self-Management Program (CDSMP). In contrast to disease-specific programs, the CDSMP was developed to increase an individual's ability to confidently manage symptoms, irrespective of the underlying chronic disease. Group classes are led by laypersons and focus on creating individual action plans to in-crease confidence for problem solving. The initial randomized controlled clinical trial and subsequent studies showed reductions in common symp-toms (e.g., pain, depression, fatigue) and in healthcare utilization (e.g., hospitalizations, emergency department use).[23]

In the early 2000s this led HHS agencies, such as the CDC and the Administration on Aging (AoA), to begin supporting the CDSMP nation-wide at community-based organizations. In 2009, as part of the Ameri-can Recovery and Reinvestment Act, we had the opportunity at HHS to invest $30 million in grants to expand the CDSMP to tens of thousands of Americans. A national study of this effort resulted in analyses show-ing improvements in health and healthcare outcome measures as well as reductions in emergency department visits and hospitalizations, equat-ing to potential net savings of $364 per participant and a national savings of $3.3 billion, if 5% of adults with one or more chronic conditions were reached.[24, 25]

In 2013, the CMS issued a report to Congress on evaluating community-based wellness and prevention programs such as the CDSMP for their effects on Medicare beneficiaries. While retrospective analyses at the time suggested that the CDSMP demonstrated reductions in unplanned hospital utilization and costs,[26] a subsequent 2018 prospective analysis of various chronic disease management programs did not demonstrate a reduction in healthcare utilization or expenditures. The authors cautioned that this may have been due to small sample sizes and a limited follow-up period, and thus further studies would be needed.[27]

If the CMS wanted to expand the CDSMP to eligible beneficiaries, it would run into some thorny issues. The DPP was expanded based on its being tested under the authorities of the CMMI. The authorities, granted in the Affordable Care Act, allow the secretary to expand Innovation Center programs that either reduce spending without reducing the quality of care, or improve the quality of care without increasing spending, as certified by the CMS and its chief actuary. Although the CMS commissioned a prospective study on a range of chronic disease management programs, it would likely need to test the CDSMP specifically on a larger scale under the authorities of the Innovation Center to see if it meets the criteria for expansion as laid out in the ACA. If the CMS does not formally test the model, the only other recourse for expansion of the CDSMP would be through an act of Congress. And getting Congress to do this would require considerable time, energy, and effort.

This entire discussion of increasing access to evidence-based community prevention programs is somewhat surreal. Why should it be so difficult to provide coverage and payment for interventions just because they occur outside the clinical setting and by nonclinical staff? If the CDSMP were a pill, this would not be a conversation. Once it was approved by the FDA for safety and efficacy, the CMS would promptly make a coverage and payment determination. And the cost of the intervention, or pill in this hypothetical case, would not be a criterion for coverage. In sum, while clinical interventions (e.g., drugs, devices) are not required to prove that they save healthcare dollars or are budget neutral, community prevention programs must seemingly meet this higher standard. Even with considerable evidence indicating that community prevention programs are effective, these programs are often not financed by payers and are poorly funded through grants. Thus, these programs are not widely available to those who could benefit from them.

In addition to the CDSMP, there are several other evidence-based community prevention programs that have demonstrated health benefits with potential cost savings.[28] For example, physical activity programs include Enhance Fitness, a program focused on sedentary older adults wishing to maintain and improve their physical functioning and to stay socially connected. A certified fitness instructor leads regular group physical activity sessions centered around stretching and flexibility, low impact aerobics, strength training, and balance. The Arthritis Foundation's Exercise Program and Tai Chi Program similarly are programs that improve functional ability, movement, and strength in individuals with arthritis and related musculoskeletal conditions.[29]

But perhaps the most promising evidence-based community prevention programs focus on falls prevention. To explain why this is requires taking a step back to understand the consequences of falls in the older adult population. Each year, millions of Americans over the age of 65, more than one out of four, experience a fall, resulting in 3 million emergency department visits and 800,000 hospitalizations. Most of the injuries occur from broken bones, such as hip fractures, and head injuries, such as traumatic brain injuries.[30] All told, 27,000 adults die from falls each year, making it the leading cause of injury-related death in older adults. Recent data also suggest that falls cost the Medicare program over $31 billion annually (as a comparison, cancer costs Medicare $36 billion annually)![31] In spite of this, there are no comprehensive programs or policies currently in place across the federal government to tackle this public health challenge.

The good news is that most falls are preventable through a combination of clinical and community-based interventions. Clinically, the CDC's STEADI (Stopping Elderly Accidents, Deaths, and Injuries) Initiative has established guidelines for healthcare providers who treat older adults at risk of falling, as well as those who have fallen in the past. The CDC estimates that for every 5,000 healthcare providers who adopt the STEADI system, over a five-year period, six million more patients could be screened for falls risk; one million falls could be prevented; and $3.5 billion in medical costs could be saved.[32]

Complementing this clinical intervention are a series of important home and community-based interventions. Home modifications, for example, are critical to reduce falls. Most homes weren't designed for older residents. In fact, only 57% of existing homes have more than one universal design element like no-step entries, single-floor living, switches and outlets reachable at any height, extrawide hallways and doors, and lever-style door and faucet handles.[33] Other features such as grab bars are generally recommended by experts to reduce falls. In 2016, the first randomized controlled trial examining the benefits of home modifications for reducing fall injury costs was published. Compared to unmodified homes, modified homes showed a reduction in the costs of home fall injuries by 33%. Societal benefits of injuries prevented were estimated to be at least six times the costs of the intervention. The cost-benefit ratio was found to be at least double for older people and increased by 60% for those with a prior history of fall injuries.[34]

In addition, evidence-based community falls prevention programs have the potential to be an important complement to clinical interventions. One program specifically, A Matter of Balance, focuses on reducing fall risk and fear of falling and improving falls self-management. The target audience is adults over the age of 60, who are led by volunteer lay leaders in a structured group intervention that includes problem-solving, skill building, and exercise training over several weeks.[35] One analysis of this program showed that for every 20 program participants, one unplanned admission for a fall was prevented and overall, participation was associated with a $938 decrease in total medical costs per year.[36]

One important consideration to note for successful clinical-community linkages is the fidelity, or ability of a community-based organization to implement evidence-based programs. This is vital for healthcare providers to have confidence in linking and referring patients to community programs; it's also vital for public and private insurers seeking to maximize the value of their investments. Over the last few years, the US Administration for Community Living has supported a Business Acumen Learning

Collaborative, where community-based organizations receive targeted technical assistance in partnering with payers and clinical entities. They engage in peer-to-peer learning in areas such as organizational culture change, business planning, marketing, contracting, and pricing services. In addition, the SCAN Foundation in California has identified core competencies for community-based organizations to promote their services and make a clear business case, deliver them effectively and profitably, and evaluate them.[37] While developing such skills is important to expand access, the very need to "sell" these programs on a payer-by-payer basis suggests that the goal of nationwide access could be a long time in coming.

The value of community prevention programs is not limited to the older population. A prime example is home-visiting programs, interventions that give pregnant women and families resources and skills to raise healthy and ready-to-learn children. Specifically, these programs support preventive health and prenatal practices as well as educate parents on infant care, child development, and positive parenting techniques.[38] Studies have shown that planned home visits by nurses result in reductions in preterm births, infant deaths, child abuse, and injury. In addition, child development measures such as language development, and over the long term, cognitive and educational outcomes also improve.[39] What's more is that researchers have found that high-fidelity home-visiting programs for high-risk families have up to a $5.70 return for every tax dollar spent, from reduced spending for healthcare and welfare services.[40] From a clinical-community linkage perspective, clinicians have two major roles in home-visiting programs—the first as a referral source of at-risk patients and families, and second as maintaining awareness of and communications with the home visiting team.

Many home-visiting programs, such as the Nurse-Family Partnership and the Home Instruction for Parents of Preschool Youngsters, are now being supported through a governmental program called the Maternal, Infant, and Early Childhood Home Visiting (MIECHV) program, administered by the Health Resources and Services Administration. In fiscal year 2017, the MIECHV program served over 156,000 parents and children in all 50 states.[41] The success of the program has been touted by both Republicans and Democrats as an example of a program that improves health and upward mobility while potentially reducing long-term government spending on programs such as Medicaid, welfare, and food stamps.[42] However, similar to other community-based prevention programs discussed in this chapter, the MIECHV program only reaches a small proportion of families who could benefit in this country, because it is only marginally financed by the healthcare system. Particularly with respect to Medicaid, which pays for roughly half of all births in the United States, few states have scaled this program to match the population's need. Both liberal and conservative health policy experts have raised the idea of the federal government, in conjunction with the private sector, incentivizing states through up-front resources to set up the program. Over time, as savings start to accrue, states could repay the government. The end result would be savings for federal and state budgets with improved early childhood health and development.[43]

The Road Forward

Moving forward, several steps are required for community prevention programs to optimally reinforce clinical care plans. First, clinicians must become more aware of the benefits of these programs and refer appropriate patients where possible. Patients also need to become aware of and increase demand for community-based prevention programs. Second, these programs need funding in order to expand their reach. Payers should become familiar with the evidence base behind these programs. While the jury is still out on whether some of these programs are cost-saving, there is less ambiguity on the benefits of most of these programs to prevent poor health outcomes.

Most importantly, a pathway needs to be developed to allow for community-based prevention programs to be deemed safe, evidence-based, and worthy of payment by Medicare and other healthcare payers. As previously mentioned, drugs, devices, and other medical interventions undergo an established process to gain approval by the FDA for their safety and efficacy; in most cases, this then triggers coverage determinations by

Medicare based on the standard of the intervention being reasonable and necessary. A similar pathway does not exist for community prevention interventions led by nonclinical personnel. The aforementioned DPP has only recently been covered by Medicare through the special authority of the CMMI. No other community-based program is currently slated for Medicare coverage (or for testing by the CMMI) even though millions of Americans stand to benefit from programs focused on areas such as falls prevention, physical activity promotion, and chronic disease self-management. Congress should intervene and create a new regulatory role for an agency such as the CDC or the Administration on Aging to certify community-based programs for safety and efficacy, akin to the FDA's approval process. Both of these agencies have significant expertise in identifying community-based prevention programs. Their certification should trigger a coverage decision by the CMS so that beneficiaries of public insurance programs have increasing access to evidence-based programs in their communities. Since most commercial insurers follow or align with Medicare coverage determinations, this would help to scale evidence-based programs. It is true that commercial insurers sometimes hesitate to invest in prevention programs because they don't believe they will reap the benefits, given consumer churn; however, the more insurers that provide coverage, the more likely they will be able to benefit collectively from a healthier population.

In addition to fee-for-service Medicare, opportunities to scale community-based prevention programs exist for Medicare Advantage plans, accountable care organizations, and state Medicaid programs. Some Medicare Advantage plans have already made strides in this area by expanding access to physical activity programs such as the SilverSneakers fitness program. These entities have opportunities to match their members with the most appropriate programs, and the CMS should think of ways to further incentivize this to occur. State Medicaid programs can now pay for community programs based on a regulatory change that occurred in 2014 allowing states to pay for evidence-based interventions by nonlicensed healthcare professionals.[44] The CMS should develop model state plan amendment templates and convene state learning collaboratives to support states in their efforts. The CMS could also incentivize Medicaid programs to offer appropriate programs to their members by increasing the federal medical assistance percentage (FMAP) for states that do so. Continued research findings demonstrating the benefits of community-based prevention programs will only help to positively influence clinicians and payers.

Clinical-community linkages can play an even larger role in support of state-based health reform efforts. The best example of this occurred in Vermont, which launched its Blueprint for Health in 2003 under the leadership of Governor Jim Douglas. The initiative is based on the premise of primary care practices supported by community health teams and connected through an integrated information technology infrastructure. Each team is staffed by a multidisciplinary group of healthcare professionals, including a registered nurse and behavioral health counselor, serving a defined set of practices and population. The teams offer not only individual care coordination, health and wellness coaching, and behavioral health counseling but also connect patients to social and economic support services in the community. Similar to other highly effective programs, there is bidirectional communication and connectivity, as referrals can start either in the clinical or community setting. The costs of these teams are borne by public and private insurers.[45] Evaluations over the last several years have demonstrated increased preventive services, fewer emergency department and inpatient visits, improved access, and cost savings.[46] A provision in the ACA required the secretary of HHS to implement a grant program for states to establish similar community health teams. Unfortunately, funds were never appropriated to scale this model. States such as North Carolina and Montana have nevertheless continued to implement this concept as part of their state reform efforts.[47, 48] More leadership from states in this regard would be welcome.

As clinical-community linkages and programs have expanded, there has been an increasing recognition that the requirement for patients to remain in a state of good health requires more than community supports to reinforce clinical care plans or influence lifestyle behaviors. The social determinants of health are a reminder that socioeconomic status and the physical environment have a substantial impact on health and premature mortality. More and more clinical-community linkages are now focused on areas such as housing, transportation, nutrition, and job training. Indeed, forward-looking healthcare entities are investing in these areas, since they recognize that, unless the basic necessities of life are attended to by vulnerable Americans, their ability to remain in optimal health will be limited. Many of these vanguard healthcare entities are also seeing return on investments from a focus on upstream social determinants. In the next chapter, we will look further upstream and examine case studies and opportunities for healthcare to improve people's overall lives in a way that impacts their underlying health status.

Social Determinants and Healthcare

Is It Time to Go Upstream?

H EALTH INSURERS are in the business of managing risk, providing financial security for consumers, and paying for healthcare services. But in 2015, Humana, one of the nation's largest health insurers, announced an additional goal: to improve the health of communities it serves by 20% by 2020.[1] The rationale, the pursuit of healthcare needs to focus on health, not just care.

And so, the company's senior leadership team set out to find a way to measure health improvement and came upon a health-related quality of life measure developed and validated by the CDC called Healthy Days. A central part of this measure assesses the number of days during the past 30 when an individual's physical health and mental health were not good. Since the measure has been associated with chronic health conditions and healthcare utilization,[2] Humana began to track the measure for its employees and also in selected communities across the country. These "Bold Goal" communities include Louisville, New Orleans, Baton Rouge, Tampa Bay, Broward County, Florida, Knoxville, and San Antonio—largely Southern cities, many experiencing significant health disparities. In each of these communities, Humana convened community nonprofit, government, physician, and business stakeholders to identify and implement clinical and community prevention interventions that help improve health outcomes. In 2016, Humana's first year of survey results showed a 2% decrease in Unhealthy Days for members across the nation and a 3% decrease across its Bold Goal communities.[3, 4] Beyond health improvement, these findings matter from a healthcare cost perspective as well. Evaluations have shown that one Unhealthy Day a month is associated with a $15.64 increase in monthly medical costs and an increase of 10.4 hospital admissions per thousand people.[5]

But, Humana researchers didn't stop there. They knew about the social determinants of health and hypothesized that these were strongly connected to the Healthy Days measure. If they could identify which determinants had the strongest link, communities could focus on these areas. After analyzing 31 different factors, two social determinants stood out to them near the top of the list: inadequate social/emotional support and food insecurity.[6] Evidence confirms that these conditions are associated with a range of chronic conditions. Specifically, social isolation, which is an objective measure of a lack of social contacts, increases the likelihood of depression, dementia, and diabetes.[7] Studies have shown that social isolation is associated with a 29% increased risk for mortality and a 59% increased risk for functional declines in activities of daily living.[8] Food insecurity leads to an increased likelihood of heart failure, high blood pressure, diabetes, asthma, and depression. It's estimated that food insecurity impacts 14% of all Americans and accounts for nearly $125 billion in direct health-related costs.[9]

Equipped with this new information, Humana refined its Bold Goal strategy and guided its communities to concentrate on these areas. As an example, San Antonio's collaborative launched a telepsychiatry pilot in primary care physician offices to increase access to behavioral health services for individuals in a remote location. A Path to Wellness program, formed in partnership with H-E-B grocery, YMCA of Greater San Antonio, and Partners in Primary Care, now addresses diabetes, nutrition, and health literacy. And the San Antonio Parks and Recreation Department created a rewards-based initiative to improve well-being by incentivizing residents to use the many parks and walks throughout the city. San Antonio witnessed the most dramatic improvement in Healthy Days in 2016, a 9% decrease in Unhealthy Days.[10]

More and more, healthcare entities are embracing the upstream factors central to disease prevention and health promotion. The experience of other developed countries tells us that higher levels of social spending are associated with better health outcomes.[11] However, the comparatively smaller investment in social spending in the United States compared to healthcare spending does not appear to be changing anytime soon. While we certainly need greater national investment in social services and upstream determinants of health, it's important that the significantly resourced healthcare sector also take initiative. A focus on the trailblazers —why they've pursued social determinants of health such as housing, nutrition, and transportation and to what degree of success—helps to understand how this trend can optimize the nation's health.

Housing

Of all the social determinants of health, none may be more significant than housing, or the lack thereof. After all, each one of us spends as much or more time in the home setting than anywhere else. Significant evidence exists that housing affordability, neighborhood conditions, and conditions within the home are all important social determinants of health.[12] The negative health impacts of unaffordable housing are particularly pronounced in children; those who are homeless or unstably housed have higher rates of mental health problems and often lack basic access to primary pediatric care. Supportive housing, which combines affordable-housing assistance with wraparound services to assist people experiencing homelessness, joblessness, disability, or health problems, has been shown to help a number of vulnerable populations, including homeless adults with mental illness and individuals with HIV/AIDS.[13] More recently, a study of elderly Medicare beneficiaries living in affordable housing with supportive services found that these individuals had lower rates of hospitalization and shorter lengths-of-stay than people in a comparison group.[14] Beyond the benefit of safe and affordable housing, the home can also serve as a vital platform for the delivery of healthcare and other critical services.

In spite of these insights, there are myriad challenges for housing in this country. First, the National Low-Income Housing Coalition estimates that there is a shortage of 7.4 million affordable and available rental units for the nation's "extremely low-income" renter households—at or below poverty or 30% of area median income (AMI). In addition, housing cost burdens have risen significantly for renters since 2008, with 11.1 million people experiencing severe cost burdens, meaning they spend more than 50% of their income on housing.[15] Second, as discussed in chapter 3, most homes in the United States have not been constructed with an aging population in mind. Only 1% of homes today have five features necessary for universal design (no-step entries, single-floor living, accessible electrical controls and switches, extrawide doorways and halls, and lever-style door and faucet handles),[16] yet over 38% of Americans 65 and older report living with a disability.[17] And third, homes in this country, particularly those that are older, are not uniformly healthy, with hazards such as lead, radon, carbon monoxide, and asthma irritants commonplace, particularly in low-income regions.

Recognizing the importance of housing to health, healthcare entities are taking matters into their own hands to meet the challenges of housing affordability. As the largest private health insurance company in the country, UnitedHealthcare has invested over $400 million in 80 affordable housing communities in 18 states since 2011. The insurer has done this by providing equity funding in partnerships with other housing developers through the use of the low-income housing tax credit (LIHTC). This has resulted in the creation of more than 4,500 new homes for low-income individuals and families, including seniors, veterans, people living with disabilities, and people struggling with homelessness.[18] What led United-Healthcare to take these steps? Almost a decade ago, UnitedHealthcare's leadership recognized that member adherence to medications and care plans were predicated upon basic necessities being met for vulnerable low-income Americans. In addition, a significant percentage of United-Healthcare's Medicaid and dually eligible members required home and community-based services (HCBS) to meet their long-term services and supports (LTSS) needs. Further, the Affordable Care Act's expansion of Medicaid created even more of an incentive to connect new members to housing over the last several years.[19]

Beyond supporting the development of affordable housing, United-Healthcare has also looked to connect its "superutilizers" with both health and housing services. One example of this is its partnership in Austin, Texas, with the Ending Community Homeless Coalition (ECHO), a non-profit that tracks individuals who have received US Department of Housing and Urban Development–funded homeless services. The two organizations matched names of individuals receiving services from both organizations and UnitedHealthcare narrowed the list to focus on people who were the most clinically at risk and with the highest rates of healthcare use. They were then able to work collaboratively to connect individuals to a usual source of healthcare and secure housing for them.[20]

UnitedHealthcare is not the only payer to recognize that investments in housing can translate into better health outcomes. As another example, over the last several years, Mercy Maricopa, a Medicaid-managed care plan in Arizona administered by Aetna, expanded housing, employment, court, and peer support services for individuals with serious mental illness (SMI) to see if addressing various social determinants of health could reduce cost and improve quality of care. Research conducted between 2014 and 2017 found that members enrolled in the supportive housing intervention experienced decreases in total cost of care of 24% after enrolling in the program. This decrease in cost was maintained when compared to a matched cohort. These members also had fewer psychiatric hospitalizations than they had before enrolling in the program.[21] Further research with a larger sample and conducted over a longer time period would provide valuable information on the effectiveness of a permanent supportive housing subsidy and services to the SMI population on health outcomes and cost.

Private sector innovation and the burgeoning evidence of housing's impact on health led the federal Center for Medicaid and CHIP Services at the Centers for Medicare and Medicaid Services to issue an informational bulletin in 2015 laying out the range of opportunities through which states could be reimbursed for providing housing-related activities and services. While the federal Medicaid program does not allow for capital funding for supportive housing nor pay for room or board, reimbursable activities include housing-transition services and individual housing and tenancy-sustaining services. In addition, through home- and community-based waivers, states may cover environmental modifications to install necessary accommodations for accessibility.[22] The Bipartisan Policy Center's Senior Health and Housing Task Force recommended that Medicaid track how states are utilizing these opportunities and also seek to quantify the impact of these services on beneficiary outcomes and health costs.[23]

Some states are going beyond these services and engaging in expanding the supply of affordable housing. For example, New York State is using its own share of Medicaid funding for housing in the form of both newly constructed supportive housing units and subsidies for use in existing units. Iowa has created a state-funded rental-subsidy program administered by the Iowa Finance Authority that specifically targets older adult Medicaid home- and community-based services recipients. These efforts will undoubtedly help inform policies of other state Medicaid programs with regard to coverage of housing-related services.[24]

Health insurers aren't the only entities that understand the connection between health and housing for optimal aging. Healthcare systems themselves see value in housing investments. As an example, Bon Secours Health System serves west Baltimore with an 88-bed acute care hospital. But what is noteworthy about the system is that it owns nearly eight times that number of affordable homes. As of 2014, Bon Secours owned 648 homes, with 530 designated for disabled seniors and 119 for families. Most of the homes have on-site service coordinators to link residents with services at the hospital and in the community. A key measure of success is to ensure that residents are able to successfully age in place so they have the support they need. Since most residents stay long-term, and most properties have long waiting lists, it is clear that Bon Secours is meeting a vital need for the population.[25]

Nutrition

Nutrition is another social determinant of health with enormous consequences, particularly given the obesity and diabetes epidemics in this country. Poor diet has emerged as a leading cause of death and disability in the United States. One recent study found that dietary factors were associated with nearly half of all deaths from heart disease, stroke, and type II diabetes—nearly 1,000 deaths each day in the United States.[26] Each of these conditions cost the healthcare system hundreds of billions of dollars each. Type II diabetes is a prime example of a consequence of the obesity epidemic. Public health researchers estimate that one in three children born in the United States after 2000 will develop diabetes;[27] annual costs for the management and treatment of diabetes are estimated to total about $327 billion in the United States.[28]

In addition to poor diet, food insecurity continues to be a reality for millions of Americans, as previously mentioned. This is why federal programs such as the Supplemental Nutrition Assistance Program (SNAP) and Meals on Wheels are so important. Serving approximately 40 million Americans each month, SNAP has reduced the percentage of American households that experience food insecurity by 12% to 19%, and SNAP participants are 20% to 50% less likely to report food insecurity than income-eligible nonparticipants. This has contributed to a variety of positive health outcomes, including improved cognitive, social, and emotional development in children, lower maternal depression, and lower rates of hospitalization and nursing home placements for individuals dually eligible for Medicare and Medicaid. The Bipartisan Policy Center's SNAP Task Force has further recommended improvements in the nutritional focus of the SNAP program through incentives for healthy foods and disincentives and restrictions of unhealthy food.[29] A recent microsimulation study of SNAP performed by researchers at Tufts University and the Harvard School of Public Health found that a combination of subsidies for fruits, vegetables, nuts, whole grains, fish, and plant-based oils and corresponding disincentives for sugar-sweetened beverages, junk food, and processed meats could yield a lifetime benefit of 940,000 fewer cardiovascular events, 147,000 fewer cases of diabetes, and nearly $42 billion in health-care cost-savings.[30]

With over 60% of Medicaid beneficiaries also SNAP participants, there is also an opportunity that, with more nutritious food choices through SNAP, one might see better health outcomes and lower preventable health-care costs in Medicaid. The Task Force thus also recommended that the Departments of Agriculture and Health and Human Services develop joint waiver authorities to encourage states to experiment with promising strategies for improving health and nutrition through SNAP and Medicaid.[31]

Meals on Wheels is another important program demonstrating the impact of food insecurity and nutrition on health and healthcare. Evidence from multiple studies exists that home-delivered meal programs improve diet quality and increase nutrient intakes.[32] In addition, a 2015 randomized-controlled trial conducted by researchers at Brown University demonstrated that individuals who received daily-delivered meals, compared to others who received frozen weekly-delivered meals or no meals, were more likely to exhibit improvements in mental health and feelings of isolation and loneliness in addition to reduction in the rate of falls.[33] The same researchers in another study found that if all states had increased by 1% the number of adults age 65 or older who received home-delivered meals, total annual savings to state Medicaid programs could have exceeded $109 million (savings would accrue from fewer older adults with long-term care needs requiring nursing home care).[34] Another more recent study looked at dually eligible adults to see if home delivery of either medically tailored meals or nontailored food reduces the use of healthcare services and medical spending. It found that, compared to nonparticipants, both groups had fewer emergency department visits and lower medical spending; the medically tailored meal group also had fewer inpatient admissions.[35]

The association between nutrition and patient health outcomes and healthcare costs has not been lost on hospitals and healthcare systems. One of the best examples is Geisinger Health System's Fresh Food Pharmacy. As a leading physician-led healthcare system situated in rural, central Pennsylvania, Geisinger is a vertically integrated system that provides both healthcare services and health insurance. This orientation provides the system an incentive to engage in delivery system reform efforts that might lead to a reduction in unnecessary costs. Located in the middle of coal country, a region with significant unemployment and poverty, Geisinger Health System sees a disproportionate number of food-insecure patients who have high rates of obesity and type II diabetes. Senior leadership recognized that local residents needed additional help with nutrition and maintaining healthy weight. So, in July 2016, Geisinger opened its first "farmacy" at one of its clinical sites of care in collaboration with the Central Pennsylvania Food Bank.[36] The pilot program focused on poorly controlled diabetic patients who screened positive for food insecurity. A multidisciplinary team establishes a nutritional counseling plan for each patient and provides enough healthy and nutritious food weekly to prepare meals twice a day for five days for the entire family. Patients also participate in diabetes self-management classes with support from pharmacists, registered dieticians, and health coaches.[37]

The results, per program leaders, have been pretty impressive. After a year in the program, participants have seen an average drop in the HbA1c levels of two points, from 9.6 before the program to 7.5. This matters because every one-point drop in HbA1c levels corresponds to a more than 20% decline in the chance of death or serious complications from diabetes, such as blindness and kidney failure, and an $8,000 reduction in annual healthcare costs.[38, 39] Specifically, with respect to return on investment, while program costs per year per patient are approximately $2,200, healthcare claims data show a drop in costs of two-thirds from average patient costs prior to the program of $8,000 to $12,000 per month. The program now serves more than 250 patients and family members and is looking to expand regionally.[40] Given the projected burden of diabetes in this country, the opportunities for scaling similar programs are substantial.

Malnutrition, more broadly, has also been a focus of healthcare providers, given that patients with malnutrition cost nearly twice as much as well-nourished patients. One accountable care organization, part of Advocate Health Care in Chicago, has started screening all patients at admission for malnutrition and providing high-risk patients oral nutritional supplementation; the ACO also provides these patients nutrition education and postdischarge nutritional support. Reportedly, within six months of launching these initiatives, the ACO reduced hospital readmissions and healthcare costs by $3,800 per patient, resulting in $4.8 million in total savings.[41]

Transportation

Just like housing and nutrition, transportation is another fundamentally important determinant to health. The ability to access healthcare services as well as access healthy foods, as previously discussed, is critical to optimal health. It is estimated that 3.6 million Americans have transportation problems that prevent them from getting to or from a doctor's appointment, and 25% of lower-income patients have missed or rescheduled appointments due to lack of transportation.[42] It's also estimated that the federal government spends more than $2.7 billion annually on nonemergency patient transportation, with national waiting times averaging 60 minutes.[43] These issues are particularly acute in geographically remote areas of the country, where there are often great distances between where residents live and where services are available. Indeed, this plays out in rural America each day for the 60 million Americans, 19% of the US population, who reside in 97% of the nation's land. While technological advances through telemedicine as well as retail clinics are important consumer-centric opportunities that should meaningfully increase access to care, they will not in and of themselves substitute for the need for transportation.

Entering this space over the last couple of years have been entrepreneurial on-demand transportation companies such as Uber and Lyft. Recently, Uber launched Uber Health to help patients and healthcare providers book rides for future outpatient appointments, and Lyft announced a partnership with Allscripts, an electronic health record vendor, to do the same and within the workflow of a provider's practice.[44] The latter's announcement is part of its overall goals of reducing care gaps caused by transportation barriers by 50% within the next two years.[45] Though non-emergency medical transportation service companies have previously existed, healthcare entities see the newer generation of partners as being more reliable, faster, and importantly, less expensive. They also see an opportunity to reduce preventable healthcare costs by ensuring that patients follow up and are compliant with care plans and medications. Large health systems such as Ascension and private health insurers such as Cigna have all inked recent deals with on-demand transportation companies.[46] In the Detroit area, the Ford Motor Company has made deals with most of the major tertiary medical centers, offering bedside-to-bedside transportation and wheelchair accessibility with a 97% on-time pickup rate.[47]

Early results from some of these partnerships are intriguing. One Anthem managed care subsidiary, CareMore Health Plan, piloted a collaboration with Lyft and found that patient waiting times dropped by 30% (12.5 minutes to 8.7 minutes) and per-ride costs by 32.4% ($31.54 to $21.32).[48] Another recent study, however, focusing on Medicaid beneficiaries in west Philadelphia demonstrated a low uptake of ridesharing, which did not decrease missed primary care appointments. Part of the issue may be that targeting ridesharing to patients with chronic health conditions where management is crucial may be most impactful and cost-effective.[49] Nevertheless, interest from the healthcare sector will likely continue to build. It's estimated that nationally, missed appointments cost healthcare providers $150 billion a year, with no-show rates as high as 30%.[50] While a financial imperative exists for healthcare entities to embrace opportunities in the transportation sector, more important from a health perspective is whether patients ultimately benefit from the services. It will be critical in the coming years to ensure that these collaborations produce, first and foremost, improved health outcomes, as opposed to simply increased healthcare sector revenue.

Finally, it is worth noting that there are a number of private sector organizations providing technical assistance to healthcare entities as they embrace the social determinants of health. Organizations such as Health Leads are helping healthcare providers meet the social service needs of their patients by utilizing college students to connect patients with the basic resources they need to stay healthy.[51] Others such as the software company Healthify help healthcare organizations find community services, track social needs, and coordinate referrals with community partners.[52] Unite US, a health and human services software company, has created a return on investment (ROI) calculator to demonstrate to hospital chief executive officers and chief financial officers that investing in social determinants of health technology can save organizations money. Specifically, the company's outcome of focus is 30-day readmissions, a metric that the CMS uses to assess the ability of hospitals to ensure postdischarge coordination of care outside the clinical setting.[53] Additional research efforts aim to integrate social determinants of health data in electronic health records.[54] All of these organizations are filling a niche in the healthcare sector, recognizing that for many healthcare providers tackling the social determinants of health is new to their business model.

Social Determinants of Health: Healthcare Initiatives

Payers led by Medicare and Medicaid have now started to incorporate a full suite of social determinants within their delivery and payment models. In the summer of 2011, with Medicare ACOs starting to proliferate across the country, several of us asked whether a broader and more holistic delivery and payment model should be tested—one focused not just on care and the clinical setting but on health and the community at large. Specifically, we envisioned a model in which healthcare entities would be accountable not just for patients they serve, as in ACOs, but for a broader population defined geographically. In addition, the model would seek to improve not only the care of patients but their actual health status. More than just doctors and hospitals working together, this model would bring social services and community providers to the table with their clinical counterparts to optimize health. Any savings would be shared by this broader coalition of entities participating in the model. Eventually it was not fully implemented in this way, but variations of this theme were subsequently supported over the years at the CMS's Innovation Center, including the launch of its Accountable Health Communities (AHC) model as well as population health efforts as part of its State Innovation Models initiative. To better connect the social determinants of health to healthcare, the CMS launched its AHC model in 2016 by funding 31 entities across the country to screen beneficiaries for social needs in the clinical care setting. The screening tool focuses on housing instability, food insecurity, transportation problems, utility help needs, and interpersonal safety. Broader issues related to employment and education are also included. Eleven entities are being funded to help connect high-risk beneficiaries with services that address their identified health-related social needs. Another 20 entities are responsible additionally for building community capacity to address the most common health-related social needs. This five-year model test is being evaluated to determine the impact of the model on quality-of-care and spending, including total healthcare costs and inpatient and outpatient healthcare utilization.[55] If successful, it could provide healthcare entities with a new set of evidence-based practices that inform them how to address social needs in a manner that leads to improved health outcomes and lower preventable healthcare costs.

In a parallel track to this development is the work of states through the State Innovation Models initiative. Several states, such as California, Michigan, Minnesota, and Washington have formed "Accountable Communities for Health," bringing together partners from health, social service, and other sectors to improve population health and clinical-community linkages within a geographic area and often with a "backbone" organization to provide coordination. Critical to the long-term sustainability of these efforts, which are currently being financed through government grants and philanthropy, will be demonstrating a reduction in preventable healthcare costs to payers. To this end, in Minnesota, for example, accountable communities for health must partner with an ACO and the state will be looking to see whether such a relationship improves the ability of the latter to improve health outcomes and control healthcare costs. In Washington, the state's accountable communities for health are geographically aligned with the state's Medicaid regional service areas, which should help care and social service coordination for vulnerable state residents.[56] And finally, in Michigan, given the important role of community health workers in addressing the social determinants of health, state health policy leaders envision health plans funding these individuals to ensure sustainability of population health efforts.[57] Evaluations of current efforts over the next several years should further inform how healthcare entities can integrate social services into their payment and business models.

Some observers have noted that Medicaid may be best positioned to address the social determinants of health, considering that several states have aligned a Medicaid application with other human service programs such as SNAP and child care assistance. Other states are allowing the use of Medicaid funds to actually deliver supportive services that impact the social determinants of health. Oregon, specifically, has gone beyond a focus on the common social determinants of health and focused on aligning its healthcare and early education systems with shared goals, staffing, and funding, given the bidirectional impact both areas have on overall child development.[58] The CMS appears receptive to providing flexibility to states to better incorporate the social determinants of health. In October 2018, it approved a North Carolina Medicaid reform demonstration program that will pilot enhanced case management services through its managed care delivery system for targeted individuals who need help addressing issues such as housing instability, transportation insecurity, food security, and interpersonal violence. The five-year demonstration will track the impact on health outcomes and total costs of care.[59]

With respect to Medicare, the Bipartisan Budget Act of 2018 enhanced flexibilities for Medicare Advantage plans to provide targeted supplementary nonmedical health-related services to improve health outcomes in beneficiaries starting in 2020, a significant step forward and one influenced by the Bipartisan Policy Center's Health project.[60] In addition, in its 2019 Medicare Advantage Final Call Letter, the CMS expanded its interpretation of "supplemental healthcare benefit" to include services that support daily maintenance to optimize quality of life and health outcomes.[61] An analysis by Avalere found that Medicare Advantage plans will offer new or enhanced supplemental benefits in 2019, such as caregiver support services, home and bathroom safety devices and modifications, and transportation services.[62] As an example, Anthem publicly rolled out a detailed "Essential Extras" or "Everyday Extras" benefits package built around food delivery, transportation, assistive devices, alternative medicine, adult day center visits, and personal home helpers. Members in select geographic areas, along with their healthcare providers, will be able to select one of the six benefits without additional charges.[63] While all these policies should help the approximately one-third of Medicare beneficiaries currently in Medicare Advantage, similar efforts are needed to support beneficiaries in traditional Medicare.

Finally, while health insurer interest in the social determinants of health will accelerate the ability of healthcare providers to address the social needs of their patients, several additional promising financing approaches exist. First, "pay for success" mechanisms, in which the private sector provides financing to implement evidence-based prevention programs in return for a payout from government if the metrics are met, is an exciting area. As an example, pay for success has been used to fund interventions that prevent childhood asthma exacerbations such as home environment risk mitigation.[64] In 2018, Congress passed the Social Impact Partnerships to Pay for Results Act (SIPPRA), which provides $100 million to state and local governments to launch new pay for success initiatives.[65] Second, some policy experts have championed "blending and braiding" government funding streams to better coordinate healthcare and social service programs. Proponents explain that this may address the "wrong pocket" problem, in which the return on investment by one sector is realized by another sector, thus disincentivizing collaboration.[66] And third, other experts have called for new community financing mechanisms to address the social determinants of health. This model envisions a trusted broker convening key community stakeholders to collectively fund evidence-based interventions that can earn a financial return and be sustained over time.[67]

Community Benefit Responsibilities of Nonprofit Hospitals

One additional opportunity for healthcare to tackle the social determinants of health lies in the community benefit requirements for nonprofit hospitals to maintain their tax-exempt status. For the last 50 years, nonprofit hospitals have maintained their charitable tax exemption by providing either free or reduced-cost clinical services or by engaging in other activities that benefit communities broadly. As part of the Affordable Care Act, an additional requirement was added for hospitals to perform a community health needs assessment every three years. Hospitals must also create a community implementation plan responding to the assessment. An analysis of hospital community health needs assessment data by George Washington University found that the top six challenges identified include access to healthcare, the food environment, education, physical activity, poverty, and transportation. While the assessments are public, there is no requirement for hospitals to disclose their implementation plans or demonstrate that their community benefit efforts are linked to their assessment findings.[68] The Internal Revenue Service (IRS) should make this a requirement.

Given the challenges hospitals are identifying, the IRS should also clarify the category of "community building" expenditures. These are activities that focus on the social determinants of health, such as physical improvements and housing, economic development, and environmental improvements. While community building activities may count as community benefits, this is an area of ambiguity that should be clarified by the IRS. If not, experts believe that since the public looks first to a hospital's community benefit activities in assessing their support of a community, hospitals may not invest in community-building activities, even though these activities may in fact be the most powerful drivers of health.[69]

A decade ago, very few healthcare entities were paying attention to upstream factors impacting health. It is now commonplace for healthcare providers and payers to acknowledge and attempt to address these factors. As best practices continue to emerge and return on investments become clearer, expect healthcare entities to embrace the social determinants of health even more.

PREVENTION *OUTSIDE* THE HEALTHCARE SETTING

[5]

Personal Responsibility or Policy, Systems, and Environmental Change?

IN RESPONSE to the Great Recession of the late 2000s, Congress passed the American Recovery and Reinvestment Act in February of 2009. Its goals were to assist Americans most impacted by the recession and also provide investments in areas such as energy, science, health, transportation, and other infrastructure to increase the nation's economic productivity. Tucked in the massive $831 billion bill[1] was the creation of a Prevention and Wellness Fund with monies allocated to support immunizations, the reduction of healthcare-associated infections, and funding for evidence-based clinical and community-based prevention and wellness strategies. Specifically, the bill language stipulated that "$650,000,000 shall be to carry out evidence-based clinical and community-based prevention and wellness strategies authorized by the Public Health Services Act, as determined by the Secretary, that deliver specific, measurable health outcomes that address chronic disease rates."[2]

The acting surgeon general at the time, Rear Admiral Steven Galson, was tasked by the HHS Office of the Secretary to determine how best to spend the monies. He asked me to lead a cross-departmental task force to develop an approach that would be most impactful from a health perspective. The task force quickly homed in on two of the most important chronic disease risk factors—tobacco use and obesity (poor nutrition and physical activity). Consideration was also given to mental health and other substance abuse disorders, but there was concern that diffusion of efforts across several prevention areas would yield potentially less powerful results. In retrospect, we know now that emotional well-being and mental health are important predictors of chronic disease risk factors.

The task force also felt strongly that both states and communities should receive funding and that communities be diverse in terms of their size, geography, and racial and ethnic make-up. The big question, of course, was what population-based interventions should communities implement? In conjunction with the task force's efforts, a group of researchers at the CDC led by Dr. Janet Collins, then director of the CDC's National Chronic Disease Prevention and Health Promotion Center, launched an ambitious project. Combing through hundreds of studies, they sought to identify specific interventions found to successfully reduce tobacco consumption, improve nutrition, and enhance physical activity. They came up with five evidence-based strategies: Media, Access, Point of decision information, Price, and Social support/services (MAPPS); the theory was that when combined, these strategies could have a profound influence on improving health behaviors by changing community environments.[3]

The work of the task force and the identification of evidence-based strategies led to the creation of Communities Putting Prevention to Work (CPPW), a three-year initiative led by the CDC to reduce morbidity, mortality, and the economic burden of chronic disease through effective prevention. Communities were provided technical assistance and resources to implement evidence-based strategies such as enhancing community infrastructure to support walking and bicycling, increasing access to physical activity for children during and after school, providing incentives to food retailers to offer healthier choices in underserved areas, limiting unhealthy food and drink availability, increasing prices for tobacco products, and increasing community access to smoking cessation services.[4]

By the end of the program, the CDC estimated that over 40 million Americans experienced increased access to physical activity opportunities and to environments with healthy food or beverage options in schools, workplaces, and other community settings. Over 27 million Americans experienced increased protections from secondhand smoke exposure in workplaces, restaurants, bars, and other public spaces. Communities performed their own evaluation efforts; for example, in Seattle, Washington, the CPPW program was directly associated with a decline in obesity prevalence in low-income school districts; in comparison, non-CPPW districts showed no such decline.[5]

Perhaps the most comprehensive effort was led by Philadelphia's health commissioner, Dr. Donald Schwarz, and the public health department's director of policy and planning, Dr. Giridhar Mallya. Leveraging CPPW dollars, they launched the Get Healthy Philly initiative in 2010 to focus on tobacco control and obesity prevention in Philadelphia.[6] Over several years, they implemented initiatives such as increasing healthy food incentives for SNAP participants, launching a Healthy Corner Store initiative, revising citywide zoning policies to increase physical activity, enacting smoke-free policies, utilizing paid media to promote healthy choices, and promoting and supporting quit attempts. While this is not attributable only to CPPW, it's notable that during the span between 2010 and 2012, adult smoking rates fell from 25.2% to 23.3% and adult obesity rates plateaued from 32.2% to 31.9% after having increased for the prior eight years.[7]

CDC researchers went further to estimate the long-term benefits of completed CPPW interventions. Their simulations suggested that if community health improvement could be sustained beyond the initial CPPW program, there would be 14,000 fewer chronic disease–related deaths from all risk factors than expected given current trends, and $2.4 billion in healthcare costs averted.[8] Long-term studies of this initiative and similar follow-on programs such as the CDC's Community Transformation Grant continue.

While many public health advocates cited CPPW's efforts as instrumental in creating conditions for Americans to make healthier choices, others saw it as an encroachment of government control over individual behavior—an example of the "nanny state" gone wild. Some accused the CDC and the program of using government dollars to lobby for changes in state and local policy, such as for tax increases for unhealthy foods or products, citing the Anti-Lobbying Act of 1919, which was amended in

2002. The CDC pushed back that there was a difference between educating policymakers about the latest scientific evidence on an intervention and lobbying for passage of specific legislation or appropriations.[9]

Over the last several years, private sector organizations have also started to champion policy, systems, and environmental changes in order to improve community health. For example, CityHealth, led by the de Beaumont Foundation and Kaiser Permanente, has set out to improve the health and well-being of residents in the 40 largest cities in the United States through policy, systems, and environmental change. Several of the policies focus on chronic disease prevention such as smoke-free indoor air, raising the minimum legal age for the sale of tobacco to 21, healthy food procurement, and adapting city infrastructure to promote physical activity.[10] As another example, Trust for America's Health "Promoting Health and Cost Control in States" project focuses on selected "best-buy" state level policies that can be adopted and implemented to promote health and control cost growth.[11]

This debate brings up a broader issue. What's the best way to promote behavior change leading to healthier choices and the prevention of chronic diseases? Certainly, individuals themselves have a role, and providing information to them about healthy behaviors is important. But is this enough? Are there societal factors that make selecting the healthy choice difficult for the average American? It's worth taking a look at a few specific examples of unhealthy behaviors and their associated prevention efforts.

Tobacco Control

Tobacco control efforts may best demonstrate why policies, systems, and environmental change are critical to the adoption of healthy behaviors. In 1964, smoking prevalence among US adults was 42%, smoking was glamorized, and cessation programs were very uncommon. In a watershed moment, Surgeon General Luther Terry released a groundbreaking report entitled *Smoking and Health: Report of the Advisory Committee of the Surgeon General of the Public Health Service*, which galvanized the nation about the harmful effects of cigarettes.[12] Over the course of the last 50 years, the combination of tobacco taxes, media counteradvertising, smoke-free policies, and smoking cessation programs have helped reduce smoking rates to a new low of 14% for adults (though rates for subpopulations such as individuals with mental illness continue to be much higher). In spite of this progress, 20 million Americans have lost their lives from smoking-related illnesses since 1964.[13]

I have been fortunate to work with a number of colleagues and mentors over the years who contributed to this effort. These include physicians like Dr. Howard Koh, who after treating countless tobacco-related cancer patients, led efforts in Massachusetts to build community coalitions advocating for antismoking policies; public health professionals such as Rosie Henson, who led efforts at the CDC's Office of Smoking and Health to ensure that all states received support from the federal government to enact antismoking policies; and economists such as Ken Warner, whose policy research impacted both domestic and global tobacco control efforts.

Policy, systems, and environmental change have been particularly important to the continued decline in adult and youth smoking rates over the last decade. In 2009, Congress approved the Children's Health Insurance Program Reauthorization Act, which increased the federal tax rate on cigarettes from 39 cents to roughly $1.00. Within the first two months alone, the number of youth smokers decreased by at least 220,000. Taxes were also increased on smokeless tobacco, and researchers estimated there were at least 135,000 fewer youth smokeless tobacco users in the immediate term.[14] Media counteradvertising has also been a focus of recent federal public health efforts. In 2012, the CDC launched a national tobacco education campaign to encourage quitting. The campaign, entitled Tips from Former Smokers (*Tips*), consisted of graphic antismoking advertisements that featured former cigarette smokers. An evaluation of the 2014 campaign showed that exposure to the campaign was associated with an estimated 1.83 million additional quit attempts, 1.73 million additional smokers intending to quit within six months, and 104,000 sustained quits of at least six months.[15]

In addition, societal norms continue to evolve in favor of promoting prevention through policy change to reduce secondhand smoke exposure. The 2014 *Surgeon General's Report: The Health Consequences of Smoking— 50 Years of Progress* included a startling finding: since 1964, approximately 2,500,000 nonsmokers have died from health problems caused by exposure to secondhand smoke.[16] It's estimated that secondhand smoke exposure causes nearly 41,000 premature deaths from heart disease and stroke annually. New evidence has linked childhood exposure to secondhand smoke to death from lung disease (COPD) decades later.[17] The Community Preventive Services Task Force has found that smoke-free policies reduce exposure to secondhand smoke, prevalence of tobacco use, tobacco consumption, initiation of tobacco use among young people, and tobacco-related morbidity and mortality, including acute cardiovascular events. Smoke-free policies also prompt smokers to consider calling quit-lines or talking to their healthcare professionals about cessation.[18]

Currently 27 states, Washington, DC, Puerto Rico, and the US Virgin Islands, plus hundreds of cities and counties, have enacted comprehensive smoke-free laws covering workplaces, restaurants, and bars. Collectively, these laws protect roughly 50% of the US population. Additional states have enacted bans in bars and restaurants, and many other state legislatures are actively considering new bans.[19] After Kansas and North Carolina implemented their respective smoke-free laws in 2010, Howard Koh and I wrote editorials in their state newspapers congratulating policymakers for providing the gift of cleaner and safer air to their residents.

Beyond implementation of known evidence-based tobacco control policies, there are several additional areas to watch moving forward. One of the most important initiatives that may help end the scourge of tobacco-related illness and death was announced in July 2017 by FDA commissioner Scott Gottlieb. The FDA is looking to develop a comprehensive regulatory framework with the aim of lowering nicotine to minimal or nonaddictive levels. By doing so, the FDA hopes to reduce addiction to cigarettes in the first place as well as make it easier for those wishing to quit (over 70% of smokers do).[20] Eliminating combustible tobacco use would be one of public health's greatest achievements. While this process may take time and trigger legal action by the industry, it may well be the single most important policy yet.

The rise of e-cigarettes is another new development that requires vigilance. In theory, trading cancer-causing combustible cigarettes for e-cigarettes should reduce significant harm from tobacco use. More studies are necessary to understand how e-cigarettes might be used as a cigarette smoking cessation tool. However, an unintended consequence of e-cigarettes has been the impact of flavorings, which appeal to youth. This is thought to have led to the rapid increase in e-cigarette use among adolescents. In fact, e-cigarettes are now the most commonly used tobacco product by youth, with more than two million middle and high school students having used them in 2017[21] (almost 40% of high school students have used e-cigarettes sometime in their life).[22] This is problematic for a number of reasons. First, nicotine addiction is particularly harmful to the developing adolescent brain. Nicotine use in adolescents can disrupt the formation of brain circuits that control attention and learning as well as increase the long-term risks for mood disorders and for permanent lowering of impulse control.[23] Second, a recent RAND Corporation study showed that adolescents who use vaping products are not only more likely to smoke cigarettes but also more likely to increase their use of both products over time.[24] In 2018, not only did e-cigarette use rise 78% among teens and 48% among middle school students, overall tobacco product use also grew 38% among teens and 29% among middle school students, reversing a decline seen over the last several years.[25] In response to these trends, in November 2018, the FDA moved to ban sweet and fruity flavored e-cigarettes from most convenience stores and gas stations and enforced new regulations on online sales, requiring that all websites install new age-verification safeguards. The FDA did not ban mint and menthol flavored e-cigarettes, since they are more popular with adult users.[26] This speaks to the balance that the FDA is trying to preserve, namely, to ensure e-cigarettes have a future as a potential harm reduction and/or smoking cessation tool while ensuring that the next generation of Americans doesn't become addicted to nicotine.

Nutrition and Obesity Prevention

The impact of policy, systems, and environmental change to improve nutrition and tackle the obesity epidemic also deserves some discussion. One prime example involves trans fats, a substance previously found in many baked goods and fried foods. As the evidence grew in the 1990s and early 2000s about the link between trans fats and coronary health disease, the FDA began requiring manufacturers to start listing trans fats on the Nutrition Facts panel of foods in 2006.[27] Despite the objections of the restaurant industry, many cities and states went further and passed legislation limiting or banning trans fats in restaurant food. One study found that three years after some New York counties banned trans fats, heart attacks and strokes fell by more than 6%.[28] In 2015, the FDA issued a final determination that trans fats are not "generally recognized as safe," meaning that they cannot be used in foods without permission from the FDA as of 2018.[29] This has nearly eliminated artificial trans fats from the US food supply.

Salt is another substance that has been linked to high blood pressure and cardiovascular disease. While recommendations to Americans from the federal government have been to limit daily sodium to 2,300 milligrams, the average adult consumes over 3,400 milligrams a day. In advance of the release of the *2010 Dietary Guidelines for Americans*, I mediated a scientific dispute between federal agencies as to whether the science justified recommendations for all adults to consume no more than 1,500 milligrams. Ultimately, it was decided that the evidence supported the recommendation only for high-risk groups (though these groups totaled 70% of the US adult population). After a 2013 report from the Institute of Medicine on sodium,[30] the *2015 Dietary Guidelines for Americans* narrowed the high-risk population to just those with high blood pressure or prehypertension.

In spite of years of recommendations, average sodium consumption has not budged, largely because of the American public's penchant for purchasing processed and prepared foods that have significant sodium content. So, in 2016, the FDA proposed voluntary guidelines for the food industry to reduce salt in the food supply. By setting targets for the gradual reduction in sodium in over 150 food categories, the FDA estimates that if the industry voluntarily reduces sodium levels based on their targets, average adult sodium consumption could drop to 3,000 milligrams a day in two years and to 2,300 milligrams a day in 10 years.[31] Subsequent modeling by researchers estimates that if the policy achieved 100% compliance with the 10-year FDA targets, 450,000 cases of cardiovascular disease could be prevented, leading to a gain of two million quality-adjusted life years (QALYs) and cost savings of approximately $40 billion over a 20-year period.[32] Current FDA leadership has signaled its intent to support setting sodium reduction targets in spite of continued industry and some congressional pushback.[33]

Perhaps the most controversial area in nutritional policy is regulating consumption of sugar-sweetened beverages. Studies are clear that these drinks provide no nutritional value and have harmful health effects. As the Bipartisan Policy Center's SNAP Task Force has noted, sugar-sweetened beverages are linked to long-term weight gain, diabetes, and coronary heart disease. Specifically, for every one to two daily servings of beverages consumed, an individual's lifetime risk of developing diabetes increases by 30%. The Task Force also noted that compared with SNAP-eligible non-participants, SNAP participants consumed 61% more sugar-sweetened beverages. A 2016 report from the Department of Agriculture found that soft drinks were the number-one purchase in terms of share of expenditures by SNAP households, although non-SNAP households were not far behind, with soft drinks being the number-two largest purchase.[34] A concerning 2018 study utilizing a beverage environment scan assessing marketing by SNAP-authorized beverage retailers found higher odds of in-store sugar-sweetened beverage marketing during SNAP benefit issuance days compared with other days of the month. The results were more pronounced in geographic areas with high SNAP enrollment.[35] Yet another study found that the majority of SNAP participants would support removing sugar-sweetened beverages as a SNAP benefit.[36]

BPC's Task Force ultimately recommended eliminating sugar-sweetened beverages from the list of items that could be purchased with SNAP benefits, in addition to incentivizing purchases for healthy foods.[37] While some external stakeholders on both sides of the aisle applauded the recommendation, the majority were either silent or outwardly opposed. Past criticisms of this idea have ranged from unfairly singling out one specific industry and class of products to singling out poor Americans (although nothing in this recommendation would preclude Americans from purchasing sugar-sweetened beverages with their own dollars). Government overreach into the sphere of what many considered to be personal choices of Americans has often been another criticism. While more recent studies suggest that restricting sugar-sweetened beverages may be inferior to a strategy of combining incentives and disincentives across a broader range of healthy and unhealthy foods,[38] the fault lines between individual choice and government intervention continue to be exposed.

A more publicized policy intervention, with respect to sugar-sweetened beverages and modeled after the tobacco movement, is a consumption tax. On this issue, we've learned quite a bit from our southern neighbor. In 2014, Mexico implemented a 1 peso per liter excise tax on sugar-sweetened beverages. Purchases of taxed beverages decreased 7.6% over the next two years, compared to previous trends. The impact was greatest for households at the lowest socioeconomic level.[39] Researchers have modeled the long-term impacts of the tax and found that the tax should result in significantly fewer cases of type II diabetes, cardiovascular events, and mortality overall.[40]

Cities across the United States watched Mexico's experience and decided to follow suit. Between 2015 and 2018, eight cities implemented a soda tax, starting with Berkeley, California.[41] One preliminary study six months after enactment of Berkeley's tax found consumption dropped by 21% versus an increase of 4% in Oakland and San Francisco. Only 2% of residents interviewed by the investigators said they went to another city to purchase sugar-sweetened beverages and avoid the tax. There was also a significant increase in water consumption in Berkeley during that time, in comparison to San Francisco and Oakland.[42] In Philadelphia, researchers at Drexel University found that within the first two months of implementing the city's tax, relative to nearby comparison cities, the odds of daily soda consumption dropped by 40% and sugary energy drink consumption dropped by 64%. There was also a 38% drop in the total number of sodas consumed over a 30-day period.[43] A working paper of the National Bureau of Economic Research assessed implementation after one year and found more mixed results. While purchases of taxed beverages fell in Philadelphia stores, Philadelphia residents increased purchases of these beverages outside the city. There was some evidence of reduction in adults' overall sugar consumption from sweetened beverages, particularly for African American adults. It also appeared that the tax substantially reduced consumption of added sugars from sweetened beverages among African American children and among children who were frequent consumers of sweetened beverages.[44] This underscores one powerful argument for sugary beverage taxes, in that by reducing risk factors for disease among people at the highest risk, this intervention has the potential to improve health equity.

Not surprisingly, the soda tax has come under criticism from several quarters. Beyond the nanny state crowd, there are those who complain of the economic consequences for small business owners in affected regions. Others criticize the methodology of early studies, noting that when one looks beyond survey studies of consumption to actual sales, there may be evidence that consumers may be purchasing soda outside city limits.[45] On its face, this argument seems much less likely for low-income populations, disproportionately exposed to advertising for sugar-sweetened beverages, who may not have the means to travel great distances to purchase groceries and food items.

Another example demonstrating the importance of policy, systems, and environmental change relates to reducing portion sizes to address obesity. Research has shown that consumers eat and drink more when they are served larger portions or packages. One specific group of researchers found that eliminating larger portions from the diet could reduce average daily energy consumed by 22% to 29% among US adults.[46] Dr. Deborah Cohen from the RAND Corporation, an expert on obesity research, has suggested that jurisdictions should establish standards for portion sizes to guide individual consumption much in the same way that there are standard servings of alcohol. She believes that these standards may have contributed to the 60% reduction in alcohol-related traffic fatalities over the past three decades.[47] She also recommends that there be maximum serving sizes set for foods that are high in calories and low in nutritional value, such as sugar-sweetened beverages.[48] This is exactly what New York City did under Mayor Michael Bloomberg. In 2012, the city passed a portion cap on sugar-sweetened beverages in food establishments regulated by the health department. It was vehemently opposed by an industry-backed group entitled New Yorkers for Beverage Choice. In spite of support from academics and public health professionals, the administration failed to build broad-based community support, particularly in low-income communities. The cap was ultimately overturned by the courts, less because of any infringement on personal freedoms and more because of procedural issues.[49]

Policy, Systems, and Environmental Change versus Individual Responsibility

So, what do all of these examples suggest about the optimal approaches to promote population-wide prevention? They demonstrate the impact of policy, systems, and environmental changes on making the healthy choice the default choice. Alternatively, what is the evidence behind individual responsibility in promoting prevention and healthy behaviors? It is mixed, at best. For example, while the "Just Say No" campaign of the 1980s coincided with graduating teenage drug use drop by 47%, one of its flagship programs called D.A.R.E., which sent local police officers into thousands of schools to warn about the dangers of drug use, was not found to be effective.[50, 51] With respect to teen pregnancy rates, which have dropped substantially since the 1990s, research has shown that the major causes for this trend have been policies that increase access to contraception.[52] In fact, many public health studies have shown that abstinence-only education programs don't succeed in reducing rates of teen pregnancies or sexually transmitted diseases.[53]

What does this mean for individual responsibility, with respect to prevention, and is there a role for it? While it's tempting to discount individual responsibility, one should be cautious in doing so. It may not be the message of individual responsibility that is incorrect but rather the unrealistic notion that the message in and of itself will result in the outcomes desired. Some researchers have encouraged a combined approach, promoting both individual responsibility with policy, systems, and environmental change.[54] The idea is that it is precisely changes through the latter that makes the former more possible.

Perhaps the best application of this philosophy with respect to obesity has been put forth by Dr. Kelly Brownell. Dr. Brownell, now dean of the Sanford School of Public Policy at Duke University, and colleagues published an important article in the journal *Health Affairs* in 2010, arguing that the lack of emphasis on changing environmental conditions was making it too difficult for Americans to exercise personal responsibility and to be free to make choices they would have otherwise wanted had there been more options available to them. The notion of "libertarian paternalism" or "optimal defaults" best describes the philosophy; it sees the opposing views as complementary to and symbiotic with maximizing health impacts.[55]

One public policy approach that exemplifies this is the consumers' right to truthful information in the form of menu labeling legislation. While labeling regulations were previously enacted in several cities and states across the country, the Affordable Care Act created a nationwide requirement for menu items at chain restaurants and other similar food establishments, as well as vending machines, to provide nutrition information. The Food and Drug Administration delayed implementation of the provision for years to help the industry, which generated significant pushback, come into compliance with the law. Finally, in 2018, the Trump administration implemented the law, requiring chain restaurants with more than 20 locations, nearly 300,000 food retail establishments nationwide,[56] to list calories on all menus and menu boards and to provide consumers with additional nutritional information such as fat and sodium levels on-site.[57] In addition, many large chain restaurants have also reduced the calorie content of new menu items and have dropped high-calorie items from their menus.[58] The FDA estimates that these rules will save approximately $8 billion in healthcare costs over the next two decades.[59] In the FDA's official statement, the agency cited new RAND research suggesting that people choose menu items with fewer calories when they have access to calorie information. In line with the philosophy of libertarian paternalism, the FDA stated, "This [nutritional information] is information Americans want or need in order to make decisions about the foods they eat so they can make more informed choices about their diets and health for themselves and their families."[60]

Another approach to merging the viewpoints of personal responsibility and broader policy changes involves behavioral economics. Through policies that incentivize individuals to make the healthy choice, behavioral change can be possible. Given some success in areas such as smoking cessation and weight loss, policymakers included a provision in the ACA for states to develop evidence-based chronic disease prevention programs that provide incentives to Medicaid beneficiaries to participate. Ten states focused on areas such as diabetes prevention and management, weight management, and smoking cessation and gave participants anywhere from $215 to $1,150 annually to participate and in some cases to improve outcomes.[61] An evaluation of the program demonstrated that financial incentives increased the likelihood of program participants receiving a preventive service. Some states also saw success in improving health outcomes, such as weight loss and smoking cessation. However, evaluators noted that there were few significant changes in total, inpatient, or emergency department Medicaid expenditures associated with the receipt of incentives.[62]

Another experiment in behavioral economics played out with the Supreme Court ruling in 2012 upholding the ACA while making Medicaid expansion optional. Several states that went on to expand Medicaid did so by adding a personal responsibility component for new enrollees. States such as Iowa and Michigan offered lower premiums and cost-sharing to beneficiaries who agreed to do a health risk assessment with their doctor.[63] Evaluations are still ongoing to assess the impact of these programs on both beneficiary health outcomes and healthcare costs. The Medicaid and CHIP Payment and Access Commission (MACPAC) has identified several strategies that make it more likely for healthy behavior incentive programs to succeed, including in-person communication to increase the likelihood of enrollment and distributing incentives immediately after completion of a healthy behavior activity. More empirical research is needed to guide future Medicaid incentive initiatives.[64]

Finally, perhaps the most high-profile provision of the Affordable Care Act involving incentives was the individual mandate. The individual shared responsibility provision of the ACA required taxpayers to have qualifying health coverage called minimum essential coverage or to make a shared responsibility payment with their federal income tax return for the months without coverage or an exemption.[65] Until its repeal in 2018, the mandate served as a lightning rod in the fight to repeal the ACA. While Democrats called Republicans hypocritical for opposing a concept that originated in conservative health policy circles, Republicans felt that the minimum essential coverage requirement was too expensive and burdensome. The shared responsibility payment, or penalty, for not having minimum essential coverage was meant to be an incentive for Americans to purchase health insurance coverage. Unfortunately, the penalty was for the most part much less than the average cost of annual health insurance coverage, thus not providing a strong incentive for many to purchase coverage; paying the penalty was the much cheaper option, particularly for those Americans who were relatively young and healthy.[66]

In conclusion, without policy, systems, and environmental changes, the prevention of chronic diseases from a population perspective would not be possible. Couched in appropriate terms, many of these changes could support greater individual choices and freedoms to make healthier choices thus complementary to and not opposed to the concept of personal responsibility. Other changes that reduce individual choices, such as bans and taxes, will always be more philosophically and politically controversial, even though the evidence of positive health impacts from many of these measures, such as tobacco taxes, are large. Public (e.g., CDC chronic disease prevention initiatives) and private sector efforts to assist communities in implementing health-promoting policy, systems, and environmental change should be strongly supported by policymakers.

Ultimately, the responsibility for prevention is all of ours. The factors that influence health extend beyond any one individual. For individuals to make healthy choices, they need to be supported by the communities they live in. No one knows this better than local public health officials. Indeed, public health professionals are on the front lines each day trying to protect and promote healthy communities. In the next chapter, we will discuss the status of the public health profession in the United States to understand its integral role in building a culture of prevention.

[6]

Why Do We Take Public Health for Granted?

Between 1900 and 1999, average life expectancy in the United States increased thirty years, from 47 to 77 years of age. In a seminal paper in the *Milbank Quarterly* around the turn of the century, it was estimated that an astounding twenty-five years of the gain in life expectancy occurred because of public health efforts, as opposed to medical care.[1] In response, the CDC embarked on an effort to document the greatest public health achievements over the last century.

Ten achievements were highlighted because of their impact on preventing death, disease, and disability. Activities included vaccinations and control of infectious diseases; motor vehicle safety and safer workplaces; decline in deaths from coronary heart disease and stroke, recognition of tobacco use as a health hazard, and safer and healthier foods; healthier mothers and babies and family planning; and fluoridation of drinking water.[2] In 2010, the CDC compiled a new list of achievements that took place between 2001 and 2010, adding activities such as childhood lead poisoning prevention, cancer prevention, and public health preparedness and response.[3]

There are several interesting observations to note from this list. First, in many cases, these activities are rather invisible to the public. Former HHS acting assistant secretary for health Dr. Karen DeSalvo appropriately has often exclaimed to the public that "public health saved your life today and you didn't even know it." Clean water and sanitation is a perfect example. Infections such as typhoid and cholera transmitted by contaminated water have been virtually eliminated by improved sanitation.[4] We take for granted that these conditions were once commonplace and now rare because of public health interventions. The same can be said about safer foods, which have resulted from decreases in microbial contamination.[5] While we occasionally still hear about food recalls, it is because we have a significantly improved surveillance system in this country. And each day we don't hear about food contamination is a day that public health is in action, working hard to protect us.

A second observation is that many of these achievements occur well beyond the healthcare setting. Take for example improvements in motor vehicle safety such as safety belts, child safety seats, and drinking and driving laws that have significantly reduced motor vehicle–related deaths. Between 2000 and 2009, in spite of more vehicle travel, the death rate related to motor vehicle travel declined over 25%.[6] Laws mandating motorcycle helmets have also been critical in reducing head trauma injuries and deaths. In 2012, Michigan governor Rick Snyder signed a bill into law repealing the state's motorcycle helmet law. Shortly thereafter, I was asked by his team to consider leading the state health department. In my deliberations, the governor's repeal of this law, which ran counter to public health evidence, weighed heavily in my decision not to move forward. Predictably, and unfortunately, the subsequent years witnessed an increase in motorcycle crash fatalities and injuries due to a lack of the use of helmets.[7]

It should be noted that the role of governmental public health has been crucial to the advances in disease prevention and health promotion. For over two hundred years, specifically since 1798, when President John Adams signed into law the "Act for the Relief of Sick and Disabled Seamen," the precursor for establishing the US Public Health Service Commissioned Corps, governmental leadership has contributed immensely to public health's achievements. Initially, these efforts were dedicated to protecting people against the spread of disease from sailors returning from abroad, and to monitoring the health of immigrants.[8] In fact, it was a small "Hygienic Laboratory" at a marine hospital on Staten Island established to detect infectious diseases in incoming passengers that eventually evolved into the National Institutes of Health.[9] The CDC started out first as the Communicable Disease Center with a small budget, with few employees, and with the sole objective of preventing the spread of malaria through mosquito eradication.[10] Other federal agencies were also initially created by Congress for a "protection" purpose, in the FDA's case to protect against adulterated and misbranded food and drugs. The shift from disease prevention to health promotion gradually occurred during the twentieth century, as epidemic diseases were brought under control by the nation.[11] Governmental public health agencies over the last 50 years have since made significant contributions to reducing mortality from chronic diseases, environmental exposures, and injury.

Given public health's achievements, it's reasonable to ask whether the public is aware of any of this. To better understand public perceptions of the influence of public health on health outcomes, researchers at Brigham Young University conducted an interesting study in 2014. They surveyed a nationally representative sample of 705 adults to determine which factors people credited for the increase in life expectancy since the mid-1800s. In open-ended responses to explaining the single most important reasons for increased life expectancy, 66% of respondents noted modern medicine, far surpassing any other explanation, such as improved education, nutrition, or sanitation. Respondents were also asked to project what life expectancy would be without modern medicine. The average response was approximately 47 years, about 32 years less than current life expectancy. The authors concluded that, given the 40-year life expectancy increase since the mid-1800s, the public attributes 80% of life expectancy gains to modern medicine and only 20% to all other factors. They surmised that these findings may be impacting societal support for funding public health and healthcare services.[12]

Part of the problem may be a lack of understanding or appreciation of what public health is exactly. In a 1996 public opinion poll about public health commissioned by the nonprofit California Center for Health Improvement, respondents were asked, "What do the words 'public health' mean to you?" Less than 4% of respondents provided answers commonly pertaining to public health such as health education, healthier lifestyles, prevention of infectious diseases, and immunizations. Eighty-three percent of respondents identified one or more issues such as the healthcare system, welfare programs, universal healthcare, health insurance, and Medicaid and Medicare.[13]

Interestingly enough, a majority of the same respondents noted several specific public health services as "top priorities," including ensuring safe drinking water, ensuring that foods are free from contamination, protecting the public from exposure to toxic chemicals, protecting the public from the spread of communicable diseases, helping treat disease and injury after natural disasters, and providing community education and counseling services about improving health. Yet, it appears that they didn't equate these activities with public health.[14]

In a more recent poll, Bob Blendon and colleagues at Harvard University sought to understand the views of Americans about the overall spending, priorities, and performance of the public health system. Based on prior surveys that demonstrated confusion in the public about what the term "public health" means, the new polling didn't even use the term, instead opting for the phrase, "improving and protecting the nation's health" when assessing attitudes about national spending in different views. The poll did include a follow-up question that delved into eleven specific public health activities.[15]

On one hand, avoiding the term "public health" seems like a missed opportunity in educating the American public about the subject. On the other hand, I admit that avoiding confusion in certain circumstances may be prudent. In 2010, while at HHS, I advocated for the change in the name of our office to the Office of the Assistant Secretary of Health from the Office of Public Health and Science. While there were eleven public health program offices within our organizational structure, the office's name didn't provide much specificity as to what it did or where these offices resided in the superstructure of the department. By changing the name to the Office of the Assistant Secretary of Health, it made it clear that the office reported to the secretary's principal public health advisor. Here the intent wasn't to remove the term "public health" for any specific purpose but rather to add organizational clarity.

Blendon's survey found one particularly interesting trend. His team broke down attitudes about federal spending on public health by party identification and asked whether the federal government should spend more, the same, or less on the eleven public health activities. For every activity, from preventing chronic diseases to preventing the spread of infectious diseases, Democrats believed that the federal government should spend more than Republicans did, and Republicans believed that the federal government should spend less.[16] While some of this can be explained by the traditional viewpoints of both parties on the role of government, there were some indications that the public lacks a complete understanding of how public health activities relate to health. For example, 58% of Republicans said the federal government should spend more money to prevent chronic diseases, such as heart disease, cancer, and arthritis. And yet, only 35% and 18% of Republicans believed that the federal government should spend more to reduce obesity and tobacco use, respectively, the two chief preventable risk factors for chronic diseases. In fact, more than a quarter and almost half of Republicans believed that the federal government should spend less on reducing obesity and reducing tobacco use, respectively.[17]

Researchers at Drexel University wanted to see if the political differences by party extended to voting records of members of Congress. They amassed public health policy recommendations from the American Public Health Association (APHA) over 15 years and tested the hypothesis that US Democratic senators were more likely to vote consistently with the recommendations in comparison to US Republican senators. They found that Democrats averaged 59.1% points higher in annual APHA voting concordance than Republicans. In addition, they found that females had a higher voting concordance than males and Northeastern senators had a higher voting concordance than Southern senators. The authors noted that the last point is particularly troubling, given that Southern states have some of the worst health outcomes.[18]

The difference in views between both political parties on public health may have reached its apex with the creation of the Prevention and Public Health Fund as part of the Affordable Care Act. The law required that the funds be used "to provide for expanded and sustained national investment in prevention and public health programs to improve health and restraining the rate of growth in private and public health care costs." It is the first mandatory funding stream dedicated to improving the public's health.[19] Over the first nine years of its existence, the Fund has supported evidence-based programs ranging from immunizations to lead poisoning prevention. However, there have been few Republican champions of the Fund to date. There are a number of possible reasons for this. First, the Fund is part of the ACA, which has been deeply unpopular among Republican lawmakers. Second, some saw the Fund originally as a "slush fund" for the HHS secretary that operated outside the confines of Congress's appropriations authority. Still others believe that the Fund has been used to advance political agendas and to lobby inappropriately for state and local policy changes.

It has not helped that both Democrats and Republicans have taken turns raiding the Fund to pursue additional objectives. Both parties have either taken, or attempted to take, dollars out of the Fund to pursue various initiatives from deficit reduction, to building the federal health insurance exchanges, to extending the Children's Health Insurance Program (CHIP), and even to extending the interest rate paid on federal student loans.[20] More recently during the 115th Congress, as part of the Republican strategy to repeal and replace the ACA, the Fund was constantly a target for elimination. It's likely that the Fund will continue to be the subject of partisan debate during annual appropriations processes.

What is missing, it seems here, is an open and honest conversation between both parties about how best to utilize the Fund. Absent this dialogue, Congress will continue to squander an opportunity to advance prevention policies. Ideally, a bipartisan, bicameral group of lawmakers led by the Senate Health, Education, Labor, and Pensions Committee and the House Energy and Commerce Committee should come together to ensure that the Fund supports an agreed-upon set of evidence-based disease prevention and health promotion activities. This is, after all, how Congress should work together as recommended by the Commission on Evidence-Based Policymaking (CEP), which was sponsored by former Speaker Paul Ryan and Senator Patty Murray.[21]

Challenges Facing Public Health

The combined result of the public's lack of familiarity with public health, along with a lack of bipartisanship supporting it, has consequences. For example, a 2018 Morning Consult poll sponsored by Research America found that only 59% of Americans strongly believed that they have benefited from the development of vaccines over the last 50 years, a 16% decrease compared to a decade ago.[22] This is in spite of the fact that over the last decade there have been even more vaccines approved by the FDA and recommended for use. The shingles (*Herpes zoster*) vaccine and the human papillomavirus (HPV) vaccine, both approved first by the FDA in 2006, are two examples of recent innovations in the field that have contributed to reductions in illness and disease burden. In 2017, a second shingles vaccine was approved that has even greater efficacy and effectiveness over a longer period of follow-up.[23] In spite of advances such as these in vaccine development, it may be that we are doing so well preventing diseases that the public has taken vaccines for granted and forgotten the severity of the illnesses being prevented. The 2015 Disneyland measles outbreak has been cited as an example of what happens when unvaccinated individuals are exposed to a virus not regularly seen any longer and thus not thought about much by the public.[24]

The Morning Consult poll's results were concerning in other ways. For example, 53% said they did not get the flu vaccine during the 2017–2018 flu season, with nearly half of those individuals saying they did not trust the flu vaccine and 40% saying they didn't feel they need it to prevent the flu.[25] While it is true that the phenomenon of circulating influenza viruses makes it difficult to precisely match vaccines with viruses, flu vaccines do provide protection. For the 2017–2018 season, the vaccine's overall effectiveness was 40% (over the last decade, vaccine effectiveness has ranged from 19% to 60%).[26] That still means a 40% reduction in people seeking medical care for the flu, which is not nothing.

Researchers at the University of Florida in Gainesville recently sought to quantify the benefits of a poorly matched influenza vaccine. They created a mathematical model of flu transmission and vaccination to estimate how much illness is prevented by a poorly effective flu vaccine. They found that, at an average flu vaccine uptake rate (43% between 2012 and 2017), a vaccine with just 20% of effectiveness could reduce 20 million infections or illnesses, as compared to no vaccine at all. This translates to 129,000 fewer hospitalizations and 61,000 fewer deaths.[27] These are significant findings and ones that, as scientists and medical professionals, we likely do a poor job of communicating to the general public. Certainly, if the public polled in the recent survey knew of this prior to responding to the survey, their responses might have been different.

Unfortunately, less than optimal uptake of the influenza vaccine in 2017–2018 may have resulted in deadly consequences. The flu season killed about 80,000 Americans, more than in any year dating back four decades (including more children than in any year since the 2009 swine flu pandemic), and experienced record-breaking levels of illness and hospitalization rates.[28] Of the several explanatory factors for the severe flu season, one is that vaccination coverage among adults was only 37.1%, the lowest rate for adults in the previous seven years.[29]

Public health itself faces additional challenges, one specifically related to its workforce. CDC leaders have described the field as one that "lacks the right number of people with the right skills in the right place at the right time." Contributing to this is an insufficient number of current workers caused by factors such as an aging workforce, economic crises causing furloughs and layoffs, and insufficient investment in training and workforce retention strategies.[30]

There have been several past attempts to estimate the size and composition of the public health workforce. The most recent comprehensive one in 2014 led by researchers at the University of Michigan used federal, state, and local data sources to provide a comprehensive assessment. The multiple data sources yielded an estimate of 290,988 public health workers in governmental agencies, 50%, 30%, and 20% of whom provide services in local, state, and federal public health settings, respectively. As a reference, the best previous analyses in 2000 estimated 450,000 public health workers in governmental and voluntary agencies in 2000 and in 2012 estimated 326,602 governmental public health workers.[31] The 2018 National Association of County and City Health Officials (NACCHO) *Forces of Change* survey confirmed recent workforce losses, estimating that local public health departments have eliminated 56,630 jobs over the past decade.[32] Another recent study suggested that almost one-quarter of the government public health workforce plans to leave or retire in coming years. In some states, over 50% of the public health workforce will be eligible to retire by 2020. While there are more schools of public health today graduating students to fill the anticipated demand, it's unclear whether these young professionals will have the mentorship needed to succeed in their roles or whether they will opt for the private sector.[33]

Reduced funding for public health is another major contributor to workforce challenges. The Great Recession shed thousands of public health jobs. Noted healthcare columnist Sarah Kliff described why all of this matters in a 2012 *Washington Post* column entitled "The Incredible Shrinking Public Health Workforce." In it, she described the consequences of downsizing for a small Massachusetts public health department trying to reduce smoking rates. Cyclical downturns in the economy led to fewer staff members working on smoking cessation, which includes conducting site visits to tobacco sellers to ensure they are complying with regulations not to sell to teenagers. In 1998, Massachusetts had one of the country's biggest tobacco cessation budgets, spending $39 million; by 2010, the budget had fallen to $6.8 million.[34]

Local budgetary pressures have strained public health in other ways. This is best evidenced by one of the most significant public health catastrophes of this decade, the Flint water crisis. Long in economic disarray, given the decline of the auto industry, the city in 2014 turned its water source to the Flint River while a new pipeline was being built to deliver water from Lake Huron to Flint. Unfortunately, city officials did not treat the water with anticorrosive agents, thus causing the lead in the pipes to leach into the water supply. It wasn't until pediatrician Dr. Mona Hanna-Attisha and other public health researchers sounded the alarm that federal and state regulators began to listen.[35] Researchers found that the incidence of elevated blood lead levels in children younger than five years more than doubled after the water source change and disadvantaged neighborhoods had the greatest elevated blood lead level increases. Lead exposure in children causes an array of health problems such as developmental delay, learning disabilities, and behavioral disorders.[36]

As terrible as this crisis has been, Flint represents only one of many cities and towns across the country facing an aging water infrastructure. As a 2016 Bipartisan Policy Center report outlined, there are over 14,000 publicly owned treatment works, or sewer systems, that serve over three-quarters of the US population. While pipes can range from 15 to 100 years old depending on conditions, some older cities, for example in the Northeast, operate with pipes that are 200 years old. With respect to the drinking water infrastructure, there are an estimated 240,000 water main breaks per year in the United States across roughly one million miles of pipes. According to the American Water Works Association, the United States would need to invest over $1 trillion over 25 years to replace all of its aging drinking water pipes alone. BPC's report correctly and bluntly stated, "The public takes for granted that when they turn on their tap, clean, safe water will come out. It is viewed more as a certainty rather than as a commodity that must be monitored, conserved, and properly valued."[37]

So how do we better support public health in this country? More robust funding would help, for starters. There are more than 3,000 state and local public health agencies across the country, all of which are strapped for resources on a daily basis. According to the national health expenditures projections for 2018, governmental public health accounted for only 2.4% of total healthcare spending.[38] Federal public health funding over the last decade has been largely flat, while state and local public health department spending has been decreasing.[39] In addition, although public health emergencies occasionally lead to an infusion of funding, these resources are rarely permanent.

What would it take to provide robust sustainable funding? The answer to that question first requires defining the services that are necessary for public health to assure the conditions that allow for all Americans to be healthy. In 2014, the Robert Wood Johnson Foundation funded the Public Health Leadership Forum, a project of RESOLVE, to do just this. Experts identified a "minimum package" of services and crosscutting capabilities that public health should be expected to deliver. They came up with services in five areas, including communicable disease control; chronic disease and injury prevention; environmental public health; maternal, child, and family health; and access to and linkage with clinical care. They also identified a series of capabilities, or processes, that are critical to maximize the impact of the services provided. Capabilities included assessment (including surveillance, epidemiology, and laboratory capacity), all hazards preparedness and response, policy development, communications, community partnership development, and organizational competencies.[40]

Researchers at the University of Kentucky took this information to then estimate the cost of providing foundational public health services to all Americans. Using cost information from existing public health agencies, they estimated that achieving full implementation of public health services would require $82 per capita. Average current expenditures for agencies were at $48, indicating an estimated resource gap of $34 per capita.[41] Basically, as a country, we would need to spend another $10 billion on public health to meet this gap.

Fortunately, there are some ideas on how to raise these dollars. The Public Health Leadership Forum recently released a white paper recommending more robust financing of governmental public health capabilities, which amount to approximately $4.5 billion of the $10 billion gap. Specifically, the group called on Congress to create a new, permanent mandatory funding source that would require a state contribution such as exists for Medicaid. The funds would be distributed to states based on population size, although the secretary of HHS would be authorized to develop a risk adjustment formula to account for different levels of need.[42] The timing of this recommendation comes at a good time, as a recent poll sponsored by the de Beaumont Foundation found that almost nine of ten registered voters believe that public health departments play an important role in the health of their community. In addition, two-thirds of Americans believe state government should ensure that every community has access to basic public health protections.[43]

How could Congress be convinced of making such an investment? One way is to frame investments in public health as investments in our nation's infrastructure. It is true that people have different definitions of the term "infrastructure," including roads, bridges, rail systems, water and sewage systems, electrical grid, telephone lines, and cell towers, to name a few.[44] The one constant among all of these things is that we expect them to work and often take for granted on a daily basis that they do work. In this context, public health is a perfect fit, and yet it is rarely included in infrastructure policy debates.

Candidates on both sides of the aisle during the 2016 presidential election campaign touted infrastructure projects. In some ways, infrastructure investments are seen as the quintessential bipartisan issue—an opportunity to increase participation in the workforce and grow the economy through a federal stimulus. And Congress does have a track record in some infrastructure areas, such as highways and water projects, to come together on a regular basis to support infrastructure investments.[45]

In this respect, viewing public health as an infrastructure program may be an easier pitch to both sides of the aisle. Not only does public health assure the conditions for individuals in a community to be healthy, it can also have spillover effects to other communities. Think about communicable diseases, environmental health, and even policies to reduce chronic disease risk factors, many of which, using Malcolm Gladwell's words, have a high "stickiness factor," compelling others to take notice and follow.

Opportunities for the Future

Dr. Karen DeSalvo has been a national leader in pointing to public health's future as one that needs to anchor the infrastructure of any community. Calling this the Public Health 3.0 vision, she and colleagues have set forth the idea that public health needs to partner with every sector of society including education, housing, transportation, and others to build the infrastructure of healthy communities. By serving in the position of "Chief Health Strategist" for a community, public health leaders can ensure a vision in which health is considered in all policies. The vision is also grounded, in that there are already today shining examples of jurisdictions across the country that are working with a multisectoral approach with public health at the center—from Allegheny County, Pennsylvania, to Nashville, Tennessee, to Spokane, Washington.[46]

Integral to spreading these successful partnerships is identifying creative funding streams to support public health services. While new mandatory funding streams, as discussed above, would be a welcome development, this isn't the only option. One new idea from Dr. DeSalvo and colleagues includes federal transformation grants for state and local health departments to evolve toward a Public Health 3.0 model. Additional opportunities include public and private health insurance payers investing in public health recognizing its contribution in keeping Americans healthy and reducing healthcare costs.[47] For example, there are quite a few opportunities through Medicare and Medicaid, such as those discussed earlier that are related to the State Innovation Model and Accountable Health Communities, to partner with public health departments to address the social determinants of health. Nonprofit hospitals should also be coordinating with public health departments on their community health needs assessment and implementation plan efforts.

As described in chapter 4, the private sector more broadly could also play a role in supporting public health by investing in "pay for success" initiatives, or social impact bonds. In select cases where there is likely to be a financial return from a public health intervention, the public health field could look to private investors to provide the funding to jumpstart an initiative. As the effort starts to yield cost savings, the investment would be paid back. Social impact bonds have a positive track record in areas such as reducing recidivism and homelessness. More recently, they have been applied to select public health issues such as reducing premature births and childhood asthma.[48] As data from these efforts accumulate, there may be more opportunities to support public health services.

Beyond directly financing public health, the business sector should have a substantial interest in partnering with public health. While the number of employer wellness programs have skyrocketed in recent years and led to the growth of an $8 billion industry, their performance has been mixed with respect to long-term health and return on investment. The most likely explanation for this is that health is impacted by more than just lifestyle behaviors; one's environment has a profound impact on health. By working with local health departments to improve community health, businesses are more likely to see a greater and more sustained return on investment from employer wellness programs. National public health organizations should partner with entities such as the US Chamber of Commerce and National Business Group on Health to catalyze local partnerships between public health departments and local chambers of commerce or businesses. Partnerships would be driven by community needs, and data from the resulting interventions would be collected to assess progress. Every local public health department should be looking to establish partnerships with local businesses to build healthy communities.

As alluded to earlier, a final necessary requirement for public health to expand its influence is to better communicate what it's all about. Former assistant secretary of health Dr. John Agwunobi once reminded me that public health is made up of two words—"public" and "health." We, in the field, do great with respect to the latter word, in that we are up to date with the latest evidence-based science. It's the former word that we either take for granted or underappreciate. Without public dialogue and understanding public perceptions and perspectives, public health officials risk not being able to implement interventions to improve population health.

Again, vaccinations come to mind. The Research America survey described earlier revealed that only 77% of Americans were confident in the government's ability to evaluate the safety of vaccines and recommend when they should be given, down from 85% a decade ago.[49] There are far too many vaccine skeptics in the United States. Yet instead of discounting their concerns, we need to do a much better job demonstrating empathy and patiently explaining the science as we know it today. I have previously called for the Trump administration to deploy the surgeon general and officers of the US Public Health Services Commissioned Corps to regions of the country where immunization rates for vaccine-preventable diseases have fallen to dangerously low levels. Through local public health campaigns, these individuals could help create constructive dialogue between scientists and individuals with vaccine concerns. Congress and the administration, in parallel, should also support increased budgets at the NIH and the CDC for vaccine safety research and better coordinate existing vaccine surveillance systems administered across the US government.[50]

As a separate example, in 2017, I wrote an article in the *American Journal of Public Health* about public health communications lessons learned from the Affordable Care Act. While there were multiple points between 2012 and 2016 when one might have expected favorability of the ACA to improve (e.g., the 2012 and 2015 Supreme Court decisions, President Obama's 2012 reelection, and the 2016 announcement of 20 million Americans covered), this did not occur for a variety of reasons. From the perspective of translating health policy issues to the American public, lessons learned for public health practitioners include the need to be more attuned to health literacy, utilize a multilevel communications approach both for the mass audience and for individuals, and provide steady, incremental communication over an extended period of time.[51]

In their seminal piece questioning whether public health and prevention are "political lightweights," researchers Rick Mayes and Thomas Oliver point to four reasons why public health sometimes fails to garner political support. These include public health benefits often being delayed and dispersed, invisible and taken for granted, costly to certain sectors, and potentially clashing with moral values or social norms.[52] While many of these same challenges exist today, it is worth looking in depth at one area of public health that has been able to transcend these issues.

While September 11, 2001, and the subsequent anthrax attacks on our country will always be one of the darkest times in American history, one of the key byproducts of these events included elevated public health emergency preparedness. In contrast to public health in general, these activities have been visible to the public and have generally benefited from bipartisan support. In the next chapter, we explore how this came to be and possible lessons for public health more broadly.

Public Health Emergency Preparedness

The Great Uniter?

I N THE SUMMER of 2005, I made the difficult decision to forego full-time medical practice in the hopes of improving population health through public service. I recall during my search phase having an introductory meeting with Dr. William Raub at the Department of Health and Human Services. Bill, as I learned, had a storied career since joining the National Institutes of Health in the 1960s. His scientific contributions along with his effective leadership and management skills led him to become the acting director of the NIH between 1989 and 1991. Thereafter, he served in the Office of the Secretary working for multiple secretaries on both sides of the aisle. When I met him, he had recently been appointed by Secretary Mike Leavitt as his science advisor.

In our meeting, I recall describing to him my healthcare interests with respect to improving access to high-quality care as well as improving overall population health. After giving me a few additional names of people across the department to speak with, he casually asked me if I would come work for him. When I asked him what he focuses on, he started to enumerate a whole range of priorities related to public health emergency preparedness. One topic related to "modalities of mass prophylaxis," honestly an area that I had never come across before. Surely, I thought at the time, I wasn't leaving full-time medical practice to focus on this topic. I recall naively thanking him and respectfully declining his offer but taking him up on introductions to others. As fate would have it, none of those leads panned out, and I was soon back at Bill's door reminding him of that job he had offered. Fortunately for me, he said the offer still stood, and I took it. It was the best career decision I ever made.

For many in public health, the early and mid-2000s was an era in which emergency preparedness issues skyrocketed to the top of the priority list. In the aftermath of the horrific events of September 11, 2001, the country was further terrorized by the anthrax attacks on news agencies and Senate offices. Twenty-two Americans were sickened, and ultimately five died. In total, more than 32,000 people took antibiotics for possible *Bacillus anthracis* exposure, and public health laboratories across the country tested more than 70,000 samples.[1] These events were followed by post-9/11 investigations suggesting that al Qaeda was interested in developing biological weapons.[2]

The perceived threat led to bipartisan support for an infusion of significant funding into public health and hospital preparedness programs to bolster surveillance, laboratory capacity, workforce, and healthcare surge capacity. In 2004, Project BioShield was created to develop a cache of medical countermeasures against the most urgent threats. Through this public-private partnership, manufacturers are provided financial incentives and liability protections by the government to produce stockpiles of medicines. By 2005, it was clear that one of our preparedness gaps was how to quickly distribute life-saving medicines to an at-risk population in the event of a biological attack, such as an anthrax attack. Bill Raub used to give the example of the bacterium *Bacillus thuringiensis*, a member of the same group of bacteria as *Bacillus anthracis*. The former is a biological pesticide that is commonly applied through a crop duster. Change the organism and change the venue, and it's pretty easy to see how a mass casualty scenario is possible.

Expanding the so-called modalities of mass prophylaxis was our job at HHS. While the traditional approach of distributing medicines was to set up points of dispensing (PODs) staffed by public health officials, it was clear that model could be overwhelmed in the event of an attack and that supplementary approaches for distributing countermeasures would be needed. One approach we considered included home stockpiling of pharmaceutical kits containing several different countermeasures to be taken only when directed by public health authorities. One particular kit, called a "MedKit" was created in partnership with CDC officials led at the time by Dr. Richard Besser and deployed in a study of 4,000 individuals in St. Louis. The study question to be answered was whether over a six-month period, households could in fact store these medicines properly versus using them when a household member became ill during a non-emergency. The initial results were promising: 97% of all study respondents returned the MedKits upon completion of the study, and 99% of the returned MedKits were intact without pills missing.[3] This demonstrated to us that individuals for the most part could be trusted not to misuse or misplace household stockpiles of pharmaceuticals to be taken only during an emergency.

Another approach that we considered involved direct residential delivery to households by the US Postal Service (USPS).[4] The idea was that postal workers would deliver antibiotics in the event of an anthrax attack to every residence within a geographic area within a single day thus reducing demand on the PODs. Given concerns of worker safety, pre-event issuance of antibiotics to postal workers and their families would be planned, akin to the MedKits model. In addition, to address security threats, postal workers would be accompanied by law enforcement officials during their routes. To test this aspect of the model, we conducted drills in Philadelphia, Seattle, and Boston in 2006 and 2007 with the USPS and local law enforcement. The success of these exercises led to support of this option in the ensuing administration. During his first term, President Obama issued an Executive Order directing HHS, the Department of Homeland Security, and the US Postal Service to establish a National USPS Medical Countermeasure dispensing model for residential delivery of medicines following a biological attack.[5] However, due to a lack of funding support for MedKits for participating postal workers and their household members, the vision of nationwide implementation of this model has still not been realized.

While all of these modalities were being considered back in 2005 in preparation for a possible future bioterror attack, another potential emergency was brewing halfway across the world. Cases of H5N1 avian influenza in humans began popping up in Thailand, Vietnam, Cambodia, and Indonesia. By October 2005, 115 people had become infected, half of whom died, and there was concern that in some cases secondary transmission from person to person had occurred.[6] Given the devastating tolls of human health and the global economy from the 1918, 1957, and 1968 influenza pandemics, pandemic preparedness became a top priority. I was asked to assist Dr. Bruce Gellin, director of the National Vaccine Program Office, and other subject matter experts in putting together the HHS Pandemic Influenza Plan. Over the next couple of weeks, we developed a strategic plan that included planning assumptions for a moderate and severe pandemic influenza scenario, a doctrine to initiate and direct response activities, and a set of key pandemic response actions and capabilities needed for implementation of an effective response. Along with this document, CDC officials helped draft detailed public health guidance to state and local partners on issues as far ranging as healthcare planning, infection control, vaccine and antiviral drug distribution, and public health communications.[7]

On November 1, 2005, at an event at the National Institutes for Health, President George W. Bush unveiled the National Strategy for Pandemic Influenza while HHS simultaneously released its Pandemic Influenza Plan. Along with this, President Bush requested a $7.1 billion emergency supplemental to implement these plans. Congress ultimately provided $3.8 billion to increase vaccine production capacity, acquire antiviral drugs, stockpile critical medical supplies, and enhance state and local preparedness. Secretary Leavitt embarked on a nationwide tour hosting state summits that brought together community leaders, and the CDC released a series of checklists to aid stakeholders in their preparation for a pandemic.[8]

These were not ordinary times. I still vividly recall an evening in Michigan that year between Christmas and New Year's being back at my childhood public library creating a visual depiction of how all of our planned interventions would impact the inverted U-shape curve of a pandemic.

Basically, through preparedness and response activities, we were trying to (1) delay the initial spread of illness, (2) delay the peak of cases, (3) reduce the peak of cases, and (4) reduce the total number of cases. Variations[9] of the visual diagram I created became such a frequently used depiction in presentations describing HHS's pandemic strategy that colleagues used to joke that I should ask for royalties!

While the H5N1 virus fortunately did not achieve sustained human-to-human transmission triggering a pandemic, the many years of intense preparedness greatly helped the response to the eventual H1N1 influenza pandemic of 2009–2010. That pandemic, which started in Mexico and quickly spread worldwide, did not consist of a virulent pandemic strain. Overall mortality due to the pandemic was not much different from what would be normally expected during a mild seasonal influenza outbreak.[10] The combination of continuity of career civil servants and scientists along with new administration officials who realized a response to the pandemic needed to be a top priority benefited HHS's response. In addition, prior investments in domestic vaccine-manufacturing capacity, antiviral stockpiling, and prior planning and coordination within and between all levels of government led to a successful response to the epidemic.

Politics of Emergency Preparedness and Response

The first decade of the twenty-first century thus saw a significant bolstering of the public health infrastructure through emergency preparedness activities. Funding levels for state and local public health and hospital preparedness along with biodefense research increased significantly after 9/11. It should be said that support for these activities was largely bipartisan. A prime example of this is the passage of the Pandemic and All-Hazards Preparedness Act of 2006 (PAHPA). Under the leadership of Senate Majority Leader Dr. Bill Frist, during the 109th Congress, the Senate Health, Education, Labor, and Pensions (HELP) Committee created a new subcommittee focused on bioterrorism and public health preparedness. This Senate subcommittee, led by Chairman Richard Burr and Ranking

Member Edward Kennedy, spent over a year examining ways to further federal programs and policies to support emergency preparedness efforts.[11]

The resulting legislation, among other things, designated the secretary of the Department of Health and Human Services as the lead federal official for public health emergency preparedness and response, and it established the position of assistant secretary for preparedness and response to advise the HHS secretary on all matters related to public health and medical preparedness and response. It also established loan repayment programs for the public health workforce, authorized near-real-time surveillance systems, and created the Biomedical Advanced Research and Development Authority (BARDA) to accelerate development of medical countermeasures.[12] The final bill was passed by unanimous consent in the Senate and without objection in the House, which speaks to the bipartisan attention given to this issue.[13]

The second decade of the twenty-first century has also seen its share of public health emergencies. While in each case Congress came to agreement on supporting an executive branch response, partisanship has increasingly reared its head. The Ebola outbreak in West Africa gradually started to spread in the spring of 2014. As it became clear that neither the countries in the region nor the World Health Organization were likely to contain the outbreak on their own, the US government ratcheted up its role and involvement. This led to a $6.2 billion emergency funding request by the Obama administration in November 2014, of which $5.4 billion was appropriated by Congress within a month.[14] However, the lead-up to the administration's request saw both parties point fingers at one another. Democrats blamed Republicans for the 2013 government sequester, which reduced research funding for an Ebola vaccine. Republicans blamed the executive branch for not allocating funds appropriately.[15] In addition, some Republicans began to criticize the public health strategy used by the administration to keep Ebola from coming onto our shores and called for a travel ban from the affected countries. However, there was little evidence that such a strategy could work, particularly a unilateral travel ban by the United States. On the contrary, it was argued that such a ban would both hurt the United States economically and impede US assistance to the afflicted countries.[16,17]

However, no public health emergency brought out partisanship more than the congressional response to the Zika virus epidemic. While sporadic outbreaks of Zika virus causing mild illness had been reported for decades, in February 2015, Brazil experienced an explosion of cases that then spread to dozens of countries in South and Central America. At the same time, health authorities observed an increase in congenital malformations as well as an increase in a neurological syndrome called Guillian-Barre, in which a person's immune system attacks their peripheral nervous system.[18] In a preliminary report published in the *New England Journal of Medicine* in March 2016, researchers found that fetal abnormalities were detected by ultrasound in 29% of women who tested positive for Zika virus (versus none in those testing negative). Abnormalities included fetal death, fetal growth restriction (microcephaly is an example of abnormal brain development), and injuries to the central nervous system.[19] Another study by researchers at the CDC and Harvard found that pregnant women infected with the virus in their first trimester had as high as a 13% chance that their child would develop microcephaly.[20]

Therefore, the primary prevention strategy to reduce harm in infants and newborns focused on reducing exposure of women of reproductive age to the virus. While the primary mode of transmission for the Zika virus is through the bite of an *Aedes aegypti* or *albopictus* mosquito, sexual transmission, in addition to intrauterine and perinatal transmission, has been documented.[21] Thus, pregnancy planning and care in areas with potential local Zika virus transmission became a critical focus for public health authorities. This was particularly true, given that the geographic range of the mosquito, largely the Southern United States, also corresponded with the highest rates of unintended pregnancy in the country.[22]

The lead-up to the arrival of the *Aedes* mosquitos to the US mainland carrying the Zika virus focused on intense public health communications. The CDC emphasized that the best way to prevent Zika was to protect against mosquito bites and that pregnant women shouldn't travel to areas with Zika.[23] While the initial cases of Zika virus disease on the US main-land were travel related, widespread transmission occurred first in Puerto Rico. Then on July 19, authorities in Miami-Dade County, Florida, an-nounced that a woman tested positive for Zika virus without a prior travel history to a country with Zika.[24] Pregnant women were advised to avoid areas with transmission, and public health authorities sprang into action to reduce mosquitos in affected areas and encourage individuals to use precautions to prevent mosquito bites.[25] Over the course of the next few months, small pockets of transmission occurred in Florida and Texas, ac-counting for 224 cases of locally acquired Zika virus disease. By the end of the year, over 5,000 total cases had been reported in the United States and over 36,000 cases in US territories.[26]

While President Obama asked Congress for $1.9 billion to fight Zika in February 2016, ultimately it took Congress seven months to appropriate funds ($1.1 billion) to support the public health response. During that delay, HHS was forced to draw down funds from various other accounts, including unspent funds earmarked for the Ebola response, to speed de-velopment of a vaccine, expand mosquito control programs, and support pregnancy care and family planning efforts.[27] Why did it take seven months for Congress to respond to the crisis? There are a number of rea-sons. First, some members of Congress called on the administration to tap into designated Ebola funding prior to the allocation of additional emergency response funds. But that was like "robbing Peter to pay Paul," particularly since continued vigilance and activities were needed to en-sure that Ebola did not reemerge in West Africa.[28] However, it became clear with time that Republicans were also uneasy that taxpayer funds for family planning might go for abortion and birth control. On the other hand, Democrats were alarmed as to what they saw were Republican at-tempts to circumvent environmental regulations so that an array of differ-ent pesticides could be used for mosquito control activities.[29] Additional differences of opinion included the amount of the funding request and whether or not it should be fully offset.[30] One obvious solution for situa-tions like this is to have a public health emergency fund that could be drawn from in the same way as the Federal Emergency Management

Agency (FEMA) draws down on the Disaster Relief Fund in the event of hurricanes and other natural disasters. Members on both sides of the aisle have supported such a fund in concept.[31] The interesting thing is that such a fund has existed for decades, it just has no money in it.

The impact of congressional inaction over the better part of seven months on the transmission of Zika virus is still being understood. What we do know is about one in seven children exposed to Zika during pregnancy was born with a Zika-associated birth defect or developed neurological deficits possibly associated with congenital Zika virus infection. These findings were reported by CDC researchers studying 1,450 children who were at least one year of age by February 1, 2018, in the US Zika Pregnancy and Infant Registry.[32] Beyond the significant impact on quality of life for each of these children and their families, it's estimated that the average lifetime costs of care for each child will be in the millions of dollars.[33] One can only wonder whether we could have reduced exposure of the virus to pregnant women by more quickly equipping public health and healthcare authorities with the tools they needed for mosquito control, public education, and family planning.

All of these examples reflect that while it often takes a crisis in Washington for lawmakers of different political persuasions to come together, this isn't always a given and responses are not always timely. Whereas a lack of attention to public health in general might lead to consequences well into the future, a lack of bipartisanship prior to and during an emergency response can have tragic consequences. Have the political parties learned their lessons?

With respect to the executive branch, one recent example provides optimism. One of the most vulnerable populations in the event of natural disasters leading to power outages has been Americans dependent on electricity-powered medical equipment. The Obama administration created the emPOWER initiative in 2015 specifically to identify the approximately 2.5 million Medicare beneficiaries reliant on medical equipment requiring electricity. By integrating this data with real-time weather data and GIS (geographic information system) data, HHS supports communities in their preparedness activities. Importantly, the initiative also allows local public health authorities to request and securely receive individual-specific information so that they can conduct outreach to at-risk beneficiaries prior to a natural disaster.[34] The Trump administration utilized the tool in preparation for Hurricane Irma in 2017 and continues to refine the emPOWER map and datasets, which have now been used in communities across all 50 states and 5 territories.[35]

With respect to Congress, the reauthorization of PAHPA has demonstrated strong bipartisanship. The legislation, which was nearly enacted in 2018, would reauthorize vital programs for public health and hospital preparedness and improve benchmarks and standards for preparedness and response. While it would also accelerate medical countermeasure advanced research and development, the legislation appears to fall short in one regard; it does not explicitly direct funding for Project BioShield to be provided by advance appropriations, as had been the case during its initial ten-year funding period from 2004 to 2014.[36] As former senators Tom Daschle and Judd Gregg argued in a 2018 Bipartisan Policy Center report on budgeting for medical countermeasures, advance funding allowed for comprehensive federal funding and a degree of certainty for private sector manufacturers of the government's commitment. In contrast, budgeting through the annual appropriations process since 2014 has led to smaller awards and greater uncertainty as to whether future funding will materialize. While advance appropriations would need to overcome statutory and procedural hurdles, it is possible, if Congress has the will. Indeed, advance appropriations are used to fund many different programs across the government, many of which do not carry a similar weight of potential consequences should they not be funded.[37]

Beyond funding for medical countermeasures, the bipartisan Blue Ribbon Study Panel on Biodefense, established in 2014 to provide recommendations for improving US biodefense, has noted the importance of high-level leadership to coordinate federal biodefense activities. Specifically, the Panel has previously recommended that biodefense leadership be provided by the vice president and through the establishment of a White House Biodefense Coordination Council. In addition, the Panel has noted the need for a comprehensive national strategic plan for biodefense in addition to an integrated dedicated budget for biodefense.[38]

It's important that these recommendations be acted upon, given that the threat of bioterrorism is not going away anytime soon. As indicated in the BPC's report, there are a number of countries that are believed either to possess or to be actively pursuing biological weapons.[39] In addition, nine out of 10 Americans surveyed are concerned that terrorists might use chemical or biological weapons against the United States, and most support increasing funding for preventive measures for biological threats.[40] Leaders and philanthropists such as Bill Gates have expressed public concern about the potential damage from a bioterrorism attack[41] and reportedly discussed this with President Donald Trump.[42]

Threats of Significant Concern

Beyond bioterrorism, there are arguably two even bigger threats that demand bipartisanship and the attention of public health leaders, namely, pandemic influenza and antimicrobial-resistant bacteria. With respect to pandemic influenza, as noted earlier, the world was quite fortunate that the H5N1 avian influenza virus did not become a pandemic and that the H1N1 swine flu virus was not severely virulent. However, most experts believe that it's not a question of if but when the next 1918-like severe influenza pandemic will occur. To that end, much has been accomplished to date to ensure that the United States has stockpiled vaccines, drugs, diagnostics, and medical devices for pandemic influenza. The most important factor in limiting mortality in the event of a severe influenza pandemic is time to produce a safe and effective vaccine. In a mock pandemic exercise hosted by the Johns Hopkins Center for Health Security in 2018, one of the chief reasons 150 million people died in the scenario was that a vaccine had not been developed within 20 months.[43] In contrast, it took about 6 months in 2009 from the first case of the H1N1 virus in the continental United States for a pandemic vaccine to start arriving in hospitals and doctors' offices.[44] Building on the H1N1 experience, HHS has further strengthened components of the vaccine production enterprise, from partnering with organizations to conduct vaccine clinical trials to partnering with companies to fill and finish vials with vaccine and prepare them for shipping. Both the H5N1 and H1N1 experiences have led to a significant increase in domestic vaccine-manufacturing capacity.[45]

Though it may not be recognized by the public as such, the annual flu season in many ways is also an exercise in pandemic preparedness.[46] Unfortunately, as discussed in chapter 6, it's a deadly exercise, in that each year thousands of Americans die from the flu. Reasons for this include poor vaccine uptake, imprecision in selecting circulating influenza viruses for inclusion in the annual seasonal influenza vaccine, lack of timely initiation of antiviral medications in individuals at higher risk for flu complications, and less than ideal compliance with nonpharmacologic interventions such as hand hygiene and avoiding contact with others while ill. These are all areas we need to improve on, both to reduce annual seasonal influenza burden and to prepare for the next pandemic influenza.

One potential game changer for seasonal influenza, and thus indirectly for pandemic influenza, is the development of a universal influenza vaccine.[47] Such a vaccine, according to the National Institute of Allergy and Infectious Diseases (NIAID), would be at least 75% effective, protect against multiple subtypes of flu, have long-lasting protection that lasts at least one year, and be suitable for all age groups. In February 2018, the NIAID released a Universal Influenza Vaccine Strategic Plan to provide a roadmap for developing such a vaccine. Agency scientists also recently commenced clinical trials of different prototype vaccines that have the potential to be effective against multiple influenza strains.[48] Early indications are that this effort will not be easy. As NIAID director Dr. Anthony Fauci explains, our immune system responds the strongest to the first flu virus we are exposed to in life—a concept referred to as imprinting. How a universal flu vaccine competes with the phenomenon of imprinting, in addition to how long protection lasts and for how many strains, are all open questions.[49]

The search for a universal vaccine has resulted in a whole of society response. This involves not just government agencies and industry but also academia and philanthropy. As an example, Bill Gates, in partnership with Google Inc. cofounder Larry Pate, recently announced a $12 million Grand Challenge to accelerate the development of a universal flu vaccine.[50] While the NIAID reportedly spent $64 billion in 2017 on developing a universal flu vaccine, some policymakers think that more resources need to go to this effort. Specifically, Senator Ed Markey has sponsored a bill that would devote $1 billion over five years toward the effort. While this sum seems large, one could argue that it pales in comparison to the $10.4 billion in annual direct medical costs and $87 billion in total economic burden of the flu.[51]

Antimicrobial resistance is the second area for which prevention and preparedness efforts are absolutely critical. As infectious disease expert Michael Osterholm has noted, the impact of an antimicrobial-resistant bacteria could be catastrophic, as routine injuries and routine healthcare procedures could become fatal. Osterholm points to a scenario where we would be going back to a time prior to the advent of antibiotics.[52]

Antibiotic resistance is already a significant problem in the United States. It's estimated that 23,000 Americans die annually from "superbugs" and more than two million people are infected.[53] In 2016, my father contracted an antibiotic-resistant bacterium after undergoing a medical procedure. Not only did he become quite ill and require hospitalization, his infection required six weeks of home intravenous antibiotics. Sadly, this story is all too common and a byproduct of a healthcare sector and agricultural sector that overprescribes antibiotics. Experts believe that one-third of oral antibiotics prescribed in outpatient facilities and emergency rooms are unnecessary. And one study found that, of the instances when antibiotics are required, in a third of cases, providers select the wrong drug, thus further increasing the likelihood of antibiotic resistance. In addition, while there's a scarcity of data on antibiotic use in animal agriculture compared to other countries, data from the FDA demonstrate an increase in antimicrobials sold or distributed for use in food-producing animals between 2009 and 2015 before a decline between 2015 and 2016.[54]

Several years ago, the CDC published a list of the top 18 drug-resistant threats to the United States. Three were identified as urgent threats, including *Clostridium difficile*, a bacterium related to antibiotic use and resistance that itself is associated with at least 500,000 illnesses and 15,000 deaths annually. Another threat, carbapenem-resistant Enterobacteriaceae (CRE), has required unearthing old antibiotics used decades ago.[55] Fortunately, the CDC has taken a multipronged and forward-leaning approach to detect, respond to, and contain antibiotic resistance as well as prevent further resistance.[56] A whole of government response was initiated in 2014 leading to an executive order from President Obama on combating antibiotic-resistant bacteria and the issuing of the first National Strategy for Combating Antibiotic-Resistant Bacteria.[57] The Trump administration has continued building momentum by launching the "AMR Challenge" in 2018 with more than a hundred commitments from organizations working together to address antibiotic resistance.[58] While developing new drugs and diagnostic tests as well as response activities to contain antibiotic-resistant bacteria are critical, perhaps the most important strategy is improving antibiotic prescribing or stewardship. The CDC has identified core elements of antibiotic stewardship in hospitals and nursing homes. This is so important, given that, amazingly, half of hospital admissions result in an antibiotic being prescribed.[59] According to the Trust for America's Health, only 20 states and Washington, DC, have 70% or more of hospitals meeting core elements of the CDC's Antibiotic Stewardship Program.[60] Thus, it's vital that the healthcare system redouble its efforts to prevent the rise of superbugs.

In conclusion, preparedness for public health emergencies, whether natural or man-made, has the potential to prevent catastrophic levels of mortality and morbidity. One requirement common to all of these threats is the need for collaboration with other countries. Indeed, global cooperation is critical to detecting, assessing, mobilizing, and responding to most public health emergencies. We live in a world and in an age where everything is interconnected. A novel infectious disease is only a plane ride away, and microbes know no borders. This is just one of many reasons why we must care about global health. In the next chapter, I discuss why global health is indeed US health.

[8]

Is Global Health US Health?

T HE KAISER FAMILY Foundation conducted a Health Tracking Poll in December 2015 and asked a provocative question to the public. What percentage of the federal budget is spent on foreign aid? The average response was that 31% of the federal budget was spent on foreign aid, of which global health is one component. I would have guessed lower, perhaps 5% to 10%. The right answer? Actually, less than 1%.[1]

It's unclear why public perception is out of touch with reality when it comes to how much is spent overseas. In some ways, the current administration's "America First" approach seizes on this perception and attempts to push policymakers to further look inward instead of outward. The notion is that we should take care of our internal challenges and let other countries deal with their respective ones. However, that logic breaks down, particularly when it comes to health. The fact of the matter is that most public health challenges faced by countries around the world are common and shared. Our safety and security are only as good as the weakest link outside our borders. There's no better example of this than infectious diseases and global health security.

Almost every emergency response discussed in the previous chapter relied on actions by countries around the world, or global organizations such as the World Health Organization (WHO). When these countries succeeded, our security was enhanced; when they failed, our security was threatened. Ebola provides a case in point. During the first few months of 2014, it was apparent that the West African countries of Guinea, Sierra Leone, and Liberia had neither a comprehensive emergency response system nor a robust underlying healthcare infrastructure to respond to the Ebola outbreak. Cases initially went undetected and then exploded, overwhelming an unprepared healthcare system that was poorly staffed and without the medicines and diagnostic tests required to manage the outbreak. The WHO and countries around the world, though initially delayed in their response, ultimately provided health personnel, technical assistance, and logistical support necessary to support the countries in controlling the outbreak.[2] (The WHO has since set up a Global Preparedness Monitoring Board to better monitor country readiness to respond to outbreaks.)[3] Fortunately, while cases also spread into Nigeria, Mali, and Senegal, a rapid public health and healthcare response contained the outbreak before it spread to more populous areas. Unfortunately, the overall epidemic still claimed 11,000 lives and the economic impact to the West African countries was $2.8 billion.[4]

The importance of ensuring that every country in the world has the ability to prevent, detect, and respond to infectious diseases is why the Global Health Security Agenda (GHSA) was launched in 2014. While the World Health Organization issued International Health Regulations back in 2005 that set requirements for all countries to prepare for public health emergencies, many countries were not keeping pace. The mission of the GHSA is to ramp up technical assistance to countries and create measurable targets to assess progress. As of January 2018, over 60 countries have joined the GHSA and completed voluntary assessments to determine gaps in health security capacity. Through the CDC and USAID (US Agency for International Development), the United States has spent approximately $700 million to assist over 30 countries in the early detection of serious infectious diseases and effective responses to outbreaks.[5]

A 2018 White House report highlights specific examples of US assistance helping countries in Africa and Asia contain threats such as avian influenza and hemorrhagic fever over the last several years. The stories are uplifting. With respect to preventing avoidable outbreaks, as an example, in Guinea, Liberia, and Sierra Leone about 38,000 healthcare workers and community health agents were trained in infection prevention and control standards and practices. In India, over a thousand laboratory technicians were trained in biosafety and biosecurity principles and applications. With respect to detecting early threats, Bangladesh now has laboratory capability to detect pathogens such as anthrax and hemorrhagic fever, while Vietnam has a real-time electronic surveillance and reporting system for 44 communicable diseases across all of its provinces and districts. With respect to rapid response, Cameroon has tested its emergency management capability through a full-scale cholera response and in addition activated its emergency response center within 24 hours to respond to a meningitis outbreak.[6]

While this progress is laudable, it's unclear whether US leadership for global health security will continue. In 2018, the CDC began to wind down operations in the majority of the countries the United States committed to working with back in 2015. The reason for this is that the initial US investment in 2014 was a one-time, five-year commitment that is slated to run out in September 2019.[7] The administration has proposed a funding cut of two-thirds in the FY19 budget and it's unclear whether other nations will pick up the slack should the United States reduce its contributions to global health security.[8] Fortunately, members of Congress are increasingly speaking out in support of sustaining US investments. It should be clear that the capability of preventing, detecting, and responding to outbreaks requires sustained infrastructure, training, and exercising over time. A one-time infusion of funding will not necessarily lead to robust capacity or tested capability. Certainly, individual countries also need to ramp up their domestic investment in emergency preparedness, as this is critical to long-term sustainability. However, the current funding impasse does not seem well thought out and is potentially risky, given the emerging infections and threats looming globally.

One positive development in the fight to achieve global health security has been the formation of several nongovernmental organizations with a mission to support preparedness efforts of low- and middle-income countries. For example, Resolve to Save Lives, an organization led by former

CDC director Dr. Tom Frieden, is providing resources and technical assistance to governments around the world to strengthen their public health infrastructure for purposes of containing outbreaks. The five-year, $225 million campaign is backed by a formidable group of philanthropies, including Bloomberg Philanthropies, the Chan Zuckerberg Initiative, and the Bill and Melinda Gates Foundation.[9]

What is unique about the effort is the situational awareness the organization provides with respect to global outbreaks. Its website, Prevent Epidemics.org, depicts a map of the world that color codes countries based on objective assessments of their level of epidemic preparedness. On the bottom of this page is a ticker that provides real-time information on worldwide outbreaks as reported by various media and platforms such as Google. In fact, on a separate page, one can visualize all the reported outbreaks occurring all over the world.[10] In this era of big data, it is a powerful tool that provides a sense of clarity and anxiety simultaneously.

Another nongovernmental organization filling a gap is the Coalition for Epidemic Preparedness Innovations, or CEPI. Launched at Davos, Switzerland, in 2017 and founded by the governments of Norway and India along with philanthropies and other investors, the organization focuses on accelerating the development of new vaccines against emerging threats.[11] Its CEO is Dr. Richard Hatchett. Richard started his career as a cancer doctor while researching radiation countermeasures. He too was a protégé of Bill Raub, and we had an opportunity to work together on biosecurity policy and pandemic preparedness.

The CEPI is developing vaccine candidates against multiple emerging infectious disease threats for which there is a high risk of a future outbreak.[12] It is also funding new and innovative platform technologies with the potential to expeditiously develop and manufacture vaccines against previously unknown pathogens so that vaccine safety testing can commence within months of the new pathogen being genetically sequenced.[13] Finally, a key goal for the CEPI is ensuring access of newly developed vaccines to low-income countries, which tend to be at highest risk from epidemic threats and have the least domestic vaccine-manufacturing capacity.

The premise of both Resolve to Save Lives and the CEPI is simple. The best way to prevent an epidemic or pandemic is to contain it at the source. If a threat can be neutralized through rapid detection and response utilizing a range of countermeasures including vaccines, then all countries win. Both of these organizations are filling gaps in global health security and working in complement to governments and multilateral organizations.

US Global Health in Action

However, stopping infectious diseases from coming to our border isn't the only reason for the United States to engage in global health efforts. The reality is that there's significant disease burden across the world, and frankly the United States has the means to do something about it. While the United States contains less than 5% of the world's population, it accounts for a quarter of worldwide GDP, or economic output. Simply put, the United States has the ability to help many people around the world attain healthier lives.

I saw the impact of US global health efforts firsthand as a member of HHS secretary Kathleen Sebelius's delegation to India in 2012. As an Indian American, I've always had a special connection with India and previously made several trips to visit family as well as to participate in public health efforts (I went to South India in the days after the Indian Ocean earthquake and tsunami in 2004 to help with medical relief efforts).

The purpose of the secretary's trip was to meet with the Indian minister of health and review health collaborations between the two countries. For the last 45 years, HHS has staffed an office in India to provide support for research and public health programs focused on HIV/AIDS, smallpox, polio, tuberculosis, malaria, influenza, maternal and child health, and noncommunicable diseases (NCDs). The programs are implemented by staff from HHS agencies such as the CDC, the FDA, and the National Institutes of Health in conjunction with their Indian counterparts.

There were numerous highlights of the trip, including a visit to a polio vaccination clinic to recognize the achievements India has made toward polio eradication; a visit to India's CDC to support establishment of a Global Disease Detection Center; and a visit to the FDA's office in India to support its relationship with the Indian government. In addition, we witnessed several US-India partnerships focused on noncommunicable diseases, a particular interest of mine, as I cochaired the US-India NCD working group.

The site visits were informative and provided on-the-ground validation of the importance of these global health efforts. There was the visit to Ballabgarh Civil Hospital, which is working with the CDC to improve influenza-like illness surveillance in India; the visit to BJ Medical College, where researchers are working with the NIH on HIV prevention interventions; and the visit to Emcure Pharmaceuticals, which exports various drugs to the United States while working closely with the FDA to ensure safe, quality manufactured products.

The most memorable moments from a prevention perspective involved children. One event was organized with the Health-Related Information Dissemination Amongst Youth-Student Health Action Network (HRIDAY). The organization trains teachers and adolescents in areas such as tobacco control, healthy diet and nutrition, regular physical activity, alcohol avoidance, mental health, and road safety. At the time, it was also conducting NIH-funded studies testing the effectiveness of youth tobacco prevention programs. I still recall three adolescents selected to describe to us how they implemented those programs in their own schools. To say that we were inspired is an understatement; there's nothing like the youth of the world promoting health that makes me more hopeful.

Similarly, our visit to a polio vaccination site, during which each of us, including the secretary, gave children oral polio drops, was equally meaningful. The achievement of polio eradication in India is an extraordinary public health story, a testament to thousands of public health workers supported by an array of nongovernmental and governmental organizations reaching almost every child in the nation. That day, we celebrated one year since India had last reported a case of polio. To this day, India remains polio-free.

Another example demonstrating the impact of US global health aid occurred during the tenure of Secretary Mike Leavitt. In a 2008 meeting with the Iraqi health minister, the secretary learned about the toll that the Iraq war had imposed on the medical profession. It turns out that in the years following the 2003 invasion and subsequent internal conflict, thousands of physicians had experienced violent events, including murder and kidnapping.[14] Beyond this, many physicians were not able to keep up with evidence-based medicine to provide optimal care to their patients. The Iraqi health minister asked the secretary whether the United States could arrange preceptorships for Iraqi physicians so they could learn from their US counterparts and establish connections.[15] The secretary agreed, and over the next six months I was part of a small team that worked to arrange for the visit of Iraqi physicians to the United States for month-long preceptorships. The preparation included identifying medical institutions across the country to host these physicians and matching physicians of varying specialties with the most appropriate experiences. We also needed to work with the State Department to coordinate their entry visas, as many of them had never previously been to the United States.

In the fall of 2008, 27 Iraqi physicians came to the United States and after a brief orientation in Washington, DC, traveled to various host sites across the country. These included academic medical centers such as Johns Hopkins Hospital and Children's National Medical Center in Washington, DC, to community health centers to Indian Health Services (IHS) hospitals.[16] While observing patient care in US facilities was a rewarding experience for the group, for many, the professional contacts they developed to assist with future patient consultations was even more important.

What I recall thinking during my time with these physicians was how they persevered through this difficult time in their nation's history. For them, each day was not only about their respective patients' survival but also their very own survival. I marveled at their courage and strength to carry on and seek further medical training. It demonstrated nothing less than an incredible devotion to their fellow Iraqi citizens and to their country. This is another example of how the United States' vast public and private sector resources have great potential to prevent disease and reduce suffering around the world.

Strategic Health Diplomacy

While the prior examples demonstrate the benefit that US expertise and resources can have on improving health all over the world, they may also be directly benefiting America's strategic interests. A healthier Indian population, soon to be the largest in the world, makes for a more prosperous democratic ally in South Asia, which is important for both US economic and national security interests. A cadre of Iraqi physicians knowledgeable about the latest in medical standards of care may help improve the quality of healthcare services for an ailing postwar population and bolster the civil infrastructure of the nation.

The concept that we can go out and improve health in the world while at the same time furthering our national security interests is called *strategic health diplomacy*. Introduced by former Senate majority leaders Tom Daschle and Dr. Bill Frist, the concept was featured in a 2015 Bipartisan Policy Center report depicting the President's Emergency Plan for AIDS Relief (PEPFAR) as a case study.[17]

The story of PEPFAR is well known in global health circles. In the late 1990s and early 2000s, Africa faced a humanitarian crisis of generational proportions, with HIV/AIDS emerging as the continent's leading cause of death.[18] In this context, President George W. Bush launched PEPFAR, a $15 billion initiative designed to provide treatment and care for those affected by the disease. Over the last 15 years, supported by multiple re-authorizations of PEPFAR and enhanced funding support, the public health impact of PEPFAR has been extraordinary. Over 14 million people are now on antiretroviral therapy and more than 2.2 million babies of HIV-positive mothers have been born free of HIV. PEPFAR has also implemented effective prevention interventions that have the potential to bend the epidemic curve in the region. Beyond HIV/AIDS, PEPFAR investment in laboratory capacity-building in Nigeria and Uganda has helped both to prevent and to contain Ebola outbreaks in the region.[19]

Less discussed about PEPFAR are the potential secondary-order effects of this global health initiative. In two sequential BPC reports in 2015 and 2018, Daschle and Frist found that PEPFAR investments have been associated with higher public opinion of the United States. Studies suggest that to influence public opinion, global health programs must focus on a widely understood need and be visible, effective, and sustained over time. PEPFAR meets all of these criteria. As their report notes, positive public opinion enhances our ability to work with other countries across a host of diplomatic issues.[20]

The senators also found that PEPFAR was associated with greater growth in worker productivity and economic development in program countries. In fact, increases in employment have been correlated with greater access to HIV/AIDS treatment. Strong and vibrant economies in turn provide our country with more reliable trading partners. Third, the senators found associations between PEPFAR and improved governance, stability, and civil society engagement.[21] A 2018 study from the Harvard Global Health Institute demonstrated that the highest per capita spending by the United States on health aid was associated with a large and immediate decline in state fragility, an index that gauges a state's vulnerability to collapse or conflict.[22] In addition, PEPFAR investments have also been associated with reductions in AIDS orphans, an important factor, given that high rates of orphaned children are considered a risk factor for state fragility.

Finally, in interviews with more than a dozen US ambassadors, the senators and BPC team found that PEPFAR enhanced diplomatic engagement. Starting a high-level conversation off with the impact of PEPFAR often provided an ice-breaker for diplomats to broach more sensitive foreign policy issues with their counterparts.[23] Through a strategic health diplomacy lens, PEPFAR thus stands out as a model program—one that has not only prevented HIV/AIDS cases and deaths but one that is linked to preventing economic and political instability and preserving US bilateral relationships.

This leads to the question of whether there are other global health challenges that could also be addressed through strategic health diplomacy. In the 2015 BPC report, three criteria were identified to select additional areas of focus: (1) the prevalence or rapidity of epidemic growth; (2) its treatment potential, or the potential for containment through prevention strategies; and (3) the strategic value of stricken areas.[24] Based on these criteria, there are two areas that I believe must be prioritized, namely, the prevention of noncommunicable diseases and the prevention of diseases due to lack of clean water and sanitation. Both deserve some discussion.

There has been so much focus and attention over the last several decades, and rightfully so, on curbing infectious diseases that many people may be surprised by this fact: more than seven out of ten deaths worldwide are due to noncommunicable diseases, conditions such as cardiovascular diseases, cancers, diabetes, and chronic respiratory diseases.[25] The vast majority of these deaths occur in low- and middle-income countries, thus dispelling the myth that these "chronic diseases" as they are called here in the United States, are only a challenge in wealthy countries with long life expectancies. In fact, these conditions are striking individuals at a much younger age in low- and middle-income countries, given trends in globalization. Exposure to chronic disease risk factors such as tobacco and alcohol use along with unhealthful foods, particularly in urban areas, are leading to increasing rates of NCDs, further straining healthcare systems that are on average significantly underfunded and already overwhelmed.[26]

Evidence shows that millions of deaths attributed to NCDs in low- and middle-income countries occur between the ages of 30 and 69 years.[27] From a strategic health diplomacy perspective, the "premature" deaths caused by NCDs have an impact on worker productivity, economic growth, and civil society stability. The World Economic Forum has projected that NCDs will lead to $21.3 trillion in losses of output in low- and middle-income countries over the next two decades ($47 trillion worldwide).[28]

In response to this global burden, the United Nations has now hosted three high-level meetings on NCDs, including mental illness, in 2011, 2014, and most recently in 2018. This is a big deal, as it is one of the few times a health issue has been brought to the highest level of the United Nations. The effort has resulted in a number of national commitments to prevent and treat NCDs and in the establishment of a comprehensive global monitoring framework for NCDs.[29] For example, all countries must consider setting national NCD targets for 2025 and have plans in place to reach these targets. NCDs have also made it into the United Nations' Sustainable Development Goals (SDGs), which are its overarching global goals, with a target to reduce, by 2030, premature mortality from non-communicable diseases by one-third.[30] While the issue has galvanized the attention of the United Nations, member countries, and civil societies, global financing initiatives similar to HIV/AIDS and vaccines have remained elusive. This is unfortunate, particularly given the fact that there is a plethora of evidence-based cost-effective interventions to address NCDs and their respective risk factors.

Many of these interventions were laid out in a seminal 2014 report on NCDs released by an independent task force of the Council on Foreign Relations. The bipartisan group, chaired by former Indiana governor Mitch Daniels and former national security advisor Thomas Donilon, identified areas specifically where US leadership could make a tremendous difference in curbing NCDs. Its highest recommendations for impact in the near term focused on primary and secondary prevention of cardiovascular disease, specifically through hypertension control; tobacco control; hepatitis B vaccination to prevent liver cancer; and human papillomavirus (HPV) vaccination and screening programs to prevent cervical cancer. The task force recommended that the United States should leverage its existing global health programs and private sector partners to provide countries with technical assistance to implement proven prevention policies, support surveillance efforts of NCD risk factors, and facilitate access to low-cost generic medications and vaccine delivery platforms.[31]

US government investments to combat global noncommunicable diseases are not officially tracked but are estimated to be less than 1% of US global health funding. The task force of the Council on Foreign Relations put it another way. The United States spends $0.02 in global health investments per each year of life lost to disability and early death from NCDs, compared to, for example, $44.17 for each year of life lost to disability and early death from HIV/AIDS.[32] The US government should urgently inventory its global NCD programs, activities, and initiatives to see which can be augmented to maximize impact. More importantly, existing global health efforts and platforms in other areas should be leveraged to find opportunities to add interventions that prevent or control NCDs where feasible.

Beyond government, global health philanthropy has also paid very little attention to NCDs. An exception is Bloomberg Philanthropies, which recently committed $800 million over six years to global health efforts centered around NCD data gathering, tobacco control, obesity prevention, and road safety.[33] In fact, former mayor Michael Bloomberg's passion to tackle NCDs has led to his being appointed by the World Health Organization as the first Global Ambassador for Noncommunicable Diseases.[34] We need more leaders in government and the private sector to follow his lead.

As staggering as the burden of NCDs is, what might be more inhumane is the lack of access to clean water, sanitation, and hygiene (WASH). As a board member of WaterAid America since 2016, I've learned a lot about this topic. Approximately 2.1 billion people don't have access to clean water, and 4.5 billion people live without a toilet.[35] Why this matters from a health perspective is that a newborn dies every minute from an infection caused by lack of safe water and an unclean environment. Diarrhea caused by dirty water and poor toilets kills a child under 5 every two minutes; in fact, it's estimated that if everyone had access to clean water, the total number of diarrheal deaths worldwide would be cut by a third.[36] As if this weren't enough, an additional concern has arisen from studies demonstrating the lack of clean water, sanitation, and lack of soap for handwashing in healthcare facilities in developing countries.[37, 38] Healthcare-associated infections from lack of clean water are a real risk and have spurred the WHO to develop an Action Plan on WASH in health facilities to provide universal access by 2030.[39]

But lack of clean water and access to sanitation impacts more than just health. It's an issue that is tied to economic growth, women's and girls' empowerment, prevention of conflict zones, agriculture policy, and environmental health policy, just to name a few areas. Water has been branded as the "new oil" in the twenty-first century, a necessity for any country aspiring to stability and prosperity.[40]

Fortunately, the US government has demonstrated a bipartisan commitment to supporting increased access to clean water and sanitation across the globe. Senator Bill Frist notably has played a leadership role in many of the initial efforts, including the passage of the Senator Paul Simon Water for the Poor Act of 2005, establishing WASH as a foreign policy priority.[41] The subsequent Senator Paul Simon Water for World Act of 2014 further supported WASH funding to some of the world's poorest countries and required the president to submit a Global Water Strategy to Congress every five years starting in 2017. The first sentence of the Strategy reads like it came out of a strategic health diplomacy playbook: "There is a growing global water crisis that may increase disease, undermine economic growth, foster insecurity and state failure, and generally reduce the capacity of countries to advance priorities that support U.S. national interests." The report lays out strategic objectives and priority actions across 17 government agencies and departments.[42]

While planning and coordination are necessary for US efforts to have an impact, they are not sufficient without adequate funding. Unfortunately, the Trump administration's budget requests have included elimination of USAID's Development Assistance Account, which funds WASH programs.[43] Fortunately, Congress has not supported slashing the budget of USAID; in fact, the Senate subcommittee overseeing USAID and Department of State budgets recommended $435 million for USAID WASH activities for fiscal year 2019, $129 million above the president's budget request.[44]

This brings us back to the broader issue of global health funding raised at the outset of this chapter. Without sufficient financial commitments, the United States will not be able to support the prevention of global infectious diseases, noncommunicable diseases, or WASH-related diseases. Further, our global health challenges will only grow in the future, with climate change due to the burning of fossil fuels resulting in global warming. Heat waves, weather-related natural disasters, outbreaks of mosquito-borne diseases, and air pollution are all increasing secondary to global warming.[45] The resulting human health impacts include conditions such as increased allergic illnesses, vector-borne diseases, mental illness, sleep loss, kidney stones, low birth weight, violence, and suicide.[46, 47] Air pollution in and of itself causes 7 million deaths worldwide every year and costs an estimated $5 trillion globally[48] (the director-general of the WHO has called air pollution the "new tobacco").[49] Reductions in CO_2 emissions are urgently required across the world to prevent the anticipated health consequences of climate change. At the same time, resources to promote climate resiliency as well as to support preparedness and response activities related to these public health events will be necessary.

The two most important takeaways from the Kaiser Family Foundation's polling of Americans' view on the US role in global health are the belief that the US government spends more than it actually does on global health and skepticism that funding will have much impact.[50] There is a significant need to educate Americans about the true amount of spending and the cost-effectiveness of proven evidence-based interventions to tackle some of the world's most pressing challenges. The majority of global health challenges directly or indirectly impact the health of Americans as well as our economic and national security interests. The United States also has a great deal it could learn from studying health innovations from abroad. For example, the deployment of community health workers by many countries to facilitate local health promotion and disease prevention is a model that is increasingly being adapted in this country. Most importantly, global health efforts should be supported because it's the right thing to do. We have the ability and means to make a difference in the world and prevent human suffering. This is a mantle of leadership that we should not cede to anyone else.

Twenty-First-Century Urgent Challenges and Promising Opportunities

THIS BOOK has been about the urgent need to emphasize and prioritize disease prevention, both within and outside the clinical setting, to improve the health of Americans. In this final chapter, I'll focus first on two health challenges facing the nation that urgently require a prevention orientation, namely, mental illness and substance abuse disorders. Second, I will discuss two promising opportunities to enable clinical and community prevention services through genomics and digital technology.

While the country has come a long way, the stigma of mental illness and substance abuse still remains. Infrequently, healthcare professionals add to the stigma by regarding mental illness and addiction as secondary ailments compared to other, physical ailments. For physicians in particular, this can partially be traced back to medical training. Outside of a few didactic pathophysiology sessions on these topics, I can only recall my psychiatry clerkship as a time when I was taught about screening for and management of these conditions. While medical school curricula have evolved in the 20 years since my medical training, the degree of attention to mental illness and addiction is disproportionally low compared to their mortality and morbidity burden.

Take for instance these statistics from the National Survey on Drug Use and Health. In 2017, nearly 20 million people over the age of 12 had a substance abuse disorder related to alcohol or illicit drug use. Specifically,

14.5 million people met criteria for an alcohol use disorder, while 7.5 million people had an illicit drug use disorder, most commonly due to marijuana use. Unfortunately, the vast majority of these individuals did not receive treatment for substance use disorders, reflecting both the lack of existing treatment infrastructure as well as a perception by many that they had no need for treatment.[1]

In addition, over 46 million adults experienced a mental illness in the past year, one-quarter of whom had a severe mental illness, meaning that their disorder substantially interfered with or limited their daily activities.[2] Individuals with severe mental illnesses such as schizophrenia, bipolar illness, and major depressive disorder often have multiple other chronic conditions and co-occurring substance use disorders, and they experience higher rates of violence, suicide, and homelessness. A lack of trained mental health professionals, insufficient treatment capacity, limited access to evidence-based treatment, and an overreliance on the criminal justice system further adds to their vulnerability.[3] All of these factors result in this population living an average of 10 to 25 years less than expected.[4]

The rise of many of these conditions partly explains why for the first time in a hundred years, the United States has experienced three consecutive years of decreasing life expectancy.[5] In particular, the epidemic of opioid overdose deaths has gripped the nation. Opioid overdose deaths now comprise two-thirds of all drug deaths in the United States, and in 2017 they approached 50,000.[6]

Deaths of Despair

In 2015, Princeton economists Anne Case and Angus Deaton published a study of middle-aged US whites showing that over a two-decade span their life expectancy decreased (results were especially pronounced for individuals with a high school diploma or less). They attributed this finding to "deaths of despair," which include drug overdoses, alcohol abuse, and suicide.[7] Similar results have been documented more recently in the Global Burden Disease 2016 study by the University of Washington's Institute of Health Metrics and Evaluation. In that study researchers found decreasing life expectancy over the last several decades in the 20–55 age group in 21 states and attributed this to drug use, cirrhosis, and self-harm.[8] These statistics are incredibly sobering. It's worth taking a moment to discuss each of these conditions from a prevention lens.

The opioid epidemic started in the late 1990s with the prescribing of a new class of pain medications marketed by the pharmaceutical sector as not having addictive properties. At the same time, some in the healthcare sector supported elevating pain as a "vital sign" and the elimination of pain as a patient quality measure. These factors led to a rapid increase in opioid prescribing, particularly during the first decade of this century. In fact, opioid prescribing amounts increased 350% between 1999 and 2015.[9] Once regulators started to more strictly limit prescribing and reformulate medicines to make them harder to abuse, many individuals with addiction shifted their consumption to heroin, which was cheaper and more readily available. More recently, synthetic opioids and fentanyl coming from China have fueled the epidemic, now resulting in more than half of total opioid overdose deaths.[10]

As I stated in prior congressional testimony to the House Committee on Oversight and Government Reform, until there is a dramatic increase in treatment capacity to care for the more than 2.1 million Americans with opioid use disorder, there will not be a meaningful reduction in overdose deaths (primary care will need to play a central role in this effort). However, prevention in the form of curbing overprescribing of opioids and curbing the illicit flow of opioids is also critical to reversing the epidemic.[11] With respect to the former, many strategies are being employed, from provider education about best prescribing practices to the use of prescription drug monitoring programs to insurance company restrictions on the duration and strength of opioid dosages. It's unclear which of these strategies are having an effect, but since 2012 there has been a 28% reduction in opioid prescribing rates.[12] Some experts worry about unintended consequences, such as individuals in refractory pain not being able to obtain opioids as well as others who may have opioid use disorder but no access to treatment being pushed into illicit opioid use. In fact, it's estimated that 80% of individuals using illicit opioids first began by misusing prescription opioids.[13] All of these concerns are worthy of ongoing monitoring as healthcare professionals attempt to right-size opioid prescribing.

Curbing the illicit flow is perhaps the single biggest challenge. So big that it takes multiple federal agencies, from the US Postal Service (USPS) to Customs and Border Protection to the Food and Drug Administration to the Drug Enforcement Administration, to identify essentially "needles in a haystack." A lethal dose of fentanyl is small enough to fit within the face of Abraham Lincoln on a penny.[14] In fiscal year 2017, the Customs and Border Patrol apprehended 1,485 pounds of fentanyl,[15] enough lethal doses for all 325 million Americans. Virtually all illicit fentanyl is coming to the United States from China, which up to recently had very poorly regulated its industry. While bilateral efforts to prevent illicit fentanyl shipments from the source have resulted in some progress, it is imperative that this issue remains a top foreign policy priority for the United States with China. The recent passage of the STOP Act, which will require the USPS to obtain advanced electronic data for 100% of shipments arriving into the United States by 2021,[16] and the recent announcement by China to schedule fentanyl-type substances as controlled substances[17] are important steps toward curbing the illicit flow of opioids into this country. Finally, more resources for federal agencies to interdict illicit opioid traffic are necessary. This includes resources for more staff at international mail facilities, more specialized canine units, and x-ray and chemical testing. This is also an area where private sector innovation to develop new technologies to detect fentanyl and its analogues is urgently needed. Recently, several federal agencies jointly launched the Opioid Detection Challenge, an initiative that offers cash prizes to innovators who develop rapid detection tools that help identify illicit opioids.[18]

Alcohol abuse is considered another death of despair, and one in particular that seems to be taken for granted in this country. Either it doesn't faze enough people or there is a lack of awareness that 88,000 Americans die each year from alcohol abuse, resulting in a quarter trillion dollars in economic costs to the United States.[19] This occurs in spite of a solid evidence base for clinical and community approaches to preventing alcohol abuse. As indicated in chapter 1, screening for alcohol abuse and brief behavioral counseling intervention is a high-value preventive service. Clinicians need to be trained in screening and brief counseling for unhealthy alcohol use and be knowledgeable about where to refer patients requiring more intensive treatment. In addition, community interventions such as decreasing the density of alcohol availability, enforcing laws prohibiting sales to minors, and raising alcohol excise taxes have been shown to reduce alcohol misuse.[20] Unfortunately, alcohol prevention policy is not prioritized at the federal level in the same way as efforts combating other substances of abuse such as illegal drugs. Some observers say this is because alcohol is a legal substance and the role for government must be more nuanced compared to illicit substances. However, it's hard not to believe that the $4 billion reduction in excise taxes brought about by the 2017 Tax Cuts and Jobs Act won't result in more consumption, and therefore more misuse, abuse, and death.[21] This comes on the heels of recent troubling findings from the National Epidemiologic Survey on Alcohol and Related Conditions. Researchers assessed changes in the prevalence of 12-month alcohol use, high-risk drinking, and alcohol use disorder between the first and second decades of this century and found increases in all three outcomes for the total US population, and especially among women, older adults, racial/ethnic minorities, and the socioeconomically disadvantaged.[22] Finally, more than 10,000 Americans still die each year from alcohol-related driving fatalities, despite the fact that they are entirely preventable. In addition to the community interventions mentioned previously, a recent report by the National Academies of Sciences, Engineering, and Medicine recommended that states should enact laws for alcohol-impaired driving at 0.05% blood alcohol concentration as well as for all-offender ignition interlock laws to reduce alcohol-impaired driving fatalities.[23] States should also consider mandatory alcohol abuse assessment or treatment after DUI conviction; although most states have this policy in place, it is not required in four out of the five worst states for alcohol-related driving deaths.[24]

Similarly, suicide is another condition that carries with it a similar stigma to the other deaths of despair. It claimed the lives of nearly 45,000 Americans in 2016;[25] for each of these deaths, there were another approximately

218 Americans who thought about committing suicide and 29 who survived a suicide attempt.[26] Over the last two decades, every state has experienced increases in suicide rates, the largest of which have occurred among Mountain and Midwest states. Too many people continue to attribute suicide deaths to mental illness, although research suggests that less than half of individuals dying by suicide had a known mental health condition. In fact, many circumstances have been linked to suicide, including relationship problems, near-term stress, substance abuse, and poor health, as well as financial problems. The CDC has provided leadership in suicide prevention by identifying specific steps that many sectors of society, including state governments, healthcare systems, employers, schools, and the media, can take to reduce the risk factors for suicide and know its warning signs.[27] This is one issue where each of us can help our fellow citizens. Helping someone at risk of suicide by connecting them to the National Suicide Prevention Lifeline at 1-800-273-TALK is an act of public service that can save a life.

Suicide prevention necessitates that we not shy away from controversial topics such as gun control. Gun violence is itself a public health epidemic, contributing to over 39,000 deaths in 2016[28] and sending nearly 8,000 kids to the emergency room annually.[29] The Venn diagrams of suicide and gun violence overlap, so that half of Americans who commit suicide do so with a gun[30] and close to 60% of all gun deaths are suicides.[31] In terms of lethality, guns have no competition. Ninety percent of people who shoot themselves die, whereas the overall rate of death from suicide attempts is 11%.[32] The Brady Campaign has persuasively argued that it is the lethality of guns, combined with the impulsivity of suicides (two-thirds of suicides occur without prior planning), that leads to guns being such a major risk factor for suicide deaths.[33]

Gun control has become a partisan issue for far too long in this country. Two factors that could change the dynamics are data and evidence. Unfortunately, the Dickey Amendment, a provision in the 1996 federal government spending bill stating that no CDC funds can be used to advocate or promote gun control, has been interpreted in a way that even gun violence research has been stymied. While the federal government's 2018 omnibus spending bill included language that the CDC has authority to conduct research on the causes of gun violence, no money has been appropriated to date for such research.[34] One study in the *Journal of the American Medical Association* compared the US mortality rate from a variety of public health causes to the amount of research funding each receives. According to the study, the amount of gun violence funding was less than 2% of the funding predicted based on the mortality rate—just $22 million versus $1.4 billion predicted.[35]

Fortunately, private sector entities have stepped up to fill in the evidence vacuum by at least collating the existing research base. In March 2018, RAND published *The Science of Gun Policy*, a seminal report that analyzes gun violence interventions on various outcomes such as suicide and violent crime. While the report demonstrated the array of research gaps, it found supportive evidence for child-access prevention laws to reduce firearm self-injuries (including suicide) and unintentional injuries and deaths among children. In addition, the study found moderate evidence that background checks can reduce firearm suicides and homicides. Other interventions, such as mandating a minimum age of 21 for purchasing firearms and prohibiting purchase of guns by individuals who have a history of involuntary commitment to a psychiatric facility, have limited evidence in reducing firearm suicides among youth and in total suicides and firearm suicides, respectively.[36]

A Focus on the Next Generation

Optimally addressing these conditions—drug and alcohol use disorders, suicides, and mental illness—requires two critical imperatives. First, we must address the root drivers of these epidemics, such as lack of employment, financial insecurity, hopelessness, and breakdowns in family structures. To this end, the Well Being Trust, a national philanthropy dedicated to advancing the mental, social, and spiritual health of the nation has called for a National Resilience Strategy to identify community-based strategies focused on prevention and early identification of risk factors.[37]

Second, prevention of these conditions must start at an early age. Quite simply, addiction is a chronic disease that often begins early in life by impacting neural pathways. Researchers at the National Institute for Drug Abuse (NIDA) as part of the Adolescent Brain Cognitive Development (ABCD) Study are now able to use cutting-edge imaging technology to demonstrate how the reward-related circuitry in the brain changes based on different experiences.[38] Along the same lines, the first onset of mental health disorders usually occurs in childhood or adolescence.[39]

For adolescents, the statistics are grim. One-third of high school students report they've had at least one drink of alcohol in the previous month, and 18% report they've had five or more drinks of alcohol in a row within a couple hours on at least one day during the last month. Marijuana use is even more rampant, as nearly 40% of high school students report they've used the substance in the past.[40] I've already discussed the dangers of adolescent nicotine addiction and the concerns of increasing e-cigarette use among this age group. With respect to mental health, 31% of high school students report feelings of sadness or hopelessness in the past year, while 17% report that they have seriously considered attempting suicide within the previous year.[41] Millions of children and youth are thought to have a serious emotional disturbance that refers to a mental, behavioral, or emotional disorder in the past year and that interferes with their daily lives and activities.[42] As an example, 13% of adolescents ages 12 to 17 report that they had at least one major depressive episode in the previous year.[43]

Scientists are now linking many adult mental illness and substance use disorders to adverse childhood experiences (ACEs). According to the Substance Abuse and Mental Health Services Administration (SAMHSA), these experiences include all forms of abuse, neglect, and violence within the home, substance misuse and mental illness within the household, parental separation or divorce, and incarcerated household members.[44] The SAMHSA and the NIDA have an important role to play in promoting evidence-based prevention programs for children and youth experiencing ACEs and early intervention programs for those misusing substances or experiencing severe mental illness.

Moving forward, critical efforts include screening for mental illness and substance use (including identifying ACEs) during pediatric care as well as supporting community-based programs at schools that address risk and protective factors for drug use and mental illness. Policy, systems, and environmental changes can also be helpful in limiting access to substances, particularly alcohol.[45] Community coalitions, including faith-based organizations, have also been shown to reduce youth substance use in communities. The best example of this is the White House Office of National Drug Control Policy's Drug-Free Communities Program. Long-term analyses have shown that communities with a grantee of this program experience declines in the past 30-day use of alcohol, tobacco, and marijuana among both middle school and high school students.[46]

Preventing youth mental illness and substance use is one of the most important challenges before this nation. In addition to the many clinical and community interventions, what happens in the home setting may be most important. Parents and caretakers of children need to role model good responsible behavior as well as find the time to talk regularly to their children about the dangers of substance use.[47] Unless clinical and community preventive strategies are not reinforced in the home setting, our country's future generations will continue to be at risk, and this is something we cannot afford.

Opportunities to Advance Prevention

I'd like finally to shift our attention to forward-looking opportunities that have the potential to further embed prevention into our daily lives. Advances in human biology and in technology will increasingly allow us to predict and therefore prevent disease.

Twenty years ago, as medical students at the University of Michigan, we were given a treat the day before Thanksgiving break, when Dr. Francis Collins came back to campus to give a guest lecture. A former University of Michigan professor of human genetics, Dr. Collins at the time was the director of the National Human Genome Research Institute. At the conclusion of his lecture, he took out his guitar and started to serenade us with a song about medical school. It turns out that Dr. Collins is a pretty accomplished guitarist and has been known to play in rock bands with fellow scientists. What we also didn't know at the time was that Dr. Collins and his team were close to mapping the entire human genome.

Over the next few years, the Human Genome Project would successfully identify and sequence the roughly 20,500 genes that influence the development and function of human beings.[48] Application of this information led to an explosion of biomedical research as well as discussion about the implications of this research. Policy issues ranged from ensuring genetic privacy to providing oversight of genetic testing, an area that was the focus of the Secretary's Advisory Committee on Genetics, Health, and Society, on which I served as an ex-officio member. Over the next several years, private companies began commercializing whole genome sequencing directly to consumers and to healthcare providers to help with diagnosis of rare diseases. Today, there are a number of significant efforts dedicated to precision medicine, a field incorporating genetic information to better prevent, diagnose, and treat human disease. One of the most ambitious efforts, the All of Us project, is being led by the National Institutes of Health and seeks to involve one million Americans to share their individual health data and genetic information to better understand why certain individuals develop certain diseases.[49]

With respect specifically to disease prevention, there has been real progress leading to clinical applications. In fact, Healthy People 2020 included genomics as a topic area for the first time. Specific objectives included recommendations consistent with the US Preventive Services Task Force that women with high-risk family history for breast, ovarian, tubal, or peritoneal cancer should learn about genetic testing for a specific genetic mutation, BRCA 1/2. Early detection of this mutation can provide women a choice of several interventions, including surgery, which have the potential to reduce their risk of cancer. A separate expert group recommends that individuals newly diagnosed with colorectal cancer be offered testing for a hereditary form of colorectal cancer called Lynch syndrome. Studies demonstrate that notifying family members of individuals testing positive can reduce the risk of hereditary colorectal cancer by about 60%.[50]

Geisinger Health System has been on the hunt to identify even more high-risk individuals through a DNA sequencing project of its patient population. It has collected the functional genome of over 90,000 patients and is now focused on identifying patients at risk for early onset cancer and cardiac events. Geisinger's former CEO Dr. David Feinberg estimated that 3% of patients carry DNA variants with a high probability of being harmful, and as more information is learned about how genetic variants impact various diseases, up to 10% to 15% of patients might be impacted. From his perspective, all of these patients and their physicians may have additional opportunities to engage in risk factor modification and disease prevention.[51]

While the inclusion of genetic information may expand the pool of patients at high risk for diseases, it may also help to increase the precision of screening tests. In pursuit of "precision prevention," researchers at the CDC and NIH are interested in utilizing an individual's genetic profile to dictate how often that person should receive a screening test for a particular condition. Individuals with higher "genetic risk scores" may need more frequent screening, while those with lower scores may need less frequent screening.[52] Individualized screening in this way could reduce unnecessary screening while targeting individuals at the highest risk. The significant reductions in the costs of performing genomic testing should also make these tests more accessible in the future.

Whereas the promise of incorporating genetic information in preventative medicine is substantial, it's also important to understand its limitations. Obesity provides a perfect example; like most chronic conditions it is affected by many genes. Genetic studies have identified more than 30 candidate genes associated with body mass index. However, each contributes only a small fraction to genetic susceptibility to obesity and even in totality contribute in a limited way to the risk for obesity. That is because of the even more important role our environment plays in causing obesity as well as, more broadly, the impact of environmental events and exposures on genetic information, an exciting field of study called epigenetics.[53] Harkening back to the book's introduction, genetic information is an important determinant of premature mortality, but it's often just one piece of the puzzle.

Finally, there is something that all Americans can do today to contribute to the role genetics plays in disease prevention. This activity involves sitting down with family members and learning about family health history. Family health history is an independent risk factor for nine out of ten of the leading causes of death.[54] In 2004, HHS surgeon general Richard Carmona launched the Surgeon General's Family History Initiative to encourage Americans to learn about conditions that may run in their family and to share these findings with their healthcare provider. An interactive web-based tool released by the Office of the Surgeon General entitled "My Family Health Portrait" allows Americans to organize their information in a privacy-secured location.[55] It's an opportunity that we should all take advantage of for ourselves and our loved ones.

A Digital Revolution

Lastly, I turn to technology and its role in disease prevention. There are now thousands of smartphone health applications focused on areas such as fitness, nutrition, mental health, and substance abuse. In addition, millions of Americans use wireless wearables such as Fitbit to track activity and vital signs. While some of these health promotion technologies have been shown in published studies to be impactful, most have not gone through the rigor of peer review. There is a nascent movement in the digital technology space to differentiate software-based products according to their level of published evidence and their desire to gain the FDA's stamp of approval for safety and efficacy. The Digital Therapeutics Alliance, a consortium founded in 2017, is trying to define industry standards and help companies with regulatory clearance.[56, 57]

For its part, the FDA has responded by releasing a Digital Health Innovation Action Plan to ensure all Americans have access to high-quality, safe, and effective digital health products.[58] Apps that are extensions of a medical device, use sensors, use patient specific information to diagnose or treat a patient, or are involved in active patient monitoring are subject to FDA regulatory oversight. On the other hand, the FDA is not enforcing requirements at this time on mobile apps that pose a low risk to patients such as those used for self-management or taking medication, for example.[59]

The regulatory clarity has helped the field move forward, specifically in the area of prevention. In 2017, the FDA approved the first smartphone app for smoking cessation. The app, developed by the startup Carrot, offers a mobile coaching program and a carbon monoxide breath sensor for at-home use. The Bluetooth-enabled sensor connects to the smartphone app and allows an individual to see how their smoking impacts carbon monoxide levels in the home. It's thought that this experiential insight combined with real-time evidence-based behavioral counseling will lead to higher cessation rates.[60]

The opioid epidemic is another area where digital technology may play an important role. In 2018, the FDA launched an innovation challenge to accelerate development of medical devices that could address aspects of the epidemic. One area of need is for innovative opioids packaging to reduce the risk of inappropriate or nonmedical use of prescription opioids.[61] In fact, securing funding for research to determine the most effective innovative packaging designs is a top priority from a 2017 report issued by the Johns Hopkins Bloomberg School of Public Health and the Clinton Foundation.[62]

One promising example comes from Intent Solutions, a technology company that has developed a smart mobile medication dispenser called TAD, short for "Take As Directed." It's a device with a biometric sensor embedded in it so only the prescribed individual can access medications. When it's time to take the medicine, an alert on an individual's smartphone prompts them to take their medicine, which is made available only in the dose prescribed. In this way, the developers claim that their technology provides the right dose at the right time and to the right patient.[63] While the technology requires further study and validation, it is the type of innovation that can theoretically prevent overuse and misuse of prescription opioids.

All of these innovations, however, face challenges beyond regulatory approval. Ultimately, purchasers of healthcare need to buy into these technologies if there is to be a market for them. Many companies are teaming up with self-employed plans to generate initial momentum. However, whether these technologies reach the millions who might benefit from them depends on convincing large public and private payers on their benefits. Take the example of Omada Health, a digital therapeutics firm, and its online Diabetes Prevention Program (DPP). The DPP was discussed at length in chapter 3 as an evidence-based clinical program that ultimately made its way into the community and was scaled through support by the CDC and now through reimbursement to community-based organizations by the Centers for Medicare and Medicaid Services and many private payers. Omada Health realized that there are millions of Americans with prediabetes who may not be able to participate, for whatever reason, in group classes at community settings like YMCAs. So, Omada created a virtual DPP online curriculum and demonstrated with results that it could meet the CDC's evidence-based standards for weight loss and diabetes prevention. Understanding that part of the success of the original DPP hinged on the group dynamics and support structure of the program, Omada Health smartly grouped participants geographically, thus creating a social network for participants and their health coaches.[64] However, while the CMS has begun paying eligible community-based programs for providing the intervention to eligible beneficiaries, it has declined to pay virtual providers, fearing that accepting self-reported weight loss as a metric for payment could leave the agency open to fraud and abuse.[65] Given that Omada and other like-minded competitors have accumulated data to validate their results, it would seem that there ought to be some way to reassure the CMS. In the balance lie millions of American lives, particularly people living in rural areas and others with transportation barriers, lacking access to an evidence-based diabetes prevention program.

T HERE ARE a number of policy recommendations in this book, but below I have chosen to underscore five that have the greatest potential to optimize health in this nation. These recommendations relate to the reasons that prevention has not been prioritized by policymakers, which I laid out in the introduction. Collectively, they call for policymakers to engage in proactive policymaking, leverage public payers, invest in public health, and encourage prevention research. Some may say that bipartisanship in politics is nice to have but not necessary. I believe that if we are to create a culture of prevention, policymakers from both sides of the aisle will need equally to provide leadership and support. Each of the following recommendations is within the grasp of the executive branch and Congress.

1 Each administration and leadership team at the Department of Health and Human Services should make disease prevention its top priority. This should be reflected in the strategic plan of the department and the annual budget submissions to the Office of Management and Budget and Congress. A limited set of specific metrics should be associated with the department's prevention goals, and these should be aligned with Healthy People. Each operating division of the department should likewise elevate prevention

in a manner consistent with the division's unique mission. Tackling the upstream determinants of health, community prevention, clinical prevention, primary care, public health, and global health should be the focus of each presidential administration. A focus on these issues does not necessitate that HHS neglect other essential functions; however, to be truly visionary and have an impact on the trajectory of our nation's health not only in the present but for years to come, it's critical that our nation's healthcare leaders spend each day not just being reactive to sickness in America but also proactive toward health and wellness.

2　Healthcare providers should be incentivized through quality measures not only to manage chronic diseases but also to prevent their occurrence in the first place. Chronic diseases account for the vast majority of deaths in the United States and the vast majority of healthcare expenditures. As healthcare moves ever so slowly from a volume- to value-based payment system, quality measures are the currency through which payment will be provided. For too long, we relied heavily on process measures of quality, while more recently outcome measures have become a focus. Moving forward, health status measures related to the incidence of chronic diseases and the prevalence of chronic disease risk factors should be developed, endorsed, and utilized by the Centers for Medicare and Medicaid Services and private payers. Attention should be given in the deployment of these measures to take into account when risk adjustment might be necessary and to prevent adverse selection. Increasing accountability of healthcare entities for health status measures will catalyze the clinical-community linkages necessary to keep vulnerable Americans healthy and reduce preventable healthcare costs.

3　A pathway needs to be developed to allow for community-based prevention programs to be deemed safe, evidence-based, and worthy of coverage and payment by Medicare and subsequently private insurers. In the present system, drugs, devices, and other medical interventions undergo an established process to gain approval by the FDA for their safety and efficacy; in most cases, this then triggers coverage determinations by Medicare based on the standard of the intervention being reasonable and necessary. A similar pathway does not exist for community interventions led by nonclinical staff, even though millions of Americans stand to benefit from evidence-based programs in areas such as falls prevention, physical activity promotion, and chronic disease self-management. Congress should step in and create a new regulatory role for agencies such as the CDC or the Administration on Aging to certify community-based programs akin to the FDA's approval process. This certification should then trigger a CMS coverage decision so that beneficiaries of public insurance programs have increasing access to evidence-based prevention programs in their communities.

4 Congress should provide robust funding for public health and global health efforts to support population health and well-being. Specific priorities include increasing funding to enhance domestic public health capabilities, boosting the existing public health emergency fund, scaling evidence-based community prevention programs, and supporting impactful global health projects.

Public health functions need to be viewed as part of our nation's infrastructure in the same way as sectors such as transportation, energy, and information technology. While it's true that too many Americans take the functions of public health for granted, public heath must also become more participatory in nature for the average citizen. The field must do a better job not only in explaining its role and how it relates to the daily activities of Americans but also in finding specific ways for Americans to support local public health efforts. Similarly, our nation's health leaders must do a much better job explaining why improving global health, beyond it being altruistic, matters to the health of Americans.

5 Federal support for prevention research is currently not prioritized and needs to be enhanced to match its potential impact. Arguably more important than moonshots to cure disease are moonshots to prevent disease in the first place. Along with basic science research

to identify opportunities for disease prevention, there needs to be more clinical, health services, and public health research in this area, given that most of the leading causes of death are largely preventable. Increased federal funding availability for prevention research from Congress will attract additional researchers into the field. This will result in more published studies and a better evidence base to deploy and scale effective interventions. More robust information on the cost-effectiveness of prevention interventions will also assist the Congressional Budget Office in being able to score future federal legislation related to prevention. A trans-HHS prevention research council should be established to identify the highest-priority research questions in the field of disease prevention and to designate lead federal agencies that would sponsor specific research.

These actions taken by policymakers could help transform the nation's health policy conversation. None of these recommendations would be easy to implement, but they are required if we're to be successful in shifting the conversation in this country from being focused on treatment instead of prevention, sickness instead of health, and being reactive instead of proactive. The healthier the population, the easier the conversations will be about downstream concerns such as access to health insurance and controlling healthcare costs. Healthier populations, by definition, should result in lower health insurance premiums and reduced use of preventable healthcare. Thus, making our nation healthier through disease prevention and health promotion needs to be the paramount goal. Our dereliction in glossing over prevention—either because we assume that prevention is too difficult or we fear that it is too intrusive in its pursuit of adapting human behavior—has real consequences. And these consequences come in the form of millions of Americans dying from preventable causes of deaths each year and millions of others suffering from preventable chronic diseases.

We can do better. In fact, we *must* do better. And the reason I'm optimistic is that there are people all across this country putting prevention into practice each and every day and leading the way. We must make sure their efforts are not only well publicized, supported, shared, and scaled but we must also communicate to them that their work in disease prevention is indeed among the most important activities to improve the nation's health. What this book is about, they already know. It's time for the rest of us, including policymakers and healthcare leaders, to catch up. Prevention must be first.

Introduction. The State of Disease Prevention

1. Steven H. Woolf, "The Price Paid for Not Preventing Diseases," in "Missed Prevention Opportunities," in *The Healthcare Imperative—Lowering Costs and Improving Outcomes*, Institute of Medicine (Washington, DC: National Academies Press, 2010).

2. "Primary, Secondary, and Tertiary Prevention," *At Work* 80 (Spring 2015), accessed December 10, 2017, https://www.iwh.on.ca/sites/iwh/files/iwh/at-work/at_work_80 _0.pdf.

3. "Primary, Secondary, and Tertiary Prevention."

4. "Primary, Secondary, and Tertiary Prevention."

5. J. Michael McGinnis, Pamela Williams-Russo, James R. Knickman, "The Case for More Active Policy Attention to Health Promotion," *Health Affairs* 21, no. 2 (March/April 2002): 78–93.

6. "Health Policy Brief: The Relative Contribution of Multiple Determinants to Health Outcomes," *Health Affairs*, August 21, 2014, https://www.healthaffairs.org /do/10.1377/hpb20140821.

7. "Health Policy Brief."

8. Macarena C. Garcia, Brigham Bastian, Lauren M. Rossen, Robert Anderson, Arialdi Minino, Paula W. Yoon, Mark Faul, et al., "Potentially Preventable Deaths among the Five Leading Causes of Death—United States, 2010 and 2014," *Morbidity and Mortality Weekly Report* 65, no. 45 (November 2016): 1245–1255.

9. Brett P. Giroir and Don Wright, "Physical Activity Guidelines for Health and Prosperity in the United States," *JAMA* 320, no.19 (November 2018): 1971–1972, doi:10.1001/jama.2018.16998.

10. Centers for Disease Control and Prevention, *State Indicator Report on Fruits and Vegetables, 2018* (Atlanta, GA: CDC, US Department of Health and Human Services, 2018).

11. "Adult Obesity Facts," CDC, last modified August 13, 2018, https://www.cdc.gov /obesity/data/adult.html.

12. "Childhood Obesity Facts," CDC, last modified August 13, 2018, https://www.cdc .gov/obesity/data/childhood.html.

13. Teresa W. Wang, Kat Asman, Andrea S. Gentzke, Karen A. Cullen, Enver Holder-Hayes, Carolyn Reyes-Guzman, Ahmed Jamal, et al., "Tobacco Product Use among Adults—United States, 2017," *Morbidity and Mortality Weekly Report* 67, no. 44 (November 2018): 1225–1232.

14. "Smoking and Tobacco Use," CDC, last modified February 20, 2018, https://www.cdc.gov/tobacco/data_statistics/fact_sheets/fast_facts/index.htm.

15. "Chronic Diseases and Health Promotion," World Health Organization (WHO), accessed January 5, 2019, https://www.who.int/chp/chronic_disease_report/part1/en/index11.html.

16. Yanping Li, An Pan, Dong D. Wang, Xiaoran Liu, Klodian Dhana, Oscar H. Franco, Stephen Kaptoge, et al., "Impact of Healthy Lifestyle Factors on Life Expectancies in the US Population," *Circulation* 138 (July 2018): 345–355, doi:10.1161/circulationaha.117.032047.

17. Anne Case and Angus Deaton, "Morbidity and Mortality in the 21st Century," Brookings Papers on Economic Activity, Spring 2017, https://www.brookings.edu/wp-content/uploads/2017/08/casetextsp17bpea.pdf.

18. Trust for America's Health and Well Being Trust, *Pain in the Nation: The Drug, Alcohol, and Suicide Crises and the Need for a National Resilience Strategy*, November 2017, https://www.tfah.org/report-details/pain-in-the-nation/.

19. "Alcohol Facts and Statistics," National Institute on Alcohol Abuse and Alcoholism, last modified August 2018, https://www.niaaa.nih.gov/alcohol-health/overview-alcohol-consumption/alcohol-facts-and-statistics.

20. Farida B. Ahmad, Lauren M. Rossen, Merianne R. Spencer, Margaret Warner, and Paul Sutton, "Provisional Drug Overdose Death Counts," National Center for Health Statistics, 2018.

21. Deborah M. Stone, Thomas R. Simon, Katherine A. Fowler, Scott R. Kegler, Keming Yuan, Kristin M. Holland, Asha Z. Ivey-Stephenson, et al., "*Vital Signs:* Trends in State Suicide Rates—United States, 1999–2016 and Circumstances Contributing to Suicide 27 States, 2015," *Morbidity and Mortality Weekly Report* 67, no. 22 (June 2018): 617–624.

22. Sherry L. Murphy, Jiaquan Xu, Kenneth D. Kochanek, and Elizabeth Arias, "Mortality in the United States, 2017," NCHS Data Brief, no. 328, Hyattsville, MD: National Center for Health Statistics, 2018.

23. "The Value of Prevention," Partnership for Prevention and Partnership to Fight Chronic Disease, accessed December 14, 2017, http://prevent.org/data/files/initiatives/valueofprevention%28pfpandpfcd%29.pdf.

24. "About the USPSTF," US Preventive Services Task Force, February 2018, accessed April 5, 2018, https://www.uspreventiveservicestaskforce.org/Page/Name/about-the-uspstf.

25. "Clinical Preventive Services," CDC, last modified January 31, 2017, https://www.cdc.gov/aging/services/index.htm.

26. Janet S. Wright, Hilary K. Wall, Matthew D. Ritchey, "Million Hearts 2022—Small Steps Needed for Cardiovascular Disease Prevention," *JAMA* 320, no.18 (November 2018): 1857–1858, doi:10.1001/jama.2018.13326.

27. Partnership for Prevention, *Preventive Care: A National Profile on Use, Disparities, and Health Profile, 2017*, http://www.prevent.org/data/files/initiatives/ncpppreventivecarereport.pdf.

28. "Recommendations for Primary Care Practice," US Preventive Services Task Force, accessed April 5, 2018, https://www.uspreventiveservicestaskforce.org/Page/Name/recommendations.

29. "About the Community Guide," Community Guide, accessed April 5, 2018, https://www.thecommunityguide.org/about/about-community-guide.

30. "The Community Guide in Action," Community Guide, accessed April 5, 2018, https://www.thecommunityguide.org/content/the-community-guide-in-action.

31. Campaign for Tobacco-Free Kids, American Heart Association, American Cancer Society Cancer Action Network, American Lung Association, Robert Wood Johnson Foundation, Americans for Nonsmokers' Rights and Truth Initiative, *Broken Promises to Our Children: A State-by-State Look at the 1998 Tobacco Settlement 20 Years Later*, December 2018, https://www.tobaccofreekids.org/what-we-do/us/statereport/.

32. George Miller, Charles Roehrig, Paul Hughes-Cromwick, and Ani Turner, "What Is Currently Spent on Prevention as Compared to Treatment?" chap. 2 in *Prevention vs. Treatment: What's the Right Balance?* (New York: Oxford University Press, 2012).

33. George Miller, Matthew Daly, and Charles Roehrig, "Tradeoffs in Cardiovascular Disease Prevention, Treatment, and Research," *Health Care Management Science* 16 (2013): 87–99.

34. Barbara A. Ormond, Brenda C. Spillman, Timothy A. Waidmann, Kyle J. Caswell, and Bodan Tereshchenko, "Potential National and State Medical Care Savings from Primary Disease Prevention," *American Journal of Public Health* 101 (2011): 157–164.

35. RAND Corporation, *Modeling the Health and Medical Care Spending of the Future Elderly*, 2008, https://www.rand.org/pubs/research_briefs/RB9324/index1.html.

36. Joshua T. Cohen, Peter J. Neumann, and Milton C. Weinstein, "Does Preventive Care Save Money? Health Economics and the Presidential Candidates," *New England Journal of Medicine* 358, no. 7 (February 2008): 661–663.

37. Joshua T. Cohen and Peter J. Neumann, *The Cost Savings and Cost-Effectiveness of Clinical Preventive Care*, Robert Wood Johnson Foundation, September 2009, https://www.rwjf.org/content/dam/farm/reports/issue_briefs/2009/rwjf46045/subassets/rwjf46045_1.

38. Cohen and Neumann, *Cost Savings*.

39. Cohen and Neumann, *Cost Savings*.

40. Michael V. Maciosek, Amy B. LaFrance, Steven P. Dehmer, Dana A. McGree, Thomas J. Flottemesch, Zack Xu, and Leif I. Solberg, "Updated Priorities among Effective Clinical Preventive Services," *Annals of Family Medicine* 15, no. 1 (January/February 2017): 14–22.

41. "The Community Guide," accessed April 25, 2018, https://www.thecommunityguide.org/.

42. Bipartisan Policy Center, *A Prevention Prescription for Improving Health and Health Care in America*, 2015, https://bipartisanpolicy.org/wp-content/uploads/2017/01/BPC-Prevention-Prescription-Report.pdf.

43. David M. Murray, Wilma Peterman Cross, Denise Simons-Morton, Jody Engel, Barry Portnoy, Jessica Wu, Paris A. Watson, et al., "Enhancing the Quality of Prevention Research Supported by the National Institutes of Health," *American Journal of Public Health* 105, no. 1 (January 2015): 9–12.

44. Murray, Cross, Simons-Morton, et al., "Enhancing the Quality of Prevention Research."

45. "Prevention Research Centers," CDC, accessed December 15, 2018, https://www.cdc.gov/prc/about-prc-program/index.htm.

46. Glenn Kessler, "Are There Really 10,000 Diseases and Just 500 'Cures'?" *Washington Post*, November 17, 2016.

47. Zosia Chustecka, "Public Health Experts Say 'Cancer Moonshot' Ignores Prevention," *Medscape Medical News*, March 21, 2016, https://www.medscape.com/view article/860685.

48. "US Cancer Moonshot Must Strike a Balance between Research and Prevention," *Nature* 539, no. 467 (November 2016), accessed December 22, 2017, https://doi.org /10.1038/539467a.

49. Farhad Islami, Ann Goding Sauer, Kimberly D. Miller, Rebecca L. Siegel, Stacey A. Fedewa, Eric J. Jacobs, Marjorie L. McCullough, et al., "Proportion and Number of Cancer Cases and Deaths Attributable to Potentially Modifiable Risk Factors in the United States," *CA: A Cancer Journal for Clinicians* 68, no. 1 (January/February 2018), accessed January 6, 2018, https://doi.org/10.3322/caac.21440.

50. Cancer Moonshot Blue Ribbon Panel, *Cancer Moonshot Blue Ribbon Panel Report 2016*, October 2016, accessed Mary 5, 2017, https://www.cancer.gov/research/key -initiatives/moonshot-cancer-initiative/blue-ribbon-panel/blue-ribbon-panel-report -2016.pdf.

51. US Department of Health and Human Services, *National Plan to Address Alzheimer's Disease, 2012*, accessed December 15, 2017, https://aspe.hhs.gov/system/files /pdf/102526/NatlPlan2012%20with%20Note.pdf.

52. National Academies of Sciences, Engineering, and Medicine, *Preventing Cognitive Decline and Dementia: A Way Forward*, 2017, https://doi.org/10.17226/24782.

53. "About Healthy People," HealthyPeople.gov, accessed December 15, 2018, https:// www.healthypeople.gov/2020/About-Healthy-People.

54. "About Healthy People."

55. Howard K. Koh, Carter R. Blakey, and Allison Y. Roper, "Healthy People 2020: A Report Card on the Health of the Nation," *JAMA* 311, no. 24 (2014): 2475–2476, doi:10.1001/jama.2014.6446.

56. J. Michael McGinnis, "Does Proof Matter? Why Strong Evidence Sometimes Yields Weak Action," *American Journal of Health Promotion* 15, no. 5 (2001): 391–396.

57. "Making Sense of Medicare's Preventive Service Benefits," Center for Medicare Advocacy, accessed January 31, 2019, https://www.medicareadvocacy.org/making -sense-of-medicares-preventive-service-benefits/.

58. Gail Wilensky, phone conversation with author, January 31, 2019.

Chapter 1. How Do You Insert Prevention into Healthcare's Value Equation?

1. Kelly Gooch, "Not Your Usual Hospital Ad: 'If our beds are filled, it means we've failed,'" *Becker's Hospital Review*, September 6, 2016, https://www.beckershospital review.com/hospital-management-administration/not-your-usual-hospital-ad-if-our -beds-are-filled-it-means-we-ve-failed.html.

2. Ruth C. Carlos, "Value-Driven Health Care: The Purchaser Perspective," *Journal of the American College of Radiology* 5, no. 6 (2008): 719–726, doi:10.1016/j.jacr.2008 .02.002.

3. Diana Manos, "Leavitt Predicts 'Travelocity' System for Healthcare Pricing,"

Healthcare IT News, September 26, 2007, https://www.healthcareitnews.com/news
/leavitt-predicts-travelocity-system-healthcare-pricing.

4. Patricia Neuman and Gretchen A. Jacobson, "Medicare Advantage Checkup," *New England Journal of Medicine* 379, no. 22 (2018): 2163–2168.

5. "Medicare Provides Continued Access to High-Quality Health Coverage Choices in 2019," CMS, accessed December 1, 2018, https://www.cms.gov/newsroom/press
-releases/medicare-provides-continued-access-high-quality-health-coverage
-choices-2019.

6. "Proposed Pathways to Success for the Medicare Shared Savings Program," CMS, accessed December 1, 2018, https://www.cms.gov/newsroom/fact-sheets/proposed
-pathways-success-medicare-shared-savings-program.

7. Virgil Dickson, "Next Generation ACOs Saved Medicare $62 Million in First Year," *Modern Healthcare*, August 27, 2018, https://www.modernhealthcare.com/article
/20180827/NEWS/180829914.

8. Virgil Dickson, "Rural ACOs That Received Loans from the CMS Succeeded," *Modern Healthcare*, September 4, 2018, https://www.modernhealthcare.com/article
/20180904/NEWS/180909985.

9. "Bundled Payments for Care Improvement (BPCI) Initiative: General Information," CMS, last modified December 11, 2018, accessed January 6, 2019, https://
innovation.cms.gov/initiatives/bundled-payments/.

10. Dylan Scott, "One of Obamacare's Big Experiments to Lower Costs Is Working Surprisingly Well," *Vox*, September 4, 2018, https://www.vox.com/policy-and
-politics/2018/9/4/17806348/obamacare-trump-bundled-payments-hospitals
-research.

11. Joshua M. Sharfstein, Sule Gerovich, Elizabeth Moriarty, and David C. Chin, *An Emerging Approach to Payment Reform: All-Payer Global Budgets for Large Safety-Net Hospital Systems*, Commonwealth Fund, August 2017.

12. Modern Healthcare, "The Physician behind Maryland's Move to Capped Hospital Payments," *Modern Healthcare*, January 25, 2014, https://www.modernhealthcare
.com/article/20140125/MAGAZINE/301259952.

13. Sharfstein et al., *Emerging Approach*.

14. Sarah Kliff, "Can Oregon Save American Health Care?" *Washington Post*, January 18, 2013.

15. "Oregon Coordinated Care Organizations," Patient-Centered Primary Care Collaborative, accessed January 15, 2018, https://www.pcpcc.org/initiative/oregon
-coordinated-care-organizations-ccos.

16. Anand K. Parekh, "Revisiting Health Care's Value Equation," *Milbank Quarterly* (online exclusive), November 2015, https://www.milbank.org/quarterly/articles
/revisiting-health-cares-value-equation/.

17. "Part C and D Performance Data," CMS, accessed January 16, 2018, https://www
.cms.gov/Medicare/Prescription-Drug-Coverage/PrescriptionDrugCovGenIn/
PerformanceData.html.

18. "Program Guidance and Specifications," CMS, accessed January 6, 2019, https://
www.cms.gov/Medicare/Medicare-Fee-for-Service-Payment/sharedsavingsprogram
/program-guidance-and-specifications.html.

19. "My Healthy Weight," Bipartisan Policy Center, accessed January 18, 2018, https://bipartisanpolicy.org/events/my-healthy-weight/.

20. Bipartisan Policy Center, *A Prevention Prescription for Improving Health and Health Care in America*, 2015, https://bipartisanpolicy.org/wp-content/uploads/2017/01 /BPC-Prevention-Prescription-Report.pdf.

21. Parekh, "Revisiting Health Care's Value Equation."

22. Parekh, "Revisiting Health Care's Value Equation."

23. Tracy Spinks (senior director, quality innovation, National Quality Forum), in discussion with the author, November 19, 2018.

24. Institute of Medicine, *Best Care at Lower Cost: The Path to Continuously Learning Health Care in America*, 2013, http://www.nationalacademies.org/hmd/Reports/2012 /Best-Care-at-Lower-Cost-The-Path-to-Continuously-Learning-Health-Care-in -America.aspx.

25. Institute of Medicine, *Best Care at Lower Cost*.

26. Institute of Medicine, *Best Care at Lower Cost*.

27. Thomas J. Flottemesch, Michael V. Maciosek, Nichol M. Edwards, Leif I. Solberg, and Ashley B. Coffield, "Cost Savings from Primary and Secondary Prevention," in "Missed Prevention Opportunities," in *The Healthcare Imperative—Lowering Costs and Improving Outcomes*, Institute of Medicine (Washington, DC: National Academies Press, 2010).

28. Michael P. Pignone, "Tertiary Prevention and Treatment Costs," in "Missed Prevention Opportunities," in *The Healthcare Imperative—Lowering Costs and Improving Outcomes*, Institute of Medicine (Washington, DC: National Academies Press, 2010).

29. Thomas Land, Donna Warner, Mark Paskowsky, Ayesha Cammaerts, LeAnn Wetherell, Rachel Kaufmann, Lei Zhang, Ann Malarcher, et al., "Medicaid Coverage for Tobacco Dependence Treatments in Massachusetts and Associated Decreases in Smoking Prevalence," PLOS ONE (2010), https://journals.plos.org/plosone/article ?id=10.1371/journal.pone.0009770.

30. Thomas Land, Nancy A. Rigotti, Douglas E. Levy, Mark Paskowsky, Donna Warner, Jo-Ann Kwass, LeAnn Wetherell, et al. "A Longitudinal Study of Medicaid Coverage for Tobacco Dependence Treatments in Massachusetts and Associated Decreases in Hospitalizations for Cardiovascular Diseases," PLOS ONE (2010), https://journals.plos.org/plosmedicine/article?id=10.1371/journal.pmed.1000375.

31. Patrick Richard, Kristina West, and Leighton Ku, "The Return on Investment of a Medicaid Tobacco Cessation Program in Massachusetts," PLOS ONE (2012), https:// journals.plos.org/plosone/article?id=10.1371/journal.pone.0029665.

32. Richard, West, and Ku, "The Return on Investment."

33. "National Asthma Education and Prevention Program," National Heart Lung and Blood Institute, accessed January 27, 2018, https://www.nhlbi.nih.gov/science /national-asthma-education-and-prevention-program-naepp.

34. "CDC's 6|18 Initiative—Evidence Summary: Control Asthma," CDC, accessed January 24, 2018, https://www.cdc.gov/sixeighteen/asthma/index.htm.

35. "CDC's 6|18 Initiative."

36. "CDC's 6|18 Initiative."

37. Anand K. Parekh, Richard A. Goodman, Catherine Gordon, Howard K. Koh, and

the HHS Interagency Workgroup on Multiple Chronic Conditions, "Managing Multiple Chronic Conditions: A Strategy for Improving Health Outcomes and Quality of Life," *Public Health Reports* 136, no. 4 (2011): 460–471.

38. RTI International, *Evaluation of Medicare Care Management for High Cost Beneficiaries (CMHCB) Demonstration: Massachusetts General Hospital and Massachusetts General Physicians Organization (MGH) Final Report*, September 2010, https://www.massgeneral.org/News/assets/pdf/FullFTIreport.pdf.

39. US Department of Health and Human Services, *Report to Congress: Evaluation of the Independence at Home Demonstration*, November 2018, https://innovation.cms.gov/Files/reports/iah-rtc.pdf.

40. "Chronic Care Management Services," CMS, accessed January 31, 2018, https://www.cms.gov/Outreach-and-Education/Medicare-Learning-Network-MLN/MLNProducts/Downloads/ChronicCareManagement.pdf.

41. Mathematica Policy Research, *Evaluation of the Diffusion and Impact of the Chronic Care Management (CCM) Services: Final Report*, 2017, https://innovation.cms.gov/Files/reports/chronic-care-mngmt-finalevalrpt.pdf.

42. Bradley Sawyer and Nolan Sroczynski, "How Do Health Expenditures Vary across the Population?" Peterson-Kaiser Health System Tracker, accessed January 31, 2018, https://www.healthsystemtracker.org/chart-collection/health-expenditures-vary-across-population/#item-start.

43. A. Mark Fendrick, Dean G. Smith, Michael E. Chernew, and Sonali N. Shah, "A Benefit-Based Copay for Prescription Drugs: Patient Contribution Based on Total Benefits, Not Drug Acquisition Cost," *American Journal of Managed Care* 7, no. 9 (2009): 861–867.

44. Jeannette Y. Wick, "New Acronym, Huge Impact: VBID," March 17, 2015, https://www.mdmag.com/medical-news/new-acronym-huge-impact-vbid.

45. University of Michigan Institute for Healthcare Policy and Innovation, *Value-Based Insurance Design: Shifting the Health Care Cost Discussion from How Much to How Well*, 2014, https://ihpi.umich.edu/sites/default/files/ihpi-vbid.pdf.

46. Michael E. Chernew, Allison B. Rosen, and A. Mark Fendrick, "Value-Based Insurance Design," *Health Affairs* 26, no. 2 (March/April 2007), https://doi.org/10.1377/hlthaff.26.2.w195.

47. University of Michigan, *Value-Based Insurance Design*.

48. Xuesong Han, K. Robin Yabroff, Gery P. Guy Jr., Zhiyuan Zheng, and Ahmedin Jemal, "Has Recommended Preventive Service Use Increased after Elimination of Cost-Sharing as Part of the Affordable Care Act in the United States?" *Preventive Medicine* 78 (2015): 85–91.

49. Amal N. Trivedi, Bryan Leyva, Yoojin Lee, Orestis A. Panagiotou, and Issa J. Dahabreh, "Elimination of Cost Sharing for Screening Mammography in Medicare Advantage Plans," *New England Journal of Medicine* 378, no. 3 (2018): 262–269.

50. "The Center for Consumer Information & Insurance Oversight—Affordable Care Act Implementation FAQs—Set 12," CMS, accessed January 9, 2019, https://www.cms.gov/CCIIO/Resources/Fact-Sheets-and-FAQs/aca_implementation_faqs12.html.

51. AARP Public Policy Institute, "Colonoscopy Barriers after the Affordable Care Act: Cost Barriers Persist for Medicare Beneficiaries," 2013, https://www.aarp.org

/content/dam/aarp/research/public_policy_institute/health/2013/colonoscopy
-screening-after-aca-insight-AARP-ppi-health.pdf.

52. "H.R.1017—Removing Barriers to Colorectal Cancer Screening Act of 2017,"
Congress.gov, accessed January 8, 2018, https://www.congress.gov/bill/115th
-congress/house-bill/1017/related-bills.

53. "Medicare Advantage Value-Based Insurance Design Model," CMS, accessed
January 8, 2018, https://innovation.cms.gov/initiatives/VBID/.

54. Laura Joszt, "TRICARE Will Implement a VBID Demonstration," *AJMC* (blog),
December 6, 2016, https://www.ajmc.com/focus-of-the-week/tricare-will-imple
ment-a-vbid-demonstration.

Chapter 2. Why Is Strengthening Primary Care So Important for Prevention?

1. "About Us," *Holy Cross Health*, accessed February 3, 2018, http://www.holycross
health.org/about-us.

2. "Holy Cross Health Network," *Holy Cross Health*, accessed February 3, 2018,
http://www.holycrosshealth.org/HCHN.

3. Anand K. Parekh, "Winning Their Trust," *New England Journal of Medicine* 364:e51
(2011), doi:10.1056/nejmp1105645.

4. "Ambulatory Care Use and Physician Office Visits," CDC, last modified May 3,
2017, accessed February 7, 2018, https://www.cdc.gov/nchs/fastats/physician-visits
.htm.

5. Mark W. Friedberg, Peter S. Hussey, and Eric C. Schneider, "Primary Care: A
Critical Review of the Evidence on Quality and Costs of Health Care," *Health Affairs*
29, no. 5 (2010): 766–772.

6. Friedberg, Hussey, and Schneider, "Primary Care."

7. David M. Levine, Bruce E. Landon, and Jeffrey A. Linder, "Quality and Experience
of Outpatient Care in the United States for Adults with or without Primary Care,"
JAMA Internal Medicine (2019): doi:10.1001/jamainternmed.2018.6716.

8. "Why Primary Care?" Health is Primary, accessed February 6, 2018, http://health
isprimary.org/learn.

9. Kimberly S. H. Yarnall, Kathryn I. Pollak, Truls Østbye, Katrina M. Krause, and
J. Lloyd Michener, "Primary Care: Is There Enough Time for Prevention?" *American
Journal of Public Health* 93, no. 4 (2003): 635–641.

10. Kimberly S. H. Yarnall, Truls Østbye, Katrina M. Krause, Kathryn I. Pollak,
Margaret Gradison, and J. Lloyd Michener, "Family Physicians as Team Leaders:
'Time' to Share the Care," *Preventing Chronic Disease* 6, no. 2 (2009): 1–6.

11. Association of American Medical Colleges, *2017 State Physician Workforce Data
Report*, 2017, https://store.aamc.org/downloadable/download/sample/sample_id/30/.

12. "New Research Shows Increasing Physician Shortages in Both Primary and
Specialty Care," Association of American Medical Colleges, accessed January 6, 2019,
https://news.aamc.org/press-releases/article/workforce_report_shortage_04112018/.

13. American College of Physicians, *Solutions to the Challenges Facing Primary Care
Medicine*, 2009, https://www.acponline.org/acp_policy/policies/solutions_challenges
_primarycare_2009.pdf.

14. Brendan Murphy, "94% Match Rate in 2018 for U.S. Allopathic Med Students,"

American Medical Association (blog), April 5, 2018, https://www.ama-assn.org
/residents-students/match/94-match-rate-2018-us-allopathic-med-students.

15. "State Practice Environment," American Association of Nurse Practitioners,
accessed January 6, 2019, https://www.aanp.org/advocacy/state/state-practice
-environment.

16. "Primary Care Health Professional Shortage Areas (HPSA)," Henry J. Kaiser Family
Foundation, accessed January 15, 2019, https://www.kff.org/other/state-indicator
/primary-care-health-professional-shortage-areas-hpsas/?currentTimeframe
=0&sortModel=%7B%22colId%22:%22Location%22,%22sort%22:%22asc%22%7D.

17. Jeanne M. Ferrante, Bijal A. Balasubramanian, Shawna V. Hudson, and Benjamin F. Crabtree, "Principles of the Patient-Centered Medical Home and Preventive
Services Delivery," *Annals of Family Medicine* 8 (2018): 108–116.

18. Michael L. Paustian, Jeffrey A. Alexander, Darline K. El Reda, Chris G. Wise,
Lee A. Green, and Michael D. Fetters, "Partial and Incremental PCMH Practice
Transformation: Implications for Quality and Costs," *Health Services Research* 49,
no. 1 (2014): 52–74.

19. Patient-Centered Primary Care Collaborative, Robert Graham Center, *The Impact
of Primary Care Practice Transformation on Cost, Quality, and Utilization*, 2017, https://
www.pcpcc.org/sites/default/files/resources/pcmh_evidence_report_08-1-17%20
FINAL.pdf.

20. Amanda R. Markovitz, Jeffrey A. Alexander, Paula M. Lantz, and Michael L.
Paustian, "Patient-Centered Medical Home Implementation and Use of Preventive
Services," *JAMA Internal Medicine* 175, no. 4 (2015): 598–606.

21. Diego Garcia-Huidobro, Nathan Shippee, Julia Joseph-DiCaprio, Jennifer M.
O'Brien, and Maria Veronica Svetaz, "Effect of Patient-Centered Medical Home on
Preventive Services for Adolescents and Young Adults," *Pediatrics* 137, no. 6 (2016),
http://pediatrics.aappublications.org/content/137/6/e20153813.

22. Mark W. Friedberg, Eric C. Schneider, Meredith B. Rosenthal, Kevin G. Volpp,
and Rachel M. Werner, "Association between Participation in a Multipayer Medical
Home Intervention and Changes in Quality, Utilization, and Costs of Care," *JAMA*
311, no. 8 (2014): 815–825.

23. "Patient-Centered Medical Home," National Committee for Quality Assurance,
accessed January 6, 2019, https://www.ncqa.org/programs/health-care-providers
-practices/patient-centered-medical-home-pcmh/.

24. "Patient-Centered Medical Home."

25. Patient-Centered Primary Care Collaborative, Robert Graham Center, *Advanced
Primary Care: A Key Contributor to Successful ACOs*, 2018, https://www.pcpcc.org
/sites/default/files/resources/PCPCC%202018%20Evidence%20Report.pdf.

26. "HRSA Health Center Program," Health Resources Services Administration,
accessed January 6, 2019, https://bphc.hrsa.gov/sites/default/files/bphc/about
/healthcenterfactsheet.pdf.

27. "HRSA Health Center Program."

28. Janet S. Wright, Hilary K. Wall, Matthew D. Ritchey, "Million Hearts 2022—Small
Steps Needed for Cardiovascular Disease Prevention," *JAMA* 320, no.18 (November
2018): 1857–1858, doi:10.1001/jama.2018.13326.

29. Sara Rosenbaum, Jennifer Tolbert, Jessica Sharac, Peter Shin, Rachel Gunsalus,

and Julia Zur, "Community Health Centers: Growing Importance in a Changing Health Care System," Kaiser Family Foundation, March 9, 2018, https://www.kff.org/report-section/community-health-centers-growing-importance-in-a-changing-health-care-system-issue-brief/.

30. Rosenbaum, Tolbert, Sharac, et al., "Community Health Centers."

31. Rosenbaum, Tolbert, Sharac, et al., "Community Health Centers."

32. Rosenbaum, Tolbert, Sharac, et al., "Community Health Centers."

33. "Who We Are," Life Planning Partners, accessed February 5, 2018, https://www.lifeplanningpartners.com/about-us/who-we-are/.

34. Carolyn McClanahan, "Community Health Centers: An Alternative Approach to Universal Healthcare," *CSA Journal* 69, no. 2 (2017), https://c.ymcdn.com/sites/www.csa.us/resource/resmgr/docs/journals/journal_69/Author/Carolyn-McClanahan.pdf.

35. Tom Murphy, "Employers Jump into Providing Care as Health Costs Rise," Associated Press, September 30, 2018.

36. Murphy, "Employers Jump into Providing Care."

37. "National Health Care Workforce Commission," American College of Physicians, accessed February 11, 2018, https://www.acponline.org/system/files/documents/advocacy/where_we_stand/assets/ii4-national-health-care-workforce.pdf.

38. Andy Lazris, Alan Roth, and Shannon Brownlee, "No More Lip Service; It's Time We Fixed Primary Care (Part Two)," *Health Affairs* (blog), November 21, 2018, https://www.healthaffairs.org/do/10.1377/hblog20181115.163117/full/.

39. Whitney L. J. Howell, "Medical Schools Develop Programs to Grow Primary Care Pipeline," *AAMC Reporter*, November 2015, https://www.aamc.org/newsroom/reporter/november2015/448954/medicalschoolsdevelopprogramstogrowprimarycarepipeline.html.

40. Howell, "Medical Schools Develop Programs."

41. James D. Reschovsky, Arkadipta Ghosh, Kate Stewart, and Deborah Chollet, *Paying More for Primary Care: Can It Help Bend the Medicare Cost Curve?* Commonwealth Fund, March 2012, https://www.commonwealthfund.org/publications/issue-briefs/2012/mar/paying-more-primary-care-can-it-help-bend-medicare-cost-curve.

42. Kerry Dooley Young, "MedPAC Mulls Ways to Boost Medicare Support for Primary Care," *Medscape Medical News*, January 12, 2018, https://www.medscape.com/viewarticle/891305.

43. Stephen Zuckerman and Dana Goin, "How Much Will Medicaid Physician Fees for Primary Care Rise in 2013? Evidence from a 2012 Survey of Medicaid Physician Fees," the Henry J. Kaiser Family Foundation, December 2012, https://kaiserfamilyfoundation.files.wordpress.com/2013/01/8398.pdf.

44. Lindsay M. Sabik, "Medicaid Physician Payment Rates and Use of Breast and Cervical Cancer Screening," abstract presented at American Society of Health Economists, June 14, 2016, https://ashecon.confex.com/ashecon/2016/webprogram/Paper4727.html.

45. Diane Alexander and Molly Schnell, *Closing the Gap: The Impact of the Medicaid Primary Care Rate Increase on Access and Health*, Federal Reserve Bank of Chicago Working Paper No. WP-2017-10, April 21, 2018, https://www.chicagofed.org/~/media/publications/working-papers/2017/wp2017-10-pdf.pdf.

46. Stephen Zuckerman, Laura Skopec, and Marni Epstein, *Medicaid Physician Fees*

after the ACA Primary Care Fee Bump, Urban Institute, March 2017, https://www
.urban.org/sites/default/files/publication/88836/2001180-medicaid-physician-fees
-after-the-aca-primary-care-fee-bump_0.pdf.

47. Stephen Petterson, Robert McNellis, Kathleen Klink, David Meyers, and Andrew
Bazemore, *The State of Primary Care in the United States: A Chartbook of Facts and
Statistics*, Robert Graham Center, 2018, accessed January 15, 2019, https://www
.graham-center.org/content/dam/rgc/documents/publications-reports/reports
/PrimaryCareChartbook.pdf.

48. Christopher F. Koller and Dhruv Khullar, "Primary Care Spending Rate—A Lever
for Encouraging Investment in Primary Care," *New England Journal of Medicine* 377,
no. 18 (2017): 1709–1711.

49. Christopher F. Koller, "Getting More Primary Care-Oriented: Measuring Primary
Care Spending," *Milbank Memorial Fund* (blog), July 31, 2017, https://www.milbank
.org/2017/07/getting-primary-care-oriented-measuring-primary-care-spending/.

50. "Senate Bill 227," Delaware General Assembly, accessed December 21, 2018,
https://legis.delaware.gov/BillDetail?legislationId=26743.

51. "Legislation and Regulation," Milbank Memorial Fund, accessed January 10,
2019, https://www.milbank.org/programs/primary-care-spend/legislation-and
-regulation/.

52. "Primary Care Collaborative Report 2019," Patient-Centered Primary Care
Collaborative, accessed January 15, 2019, https://www.pcpcc.org/resource/primary
-care-collaborative-report-2019.

53. Michael H. Bailit, Mark W. Friedberg, and Margaret L. Houy, *Standardizing the
Measurement of Commercial Health Plan Primary Care Spending*, Milbank Memorial
Fund, 2017, accessed January 15, 2019, https://www.milbank.org/wp-content/uploads
/2017/07/MMF-Primary-Care-Spending-Report.pdf.

Chapter 3. Where Should Healthcare Look outside the Walls
of the Clinical Setting?

1. Northwestern University, "Chicago's South Side Suffers Most from Unhealthy
Neighborhoods," *ScienceDaily*, August 15, 2011, www.sciencedaily.com/releases/2011
/08/110815143925.htm.

2. Gillian Feldmeth and Stacy Tessler Lindau, "Community Rx: How the South Side
of Chicago Is Connecting Health Care to Self-Care," *Trust for America's Health* (blog),
October 7, 2014, https://www.tfah.org/health-issues/prevention_story/communityrx
-how-the-south-side-of-chicago-is-connecting-health-care-to-self-care.

3. Feldmeth and Lindau, "Community Rx."

4. Health IT Success Stories, "Dr. Long Uses Health IT to Connect Patients to Community Resources," *HealthIT.gov* (blog), March 24, 2014, https://archive.healthit.gov
/providers-professionals/dr-long-uses-health-it-connect-patients-community
-resources.

5. Stacy T. Lindau, Jennifer Makelarski, Emily Abramsohn, David G. Beiser, Veronica
Escamilla, Jessica Jerome, Daniel Johnson, et al., "CommunityRx: A Population
Health Improvement Innovation That Connects Clinics to Communities," *Health
Affairs* 35, no. 11 (2016), https://doi.org/10.1377/hlthaff.2016.0694.

6. Jodi Summers Holtrop, Steven A. Dosh, Trissa Torres, and Yeow Meng Thum, "The Community Health Educator Referral Liaison (CHERL): A Primary Care Practice Role for Promoting Healthy Behaviors," *American Journal of Preventive Medicine* 35, no. 5 (supp) (2008), https://doi.org/10.1016/j.amepre.2008.08.012.

7. "Automated Clinician Prompts and Referrals Facilitate Access to Counseling Services, Leading to Positive Behavior Changes among Patients," AHRQ Health Care Innovations Exchange, last modified July 6, 2014, accessed March 5, 2018, https://innovations.ahrq.gov/profiles/automated-clinician-prompts-and-referrals-facilitate-access-counseling-services-leading.

8. Deborah S. Porterfield, Laurie W. Hinnant, Heather Kane, Joseph Horne, Kelly McAleer, and Amy Roussel, "Linkages between Clinical Practices and Community Organizations for Prevention," *American Journal of Preventive Medicine* 42, no. 6S2 (2012): S163–S171.

9. Agency for Healthcare Research and Quality, "AHRQ Updates on Primary Care Research: Clinical-Community Relationships," *Annals of Family Medicine* 11, no. 6 (2013): 584–585.

10. Ronald G. Victor, Kathleen Lynch, Ning Li, Ciantel Blyler, Eric Muhammad, Joel Handler, Jeffrey Brettler, et al., "A Cluster-Randomized Trial of Blood-Pressure Reduction in Black Barbershops," *New England Journal of Medicine* 378, no. 14 (2018): 1291–1301.

11. Association of State and Territorial Health Officials, *Community-Clinical Linkages to Improve Hypertension Identification, Management, and Control*, 2015, http://www.astho.org/Prevention/Community-Clinical-Linkages-Issue-Brief/.

12. "Diabetes Prevention Program," National Institute of Diabetes and Digestive and Kidney Diseases, accessed March 4, 2019, https://www.niddk.nih.gov/about-niddk/research-areas/diabetes/diabetes-prevention-program-dpp.

13. "Diabetes Prevention Program."

14. William H. Herman, "The Economics of Diabetes Prevention," *Medical Clinics of North America* 95, no. 2 (2011), doi:10.1016/j.mcna.2010.11.010.

15. "For a Better Us," YMCA of San Francisco, accessed January 17, 2019, https://www.ymcasf.org/about.

16. Ronald T. Ackermann, Emily A. Finch, Edward Brizendine, Honghong Zhou, and David G. Marrero, "Translating the Diabetes Prevention Program into the Community—The DEPLOY Pilot Study," *American Journal of Preventive Medicine* 35, no. 4 (2008), doi:10.1016/j.amepre.2008.06.035.

17. Jeffrey A. Katula, Caroline S. Blackwell, Erica L. Rosenberger, and David C. Goff, Jr., "Translating Diabetes Prevention Programs—Implications for Dissemination and Policy," *North Carolina Medical Journal* 72, no. 5 (2011): 405–408.

18. "National Diabetes Prevention Program," CDC, last modified August 15, 2017, accessed March 5, 2018, https://www.cdc.gov/diabetes/prevention/about/index.html.

19. "Diabetes Prevention Program (DPP)," National Institute of Diabetes and Digestive and Kidney Diseases, https://www.niddk.nih.gov/about-niddk/research-areas/diabetes/diabetes-prevention-program-dpp.

20. "Medicare Diabetes Prevention Program (MDPP) Expanded Model," CMS, last modified January 7, 2019, accessed January 17, 2019, https://innovation.cms.gov/initiatives/medicare-diabetes-prevention-program/.

21. "Certification of Medicare Diabetes Prevention Program," CMS Office of the Actuary, accessed March 5, 2018, https://www.cms.gov/Research-Statistics-Data-and -Systems/Research/ActuarialStudies/Downloads/Diabetes-Prevention-Certification -2016-03-14.pdf.

22. Centers for Disease Control and Prevention, *National Diabetes Statistics Report, 2017,* 2017, https://www.cdc.gov/diabetes/pdfs/data/statistics/national-diabetes -statistics-report.pdf.

23. Kate Lorig, "Chronic Disease Self-Management Program: Insights from the Eye of the Storm," *Frontiers in Public Health* 2 (2014): 253.

24. Marcia G. Ory, SangNam Ahn, Luohua Jiang, Matthew Lee Smith, Philip L. Ritter, Nancy Whitelaw, and Kate Lorig, "Successes of a National Study of the Chronic Disease Self-Management Program: Meeting the Triple Aim of Health Care Reform," *Medical Care* 51, no. 11 (2013): 992–998.

25. SangNam Ahn, Rashmita Basu, Matthew Lee Smith, Luohua Jiang, Kate Lorig, Nancy Whitelaw, and Marcia G. Ory, "The Impact of Chronic Disease Self-Management Programs: Healthcare Savings through a Community-Based Intervention," *BMC Public Health* 13, no. 1 (2013), https://doi.org/10.1186/1471-2458-13-1141.

26. Centers for Medicare and Medicaid Services, *Report to Congress: The Centers for Medicare and Medicaid Services' Evaluation of Community-Based Wellness and Prevention Programs under Section 4202 (b) of the Affordable Care Act,* 2009, https://innovation .cms.gov/Files/reports/CommunityWellnessRTC.pdf.

27. Acumen, LLC, *Wellness Prospective Evaluation Final Report,* 2018, https://down loads.cms.gov/files/cmmi/community-basedwellnessandprevention-finalreport.pdf.

28. Centers for Medicare and Medicaid Services, *Report to Congress,* https://inno vation.cms.gov/Files/reports/CommunityWellnessRTC.pdf.

29. "Highest Tier Evidence-Based Health Promotion/Disease Prevention Programs," National Council on Aging, last modified January 2019, accessed January 18, 2019, https://www.ncoa.org/resources/ebpchart/.

30. "Important Facts about Falls," CDC, last modified February 10, 2017, accessed March 8, 2018, https://www.cdc.gov/homeandrecreationalsafety/falls/adultfalls.html.

31. Gwen Bergen, Mark R. Stevens, and Elizabeth R. Burns, "Falls and Fall Injuries among Adults Aged ≥65 Years—United States, 2014," *Morbidity and Mortality Weekly Report* 65 (2016): 993–998.

32. Grant Baldwin, Matt Breiding, and David Sleet, "Using the Public Health Model to Address Unintentional Injuries and TBI: A Perspective from the Centers for Disease Control and Prevention (CDC)," *NeuroRehabilitation* 39, no. 3 (2016): 345–349.

33. Joint Center for Housing Studies of Harvard University, *Housing America's Older Adults: Meeting the Needs of an Aging Population,* 2014, http://www.jchs.harvard.edu /sites/default/files/jchs-housing_americas_older_adults_2014_1.pdf.

34. Michael D. Keall, Nevil Pierse, Philippa Howden-Chapman, Jagadish Guria, Chris W. Cunningham, and Michael G. Baker, "Cost-Benefit Analysis of Fall Injuries Prevented by a Programme of Home Modifications: A Cluster Randomised Controlled Trial," *Injury Prevention* 23, no. 1 (2017): 22–26.

35. "Highest Tier Evidence-Based Health Promotion/Disease Prevention Programs."

36. Centers for Medicare and Medicaid Services, *Report to Congress,* https:// innovation.cms.gov/Files/reports/CommunityWellnessRTC.pdf.

37. Anand Parekh and Robert Schreiber, "How Community-Based Organizations Can Support Value-Driven Health Care," *Health Affairs* (blog), July 10, 2015, https://www.healthaffairs.org/do/10.1377/hblog20150710.049256/full.

38. "Home Visiting," Health Resources and Services Administration (HRSA), accessed March 17, 2018, https://mchb.hrsa.gov/maternal-child-health-initiatives/home-visiting-overview.

39. Topher Spiro and Lanhee J. Chen, "Sending Nurses to Work with Poor Moms Helps Kids. So Why Don't We Do More of It?" *Washington Post*, April 5, 2016.

40. RAND Corporation, *Early Childhood Interventions—Proven Results, Future* Promise, 2005, https://www.rand.org/content/dam/rand/pubs/monographs/2005/RAND_MG341.pdf.

41. "Home Visiting," HRSA.

42. Spiro and Chen, "Sending nurses."

43. Spiro and Chen, "Sending nurses."

44. "Update on Preventive Services Initiatives," Center for Medicaid and CHIP Services Information Bulletin, accessed January 18, 2019, https://www.medicaid.gov/federal-policy-guidance/downloads/cib-11-27-2013-prevention.pdf.

45. Christina Bielaszka-DuVernay, "Vermont's Blueprint for Medical Homes, Community Health Teams, and Better Health at Lower Cost," *Health Affairs* 30, no. 3 (2011): 383–386.

46. "Vermont Blueprint for Health," Patient-Centered Primary Care Collaborative, accessed March 11, 2018, https://www.pcpcc.org/initiative/vermont-blueprint-health.

47. The Association of State and Territorial Health Officials, *Community Health Teams Issue Report*, http://www.astho.org/Programs/Access/Primary-Care/_Materials/Community-Health-Teams-Issue-Report/.

48. Mary Takach and Jason Buxbaum, *Care Management for Medicaid Enrollees through Community Health Needs*, Commonwealth Fund, 2013, https://www.commonwealthfund.org/sites/default/files/documents/___media_files_publications_fund_report_2013_may_1690_takach_care_mgmt_medicaid_enrollees_community_hlt_teams_520.pdf.

Chapter 4. Social Determinants and Healthcare

1. Bruce D. Broussard, "Humana CEO: We're Going to Make the Communities We Serve 20% Healthier," *Forbes*, April 6, 2015, https://www.forbes.com/sites/matthewherper/2015/04/06/humana-ceo-were-going-to-make-the-communities-we-serve-20-healthier/.

2. Tristan Cordier, S. Lane Slabaugh, Eric Havens, Jonathan Pena, Gil Haugh, Vipin Gopal, Andrew Renda, et al., "A Health Plan's Investigation of Healthy Days and Chronic Conditions," *American Journal of Managed Care* 23, no. 10 (2017): e323-e330.

3. Tristan Cordier, Yongjia Song, Jesse Cambon, Gil S. Haugh, Mark Steffen, Patty Hardy, Marnie Staehly, et al., "A Bold Goal: More Healthy Days through Improved Community Health," *Population Health Management* 21, no. 3 (2018), https://doi.org/10.1089/pop.2017.0142.

4. Humana, *2017 Progress Report—Bold Goal*, 2017, http://populationhealth.humana.com/documents/Humana_BoldGoal_2017_ProgressReport-v2.pdf.

5. Humana, *2017 Progress Report—Bold Goal*.

6. Cordier, et al., "A Bold Goal."

7. Humana, *2017 Progress Report—Bold Goal*.

8. Bipartisan Policy Center, *Rural Aging: Health and Community Policy Implications for Reversing Social Isolation*, 2018, https://bipartisanpolicy.org/wp-content/uploads/2018/07/Rural-Aging-Health-and-Community-Policy-Implications-for-Reversing-Social-Isolation.pdf.

9. Humana, *2017 Progress Report—Bold Goal*.

10. Humana, *2017 Progress Report—Bold Goal*.

11. Elizabeth H. Bradley, Benjamin R. Elkins, Jeph Herrin, and Brian Elbel, "Health and Social Services Expenditures: Associations with Health Outcomes," *BMJ Quality & Safety* 20 (2011): 826–831.

12. Paula Braveman, Mercedes Dekker, Susan Egerter, Tabashir Sadegh-Nobari, and Craig Pollack, "Housing and Health," Robert Wood Johnson Foundation, 2011, https://www.rwjf.org/content/dam/farm/reports/issue_briefs/2011/rwjf70451.

13. Bipartisan Policy Center, *Building the Case: Low-Income Housing Tax Credits and Health*, 2017, https://bipartisanpolicy.org/wp-content/uploads/2017/11/BPC-Health-Building-the-Case-Low-Income-Housing-Tax-Credits-and-Health.pdf.

14. Michael K. Gusmano, Victor G. Rodwin, and Daniel Weisz, "Medicare Beneficiaries Living in Housing with Supportive Services Experienced Lower Hospital Use Than Others," *Health Affairs* 37, no. 10 (2018), https://doi.org/10.1377/hlthaff.2018.0070.

15. Bipartisan Policy Center, *Building the Case*.

16. Joint Center for Housing Studies of Harvard University, *Housing America's Older Adults*, http://www.jchs.harvard.edu/sites/default/files/jchs-housing_americas_older_adults_2014_1.pdf.

17. Wan He and Luke J. Larsen, *Older Americans with a Disability: 2008–2012 American Community Survey Reports*, US Department of Health and Human Services and US Department of Commerce, 2014, https://www2.census.gov/library/publications/2014/acs/acs-29.pdf.

18. "UnitedHealthcare's Investments in Affordable Housing to Help People Achieve Better Health Surpass $400 Million," *Business Wire*, March 26, 2019, https://www.businesswire.com/news/home/20190326005726/en/.

19. Corianne Payton Scally, Elaine Waxman, and Ruth Gourevitch, *A National Insurer Goes Local: Emerging Strategies for Integrating Health and Housing*, Urban Institute, 2017, https://www.urban.org/sites/default/files/publication/91966/2001419_uhc_case_study_3.pdf.

20. Scally, Waxman, and Gourevitch, *A National Insurer Goes Local*.

21. NORC at the University of Chicago, *The Impact of Housing Programs and Services on Health Care Costs, Quality, and Member Experience*, 2018, https://www.mercymaricopa.org/assets/pdf/news/NORC-Housing-Report.pdf.

22. "Coverage of Housing-Related Activities and Services for Individuals with Disabilities," Center for Medicaid and CHIP Services Informational Bulletin, accessed April 4, 2018, https://www.medicaid.gov/federal-policy-guidance/downloads/cib-06-26-2015.pdf.

23. Bipartisan Policy Center. *Healthy Aging Begins at Home*, 2016, https://bipartisanpolicy.org/wp-content/uploads/2016/05/BPC-Healthy-Aging.pdf.

24. Bipartisan Policy Center, *Healthy Aging.*

25. Bipartisan Policy Center, *Healthy Aging.*

26. Renata Micha, Jose L. Peñalvo, Frederick Cudhea, Fumiaki Imamura, Colin D. Rehm, and Dariush Mozaffarian, "Association between Dietary Factors and Mortality from Heart Disease, Stroke, and Type 2 Diabetes in the United States," *JAMA* 317, no. 9 (2017): 912–924.

27. K. M. Venkat Narayan, James P. Boyle, Theodore J. Thompson, Stephen W. Sorensen, and David F. Williamson, *JAMA* 290, no. 14 (2003): 1884–1980.

28. American Diabetes Association, "Economic Costs of Diabetes in the U.S. in 2017," *Diabetes Care* (2018), https://doi.org/10.2337/dci18-0007.

29. Bipartisan Policy Center, *Leading with Nutrition: Leveraging Federal Programs for Better Health*, 2018, https://bipartisanpolicy.org/wp-content/uploads/2018/03/BPC -Health-Leading-With-Nutrition.pdf.

30. Dariush Mozaffarian, Junxiu Liu, Stephen Sy, Yue Huang, Colin Rehm, Yujin Lee, Parke Wilde, et al., "Cost-Effectiveness of Financial Incentives and Disincentives for Improving Food Purchases and Health through the US Supplemental Nutrition Assistance Program (SNAP): A Microsimulation Study," *PLoS Med* 15, no. 10 (2018), https:// journals.plos.org/plosmedicine/article?id=10.1371%2Fjournal.pmed.1002661.

31. Bipartisan Policy Center, *Leading with Nutrition.*

32. H. Zhu and R. An, "Impact of Home-Delivered Meal Programs on Diet and Nutrition among Older Adults: A Review," *Nutrition and Health* 22, no. 2 (2013): 89–103.

33. Kali S. Thomas and David Dosa, *More Than a Meal: Pilot Research Study*, Meals on Wheels America, 2015, https://www.mealsonwheelsamerica.org/learn-more /research/more-than-a-meal/pilot-research-study.

34. Kali S. Thomas and Vincent Mor, "Providing More Home-Delivered Meals Is One Way to Keep Older Adults with Low Care Needs Out of Nursing Homes," *Health Affairs* 32, no. 10 (2013): 1796–1802.

35. Seth A. Berkowitz, Jean Terranova, Caterina Hill, Toyin Ajayi, Todd Linksy, Lori W. Tishler, Darren A. DeWalt, "Meal Delivery Programs Reduce the Use of Costly Health Care in Dually Eligible Medicare and Medicaid Beneficiaries," *Health Affairs* 37, no. 4 (2018), 535–542.

36. "Fresh Food Farmacy," Geisinger Health System, accessed April 25, 2018, https:// www.geisinger.org/freshfoodfarmacy/our-purpose.

37. Andrea T. Feinberg, Jonathan R. Slotkin, Allison Hess, and Alistair R. Erskine, "How Geisinger Treats Diabetes by Giving Away Free, Healthy Food," Harvard Business Review, October 25, 2017, https://hbr.org/2017/10/how-geisinger-treats -diabetes-by-giving-away-free-healthy-food.

38. Dan Ochwat, "Grassroots Geisinger Initiative Addresses Community Health," *Hospitals and Health Networks*, March 2, 2017, https://www.hhnmag.com/articles /8068-geisinger-addresses-community-health.

39. Feinberg et al., "How Geisinger Treats Diabetes."

40. Feinberg et al., "How Geisinger Treats Diabetes."

41. Jacqueline LaPointe, "How Addressing Social Determinants of Health Cuts Healthcare Costs," *RevCycle Intelligence*, June 25, 2018, https://revcycleintelligence .com/news/how-addressing-social-determinants-of-health-cuts-healthcare-costs.

42. Tracey Walker, "Five Things to Know about the Uber and Lyft Provider Partner-

ships," Managed Healthcare Executive, March 9, 2018, https://www.instamed.com /news-and-events/managed-healthcare-executive-mar9/.

43. Brian W. Powers, Scott Rinefort, and Sachin H. Jain, "Nonemergency Medical Transportation—Delivering Care in the Era of Lyft and Uber," *JAMA* 316, no. 9 (2016): 921–922.

44. Marco della Cava, "Lyft Deal with Allscripts Lets 180,000 Doctors Call Rides for Their Patients," *USA Today*, March 5, 2018, https://www.usatoday.com/story/tech /2018/03/05/lyft-deal-allscripts-lets-180-000-doctors-call-rides-their-patients /389122002/.

45. Sara Heath, "BCBS Targets Medical Transportation, Social Determinants of Health," *PatientEngagementHIT*, March 19, 2018, https://patientengagementhit.com /news/bcbs-targets-medical-transportation-social-determinants-of-health.

46. Clive Riddle, "Recent Uber and Lyft Healthcare Transportation Collaborations," *MCOL* (blog), December 1, 2017, http://www.mcolblog.com/kcblog/2017/12/1 /recent-uber-and-lyft-healthcare-transportation-collaboration.html.

47. Kurt Nagl, "Ford Expands GoRide Medical Transport Service with Detroit Medical Center Partnership," *Modern Healthcare*, September 4, 2018, https://www .modernhealthcare.com/article/20180904/NEWS/180909991.

48. Powers et al., "Nonemergency Medical Transportation," 921–922.

49. Carolyn Y. Johnson, "Uber and Lyft Think They Can Solve One of Medicine's Biggest Problems," *Washington Post*, March 1, 2018, https://www.washingtonpost .com/.

50. Cava, "Lyft Deal with Allscripts."

51. Seth A. Berkowitz, Amy Catherine Hulberg, Sara Standish, Gally Reznor, Steven J. Atlas, "Addressing Unmet Basic Resource Needs as Part of Chronic Cardiometabolic Disease Management," *JAMA Internal Medicine* 177, no. 2 (2017): 244–252.

52. "Healthify—Ensuring End-to-End Care to Resolve the Social Determinants of Health," Healthify, accessed April 25, 2018, https://www.healthify.us/platform.

53. Ara Ohanian and Daniel McConnell, "The ROI of Addressing Social Determinants of Health," *AJMC*, January 11, 2018, https://www.ajmc.com/contributor/ara -ohanian/2018/01/the-roi-of-addressing-social-determinants-of-health.

54. Sheri Porter, "Researchers Test EHR Tools That Document Social Determinants," *AAFP News*, September 19, 2018, https://www.aafp.org/news/practice-professional -issues/20180919ehrsdoh.html.

55. "Accountable Health Communities Model," CMS, accessed April 28, 2018, https:// innovation.cms.gov/initiatives/ahcm.

56. Anna Spencer and Bianca Freda, *Advancing State Innovation Model Goals through Accountable Communities for Health*, Center for Health Care Strategies, Inc., 2016, https://www.chcs.org/media/SIM-ACH-Brief_101316_final.pdf.

57. Marianne Udow-Phillips, email communication with author, November 24, 2018.

58. Katharine Witgert, "Why Medicaid Is the Platform Best Suited for Addressing Both Health Care and Social Needs," *Health Affairs* (blog), September 7, 2017, https:// www.healthaffairs.org/do/10.1377/hblog20170907.061853/full.

59. Seema Verma, "CMS Approves North Carolina's Innovative Medicaid Demonstration to Help Improve Health Outcomes," *Health Affairs* (blog), October 24, 2018, https://www.healthaffairs.org/do/10.1377/hblog20181024.406020/full.

60. Bipartisan Policy Center, *Improving Care and Lowering Costs for Chronic Care Beneficiaries: Implementing the Bipartisan Budget Act*, 2018, https://bipartisanpolicy.org/wp-content/uploads/2018/08/Improving-Care-and-Lowering-Costs-for-Chronic-Care-Beneficiaries-Implementing-the-Bipartisan-Budget-Act.pdf.

61. "2019 Medicare Advantage and Part D Rate Announcement and Call Letter," CMS, accessed April 28, 2018, https://www.cms.gov/newsroom/fact-sheets/2019-medicare-advantage-and-part-d-rate-announcement-and-call-letter.

62. "Medicare Advantage Beneficiaries Will See a Jump in New Supplemental Benefit Offerings in 2019," Avalere Health, accessed January 10, 2019, https://avalere.com/press-releases/medicare-advantage-beneficiaries-will-see-a-jump-in-new-supplemental-benefit-offerings-in-2019.

63. Robert Holly, "Anthem Adds Home Care Benefits under Relaxed Medicare Advantage Rule," Home Health Care News, October 1, 2018, https://homehealthcarenews.com/2018/10/anthem-adds-home-care-benefits-under-relaxed-medicare-advantage-rule/.

64. Paula M. Lantz, George Miller, Corwin N. Rhyan, Sara Rosenbaum, Leighton Ku, and Samantha Iovan, "Pay for Success Financing and Home-Based Multicomponent Childhood Asthma Interventions: Modeling Results from the Detroit Medicaid Population," *Milbank Quarterly* 96, no. 2 (2018): doi:10.1111/1468-0009.12325.

65. S. 963 (115th): Social Impact Partnerships to Pay for Results Act, https://www.govtrack.us/congress/bills/115/s963.

66. Stuart Butler and Marcella Cabello, "An Antidote to the 'Wrong Pockets' Problem?" Urban Institute's Pay for Success Initiative (PFSI) and the Brookings Institution-hosted Braiding and Blending Working Group (blog), October 8, 2018, https://pfs.urban.org/pay-success/pfs-perspectives/antidote-wrong-pockets-problem.

67. Len M. Nichols and Lauren A. Taylor, "Social Determinants as Public Goods: A New Approach to Financing Key Investments in Healthy Communities," *Health Affairs* 37, no. 8 (2018): 1223–1230.

68. Sara Rosenbaum, Maureen Byrnes, Sara Rothenberg, and Rachel Gunsalus, *Improving Community Health through Hospital Community Benefit Spending: Charting a Path to Reform*, Milken Institute School of Public Health, George Washington University, 2016, https://publichealth.gwu.edu/sites/default/files/downloads/research/Improving%20Commnity%20Health%20through%20Hospital%20Community%20Benefit%20Spending%20Release.pdf.

69. Rosenbaum, Byrnes, Rothenberg, and Gunsalus, *Improving Community Health*.

Chapter 5. Personal Responsibility or Policy, Systems, and Environmental Change?

1. "American Recovery and Reinvestment Fund of 2009," Wikipedia, last modified January 4, 2019, https://en.wikipedia.org/wiki/American_Recovery_and_Reinvestment_Act_of_2009.

2. Pub.L. 111–5, https://www.govinfo.gov/content/pkg/PLAW-111publ5/html/PLAW-111publ5.htm.

3. "MAPPS Interventions for Communities Putting Prevention to Work," CDC,

accessed May 4, 2018, https://www.cdc.gov/chronicdisease/recovery/PDF/MAPPS _Intervention_Table.pdf.

4. "The Communities Putting Prevention to Work (CPPW) Program: Summary and Short- and Long-Term Findings and Benefits," CDC, accessed May 8, 2018, https://www.cdc.gov/nccdphp/dch/programs/communitiesputtingpreventiontowork/pdf /dch_cppw_outcomes_summary_20dec2015.pdf.

5. "The Communities Putting Prevention to Work (CPPW) Program."

6. "America Watches as Philadelphia Battles Obesity," *Governing*, August 2013, http://www.governing.com/topics/health-human-services/gov-america-watches-as-philly -battles-obesity.html.

7. Giridhar Mallya, "Making the Healthy Choice, the Easy Choice: Tobacco Control and Obesity Prevention in Philadelphia," for Dialogue4Health, Public Health Institute, November 2014, http://www.dialogue4health.org/uploads/resources/Mallya _111314.pdf.

8. "The Communities Putting Prevention to Work (CPPW) Program."

9. Stuart Butler, "Obamacare's Slush Fund Fuels a Broader Lobbying Controversy," *Forbes*, May 30, 2013, https://www.forbes.com/sites/realspin/2013/05/30/obamacares -slush-fund-fuels-a-broader-lobbying-controversy/.

10. "New CityHealth Report Shows City Leaders are Putting Policies in Place to Help Residents Thrive," CityHealth, accessed May 29, 2018, http://www.cityhealth.org /press-release-2018-report.

11. "Promoting Health and Cost Control in States," Trust for America's Health, accessed January 31, 2019, https://www.tfah.org/initiatives/promoting-health-cost -control-states-phaccs/.

12. US Department of Health and Human Services, *The Health Consequences of Smoking: 50 Years of Progress—A Report of the Surgeon General*, 2014, https://www .surgeongeneral.gov/library/reports/50-years-of-progress/full-report.pdf.

13. US Department of Health and Human Services, *The Health Consequences of Smoking*.

14. Jidong Huang and Frank J. Chaloupka IV, *The Impact of the 2009 Federal Tobacco Excise Tax Increase on Youth Tobacco Use*, National Bureau of Economic Research, 2012, https://www.nber.org/papers/w18026.

15. Linda J. Neff, Deesha Patel, Kevin Davis, William Ridgeway, Paul Shafer, and Shanna Cox, "Evaluation of the National Tips from Former Smokers Campaign: The 2014 Longitudinal Cohort," *Preventing Chronic Disease* 13 (2016), http://dx.doi.org/10 .5888/pcd13.150556.

16. US Department of Health and Human Services, *Health Consequences*.

17. W. Ryan Diver, Eric J. Jacobs, and Susan M. Gapstur, "Secondhand Smoke Exposure in Childhood and Adulthood in Relation to Adult Mortality among Never Smokers," *American Journal of Preventive Medicine* 55, no. 3 (2018): 345–352.

18. "Tobacco Use and Secondhand Smoke Exposure: Smoke-Free Policies," Community Guide, accessed May 5, 2018, https://www.thecommunityguide.org/findings /tobacco-use-and-secondhand-smoke-exposure-smoke-free-policies.

19. "STATE System Smokefree Indoor Air Fact Sheet," CDC, accessed January 6, 2019, https://chronicdata.cdc.gov/Legislation/STATE-System-Smokefree-Indoor -Air-Fact-Sheet/vgq2-kkcg.

20. "FDA Announces Comprehensive Regulatory Plan to Shift Trajectory of Tobacco-Related Disease, Death," Food and Drug Administration, accessed January 8, 2019, https://www.fda.gov/NewsEvents/Newsroom/PressAnnouncements/ucm568923.htm.

21. Teresa W. Wang, Andrea Gentzke, Saida Sharapova, Karen A. Cullen, Bridget K. Ambrose, and Ahmed Jamal, "Tobacco Product Use among Middle and High School Students—United States, 2011–2017," *Morbidity and Mortality Weekly Report* 67, no. 22 (2018): 629–633.

22. Tushar Singh, Sara Kennedy, Kristy Marynak, Alexander Persoskie, Paul Melstrom, and Brian A. King, "Characteristics of Electronic Cigarette Use among Middle and High School Students—United States, 2015," *Morbidity and Mortality Weekly Report* 65, no. 5051 (2016): 425–429.

23. "Health Care Professionals: Educate Your Young Patients about the Risks of E-cigarettes," CDC, accessed January 7, 2019, https://e-cigarettes.surgeongeneral.gov/documents/SGR_E-Cig_Health_Care_Provider_Card_508.pdf.

24. Michael Stephen Dunbar, Jordan P. Davis, Anthony Rodriguez, Joan Tucker, Rachana Seelam, and Elizabeth J. D'Amico, *Disentangling Within- and Between-Person Effects of Shared Risk Factors on E-cigarette and Cigarette Use Trajectories from Late Adolescence to Young Adulthood*, RAND Corporation, 2018, https://www.rand.org/pubs/external_publications/EP67710.html.

25. Karen A. Cullen, Bridget K. Ambrose, Andrea S. Gentzke, Benjamin J. Apelberg, Ahmed Jamal, and Brian A. King, "*Notes from the Field:* Use of Electronic Cigarettes and Any Tobacco Product among Middle and High School Students—United States, 2011–2018," *Morbidity and Mortality Weekly Report* 67, no. 45 (2018): 1276–1277.

26. "Statement from FDA Commissioner Scott Gottlieb, M.D., on Proposed New Steps to Protect Youth by Preventing Access to Flavored Tobacco Products and Banning Menthol in Cigarettes," Food and Drug Administration, accessed December 4, 2018, https://www.fda.gov/NewsEvents/Newsroom/PressAnnouncements/ucm625884.htm.

27. Kelly D. Brownell and Jennifer L. Pomeranz, "The Trans-Fat Ban—Food Regulation and Long-Term Health," *New England Journal of Medicine* 370, no. 19 (2014): 1773–1775.

28. Eric J. Brandt, Rebecca Myerson, Marcelo Coca Perraillon, and Tamar S. Polonsky, "Hospital Admissions for Myocardial Infarction and Stroke before and after the Trans-Fatty Acid Restrictions in New York," *JAMA Cardiology* 2, no. 6 (2017): 627–634.

29. Maggie Fox, "Trans Fat Ban Saved Lives in New York, Study Shows," *NBC News*, April 12, 2017, https://www.nbcnews.com/health/health-news/trans-fat-ban-saved-lives-new-york-study-shows-n745631.

30. Institute of Medicine, *Sodium Intake in Populations: Assessment of Evidence*, 2013, http://www.nationalacademies.org/hmd/Reports/2013/Sodium-Intake-in-Populations-Assessment-of-Evidence.aspx.

31. Sabrina Tavernise, "F.D.A. Proposes Guidelines for Salt Added to Food," *New York Times*, June 1, 2016, https://www.nytimes.com/2016/06/02/health/fda-salt-guidelines-processed-foods-restaurants.html.

32. George Smith, "Research Finds FDA Voluntary Salt Reduction Scheme Could Save Lives and Money," *New Food*, April 13, 2018, https://www.newfoodmagazine

.com/news/66073/fda-voluntary-salt-reduction-scheme-could-save-millions-of-lives/.

33. Helena Bottemiller Evich and Liz Crampton, "Trump's FDA Presses Obama-Era Nutrition Policy," *POLITICO*, March 29, 2018, https://www.politico.com/story/2018/03/29/trumps-fda-salt-reduction-491256.

34. Bipartisan Policy Center, *Leading with Nutrition*.

35. Alyssa J. Moran, Aviva Musicus, Mary T. Gorski Findling, Ian F. Brissette, Ann A. Lowenfels, S. V. Subramanian, and Christina A. Roberto, "Increases in Sugary Drink Marketing during Supplemental Nutrition Assistance Program Benefit Issuance in New York," *American Journal of Preventive Medicine* 55, no. 1 (2018): 55–62.

36. Bipartisan Policy Center, *Leading with Nutrition*.

37. Bipartisan Policy Center, *Leading with Nutrition*.

38. Dariush Mozaffarian, Junxiu Liu, Stephen Sy, Yue Huang, Colin Rehm, Yujin Lee, Parke Wilde, et al., "Cost-Effectiveness of Financial Incentives and Disincentives for Improving Food Purchases and Health through the US Supplemental Nutrition Assistance Program (SNAP): A Microsimulation Study," *PLoS Med* 15, no. 10 (2018), https://journals.plos.org/plosmedicine/article?id=10.1371%2Fjournal.pmed.1002661.

39. M. Arantxa Colchero, Juan Rivera-Dommarco, Barry M. Popkin, and Shu Wen Ng, "In Mexico, Evidence of Sustained Consumer Response Two Years after Implementing a Sugar-Sweetened Beverage Tax," *Health Affairs* 36, no. 3 (2017): 564–571.

40. Luz Maria Sánchez-Romero, Joanne Penko, Pamela G. Coxson, Alicia Fernández, Antoinette Mason, Andrew E. Moran, Leticia Ávila-Burgos, et al., "Projected Impact of Mexico's Sugar-Sweetened Beverage Tax Policy on Diabetes and Cardiovascular Disease: A Modeling Study," *PLoS Med* 13, no. 11 (2016), https://doi.org/10.1371/journal.pmed.1002158.

41. Beverly Bird, "What Is the Soda Tax and Which Cities Have One?" *The Balance*, November 25, 2018, https://www.thebalance.com/soda-tax-and-which-cities-have-one-4151209.

42. Jeanine Barone, "Expert Q&A—Why Soda Taxes Work," *Berkeley Wellness*, October 12, 2017, http://www.berkeleywellness.com/healthy-community/health-care-policy/article/why-soda-taxes-work.

43. Yichen Zhong, Amy H. Auchincloss, Brian K. Lee, and Genevieve P. Kanter, "The Short-Term Impacts of the Philadelphia Beverage Tax on Beverage Consumption," *American Journal of Preventive Medicine* 55, no. 1 (2018): 26–34.

44. John Cawley, David Frisvold, Anna Hill, and David Jones, "The Impact of the Philadelphia Beverage Tax on Purchases and Consumption by Adults and Children," National Bureau of Economic Research, 2018, https://www.nber.org/papers/w25052.

45. Jesse Hirsch, "Soda Tax May Cut Sugary Drink Consumption, New Study Finds," *Consumer Reports*, April 12, 2018, https://www.consumerreports.org/soda/soda-tax-may-cut-sugary-drink-consumption-new-study-finds/.

46. Theresa M. Marteau, Gareth J. Hollands, Ian Shemilt, and Susan A. Jebb, "Downsizing: Policy Options to Reduce Portion Sizes to Help Tackle Obesity," *BMJ* 351 (2015), https://doi.org/10.1136/bmj.h5863.

47. Deborah A. Cohen, "Bloomberg Right That Portion Control Works," *RAND Corporation* (blog), June 11, 2012, https://www.rand.org/blog/2012/06/bloomberg-right-that-portion-control-works.html.

48. Deborah Cohen and Lila Rabinovich, "Addressing the Proximal Causes of Obesity: The Relevance of Alcohol Control Policies," *Preventing Chronic Disease* 9 (2012), http://dx.doi.org/10.5888/pcd9.110274.

49. Paul M. Kelly, Anna Davies, Alexandra J. M. Greig, and Karen K. Lee, "Obesity Prevention in a City State: Lessons from New York City during the Bloomberg Administration," *Frontiers in Public Health* 4, no. 60 (2016), https://doi.org/10.3389/fpubh.2016.00060.

50. Brian Blake, "Nancy Reagan's 'Just Say No' Campaign Helped Halve Number of Teens on Drugs," *Hudson Institute* (blog), March 11, 2016, https://www.hudson.org/research/12306-nancy-reagan-s-just-say-no-campaign-helped-halve-number-of-teens-on-drugs.

51. Matthew Perrone, "Fact Check: 'Just Say No' Anti-Drug Campaigns Have Shown Little Success in Past," *Associated Press*, October 27, 2017, https://apnews.com/e69a1caee149413b89b6ba7f2cb3634f.

52. John S. Santelli, Laura Duberstein Lindberg, Lawrence B. Finer, and Susheela Singh, "Explaining Recent Declines in Adolescent Pregnancy in the United States: The Contribution of Abstinence and Improved Contraceptive Use," *American Journal of Public Health* 97, no. 1 (2007): 150–156.

53. Sarah McCammon, "Abstinence-Only Education Is Ineffective and Unethical, Report Argues," *NPR*, August 23, 2017, https://www.npr.org/sections/health-shots/2017/08/23/545289168/abstinence-education-is-ineffective-and-unethical-report-argues.

54. Harald Schmidt, "Personal Responsibility in the NHS Constitution and the Social Determinants of Health Approach: Competitive or Complementary?" *Health Economics, Policy and Law* 4 (2009): 129–138.

55. Kelly D. Brownell, Rogan Kersh, David S. Ludwig, Robert C. Post, Rebecca M. Puhl, Marlene B. Schwartz, and Walter C. Willett, "Personal Responsibility and Obesity: A Constructive Approach to a Controversial Issue," *Health Affairs* 29, no. 3 (2010): 379–387.

56. Trust for America's Health and Robert Wood Johnson Foundation, "The State of Obesity 2018: Better Policies for a Healthier America," 2018, https://www.tfah.org/report-details/the-state-of-obesity-2018/.

57. "Statement from FDA Commissioner Scott Gottlieb, M.D., on the Public Health Benefits from Enactment of Menu Labeling," Food and Drug Administration, accessed May 18, 2018, https://www.fda.gov/NewsEvents/Newsroom/PressAnnouncements/ucm606694.htm.

58. Sara N. Bleich, "A Road Map for Sustaining Healthy Eating Behavior," *New England Journal of Medicine* 379, no. 6 (2018): 507–508.

59. Trust for America's Health, "The State of Obesity 2018."

60. "Statement from FDA Commissioner, Scott Gottlieb, M.D., on the Public Health Benefits from Enactment of Menu Labeling."

61. Medicaid and CHIP Payment and Access Commission (MACPAC), *The Use of Healthy Behavior Incentives in Medicaid*, 2016, https://www.macpac.gov/wp-content/uploads/2016/08/The-Use-of-Healthy-Behavior-Incentives-in-Medicaid.pdf.

62. RTI International, *Medicaid Incentives for Prevention of Chronic Diseases*, 2017, https://downloads.cms.gov/files/cmmi/mipcd-finalevalrpt.pdf.

63. Phil Galewitz, "Michigan's Obamacare Wrinkle: 'Personal Responsibility,'" *Kaiser Health News*, June 7, 2014, https://www.usatoday.com/story/news/nation/2014/06/07/michigan-obamacare-medicaid-personal-responsbility/9728005/.

64. MACPAC, "The Use of Healthy Behavior Incentives in Medicaid."

65. "Individual Shared Responsibility Provision," Internal Revenue Service, accessed May 15, 2018, https://www.irs.gov/affordable-care-act/individuals-and-families/individual-shared-responsibility-provision.

66. "How Behavioral Economics Could Solve America's Health Care Woes" (interview with Kevin Volpp), Knowledge@Wharton, the Wharton School, University of Pennsylvania, accessed May 16, 2018, http://knowledge.wharton.upenn.edu/article/four-general-principles-health-care-reform/.

Chapter 6. Why Do We Take Public Health for Granted?

1. "Ten Great Public Health Achievements—United States, 1900–1999," *Morbidity and Mortality Weekly Report* 48, no. 12 (1999): 241–243.

2. "Ten Great Public Health Achievements, 1900–1999."

3. "Ten Great Public Health Achievements—United States, 2001–2010," *Morbidity and Mortality Weekly Report* 60, no. 19 (2011): 619–623.

4. "Ten Great Public Health Achievements, 1900–1999," 241–243.

5. "Ten Great Public Health Achievements, 1900–1999," 241–243.

6. "Ten Great Public Health Achievements, 2001–2010," 619–623.

7. Ted Roelofs, "Live Free and Die: Michigan's Motorcycle Helmet Law Four Years Later," *Bridge Magazine*, June 6, 2016, https://www.mlive.com/politics/index.ssf/2016/06/live_free_and_die_michigans_mo.html.

8. "Commissioned Corps of the U.S. Public Health Service," US Department of Health and Human Services, accessed June 15, 2018, https://www.usphs.gov/aboutus/history.aspx.

9. "A Brief History of Public Health," Boston University School of Public Health, accessed June 16, 2018, http://sphweb.bumc.bu.edu/otlt/MPH-Modules/PH/PublicHealthHistory/publichealthhistory8.html.

10. "Our History—Our Story," CDC, accessed June 16, 2018, https://www.cdc.gov/about/history/index.html.

11. "A Brief History," Boston University.

12. Gordon B. Lindsay, Ray M. Merrill, and Riley J. Hedin, "The Contribution of Public Health and Improved Social Conditions to Increased Life Expectancy: An Analysis of Public Awareness," *Journal of Community Medicine & Health Education* 4, no. 5 (2014), doi:10.4172/2161-0711.1000311.

13. "Public Opinion about Public Health—California and the United States, 1996," *Morbidity and Mortality Weekly Report* 47, no. 4 (1998): 69–73.

14. "Public Opinion about Public Health."

15. Robert J. Blendon, John M. Benson, Gillian K. SteelFisher, and John M. Connolly, "Americans' Conflicting Views about the Public Health System, and How to Shore Up Support," *Health Affairs* 29, no. 11 (2010): 2033–2040.

16. Blendon, Benson, SteelFisher, and Connolly, "Americans' Conflicting Views."

17. Blendon, Benson, SteelFisher, and Connolly, "Americans' Conflicting Views."

18. Jonathan Purtle, Neal D. Goldstein, Eli Edson, and Annamarie Hand, "Who Votes for Public Health? U.S. Senator Characteristics Associated with Voting in Concordance with Public Health Policy Recommendations (1998–2013)," *SSM Population Health* 3 (2017): 136–140.

19. "Prevention and Public Health in the Affordable Care Act: 911 for America's Health," Trust for America's Health, accessed June 15, 2018, https://www.tfah.org/wp-content/uploads/archive/health-issues/2017/01/Prevention-and-Public-Health-in-the-Affordable-Care-Act.pdf.

20. "The Incredible Shrinking Prevention Fund," *Washington Post*, April 19, 2013, https://www.washingtonpost.com/.

21. "About CEP," Commission on Evidence-Based Policymaking, accessed June 14, 2018, https://www.cep.gov/about.html.

22. Mary Woolley, "Public Confidence in Vaccines Dips; More Education Is Needed," *Morning Consult*, June 5, 2018, https://morningconsult.com/opinions/public-confidence-vaccines-dips-more-education-needed/.

23. Susan Scutti, "CDC Recommends New Shingles Vaccine to Replace Older One," *CNN*, October 26, 2017, https://www.cnn.com/2017/10/25/health/cdc-new-shingles-vaccine/index.html.

24. Lisa Aliferis, "Disneyland Measles Outbreak Hits 59 Cases and Counting," *NPR*, January 22, 2015, https://www.npr.org/sections/health-shots/2015/01/22/379072061/disneyland-measles-outbreak-hits-59-cases-and-counting.

25. Woolley, "Public Confidence."

26. Lena H. Sun, "Flu Broke Records for Deaths, Illnesses in 2017–2018, New CDC Numbers Show," *Washington Post*, September 27, 2018, https://www.washingtonpost.com/national/health-science/last-years-flu-broke-records-for-deaths-and-illnesses-new-cdc-numbers-show/2018/09/26/97cb43fc-c0ed-11e8-90c9-23f963eea204_story.html.

27. Pratha Sah, Jan Medlock, Meagan C. Fitzpatrick, Burton H. Singer, and Alison P. Galvani, "Optimizing the Impact of Low-Efficacy Influenza Vaccines," *PNAS* 115, no. 20 (2018): 5151–5156.

28. Susan Scutti, "Flu Season Deaths Top 80,000 Last Year, CDC says," *CNN*, September 27, 2018, https://www.cnn.com/2018/09/26/health/flu-deaths-2017--2018-cdc-bn/index.html.

29. Lena H. Sun, "Drop in Adult Flu Vaccinations May Be a Factor in Last Season's Record-Breaking Deaths, Illnesses," *Washington Post*, October 26, 2018, https://www.washingtonpost.com/health/2018/10/25/drop-adult-flu-vaccinations-may-be-factor-last-seasons-record-breaking-deaths-illnesses/.

30. Patricia Drehobl, Beth H. Stover, and Denise Koo, "On the Road to a Stronger Public Health Workforce—Visual Tools to Address Complex Challenges," *American Journal of Preventive Medicine* 47 (2014): S280–S285.

31. Angela J. Beck, Matthew L. Boulton, and Fátima Coronado, "Enumeration of the Governmental Public Health Workforce, 2014," *American Journal of Preventive Medicine* 47, no. 5 (2014): S306–S313.

32. National Association of County and City Health Officials, *2018 Forces of Change in America's Local Public Health System*, 2018, http://nacchoprofilestudy.org/wp-content/uploads/2018/12/2018-Forces-of-Change-Main-Report.pdf.

33. Jonathon P. Leider, Fátima Coronado, Angela J. Beck, and Elizabeth Harper, "Reconciling Supply and Demand for State and Local Public Health Staff in an Era of Retiring Baby Boomers," *American Journal of Preventive Medicine* 54, no. 3 (2018): 334–340.

34. Sarah Kliff, "The Incredible Shrinking Public Health Workforce," *Washington Post*, July 6, 2012, https://www.washingtonpost.com/news/wonk/wp/2012/07/06/the -incredible-shrinking-public-health-workforce/.

35. "Flint Water Crisis Fast Facts," *CNN*, accessed January 25, 2019, https://www.cnn .com/2016/03/04/us/flint-water-crisis-fast-facts/index.html.

36. Mona Hanna-Attisha, Jenny LaChance, Richard Casey Sadler, and Allison Champney Schnepp, "Elevated Blood Lead Levels in Children Associated with the Flint Drinking Water Crisis: A Spatial Analysis of Risk and Public Health Response," *American Journal of Public Health* 106, no. 2 (2016): 283–290.

37. Bipartisan Policy Center. *America's Aging Water Infrastructure*, 2016, https://cdn .bipartisanpolicy.org/wp-content/uploads/2016/09/BPC-Aging-Water-Infrastruc ture.pdf.

38. Gigi A. Cuckler, Andrea M. Sisko, John A. Poisal, Sean P. Keehan, Sheila D. Smith, Andrew J. Madison, Christian J. Wolfe, et al., "National Health Expenditure Projections, 2017–26: Despite Uncertainty, Fundamentals Primarily Drive Spending Growth," *Health Affairs* 37, no. 3 (2018), https://doi.org/10.1377/hlthaff.2017.1655.

39. Trust for America's Health, *A Funding Crisis for Public Health and Safety: State-by-State Public Health Funding and Key Facts and Recommendations*, 2018, https://www .tfah.org/report-details/a-funding-crisis-for-public-health-and-safety-state-by-state -and-federal-public-health-funding-facts-and-recommendations/.

40. RESOLVE—Public Health Leadership Forum, *Defining and Constituting Foundational "Capabilities" and "Areas,"* 2014, http://www.resolv.org/site-foundational-ph -services/files/2014/04/V-1-Foundational-Capabilities-and-Areas-and-Addendum .pdf.

41. Cezar Brian C. Mamaril, Glen P. Mays, Douglas Keith Branham, Betty Bekemeier, Justin Marlowe, and Lava Timsina, "Estimating the Cost of Providing Foundation Public Health Services," *Health Services Research* 53, Suppl 1, no. 3 (2017), http://dx .doi.org/10.1111/1475-6773.12816.

42. RESOLVE—Public Health Leadership Forum, *Developing a Financing System to Support Public Health Infrastructure*, 2018, http://www.resolv.org/site-healthleadership forum/files/2018/11/PHLF_developingafinancingsystemtosupportpublichealth.pdf.

43. Mark Miller, "National Survey Reveals Strong Bipartisan Support for Public Health," *de Beaumont Foundation* (blog), October 30, 2018, https://www.debeau mont.org/news/national-survey-2018/.

44. Joseph A. Davis, "Trump, Congress Face Test on Infrastructure Politics, Funding," *SEJournal Online*, February 21, 2018, https://www.sej.org/publications/back grounders/trump-congress-face-test-infrastructure-politics-funding.

45. Davis, "Trump, Congress Face Test."

46. Office of the Assistant Secretary for Health, US Department of Health and Human Services, *Public Health 3.0—A Call to Action to Create a 21st Century Public Health Infrastructure*, 2016, https://www.healthypeople.gov/sites/default/files /Public-Health-3.0-White-Paper.pdf.

47. Office of the Assistant Secretary for Health, US Department of Health and Human Services, *Public Health 3.0.*

48. Frederick Isasi, Hemi Tewarson, Kate Johnson, and Aidan Renaghan, National Governor's Association Center for Best Practices, *Social Impact Bonds for Public Health Programs: An Overview*, 2015, https://classic.nga.org/files/live/sites/NGA/files/pdf/2015/1508SocialImpactBondsPublicHealthPrograms.pdf.

49. Woolley, "Public Confidence."

50. Anand Parekh, "What Trump Can Do on Vaccines," *US News & World Report*, April 11, 2017, https://www.usnews.com/opinion/policy-dose/articles/2017-04-11/3-ways-donald-trump-and-congress-can-support-vaccine-safety.

51. Anand K. Parekh, "Public Health Communications: Lessons Learned from the Affordable Care Act," *American Journal of Public Health* 107, no. 5 (2017): 639–641.

52. Rick Mayes, Thomas R. Oliver, "Chronic Disease and the Shifting Focus of Public Health: Is Prevention Still a Political Lightweight?" *Journal of Health Politics, Policy and Law* 37, no. 2 (2012): 181–200.

Chapter 7. Public Health Emergency Preparedness

1. Trust for America's Health, *Ready or Not? Protecting the Public's Health from Diseases, Disasters and Bioterrorism*, 2017, https://www.tfah.org/report-details/ready-or-not-2017/.

2. Bootie Cosgrove-Mather, "Al Qaeda's Bio Weapons," *CBS News*, April 1, 2005, https://www.cbsnews.com/news/al-qaedas-bio-weapons/.

3. Mary Beth Hansen and Luciana Borio, "The Use of MedKits to Augment Rapid Distribution of Antibiotics after an Anthrax Attack," *Johns Hopkins School of Public Health Center for Health Security* (blog), March 14, 2018, http://www.centerforhealthsecurity.org/resources/cbn/articles/2008/cbnreport_03142008.html.

4. "Postal Model for Medical Countermeasures Delivery and Distribution," Office of the Assistant Secretary for Preparedness and Response, US Department of Health and Human Services, accessed July 15, 2018, https://www.phe.gov/preparedness/planning/postal/Pages/default.aspx.

5. "Postal Model for Medical Countermeasures."

6. US Department of Health and Human Services, *HHS Pandemic Influenza Plan*, 2005, https://www.cdc.gov/flu/pdf/professionals/hhspandemicinfluenzaplan.pdf.

7. US Department of Health and Human Services, *HHS Pandemic Influenza Plan*.

8. Statement by John Agwunobi, Assistant Secretary for Health, US Department of Health and Human Services on Avian Influenza Funding and State and Local Preparedness before the Subcommittee on Labor, Health and Human Services, Education, and Related Agencies, Committee on Appropriations, United States Senate, January 31, 2006, https://www.hsdl.org/?view&did=471744.

9. "FIGURE 1. Goals for Community Mitigation for Pandemic Influenza," CDC, accessed July 14, 2018, https://pbs.twimg.com/media/DX3FxTTXcAEOzdk.jpg.

10. Sundar S. Shrestha, David L. Swerdlow, Rebekah H. Borse, Vimalanand S. Prabhu, Lyn Finelli, Charisma Y. Atkins, Kwame Owusu-Edusei, et al., "Estimating the Burden of 2009 Pandemic Influenza A (H1N1) in the United States (April 2009–April 2010)," *Clinical Infectious Diseases* 52, no. 1 (2011): S75–S82.

11. "Burr Introduces Bipartisan Bill to Improve Nation's Public Health and Medical Response to Disasters," Office of US Senator Richard Burr, accessed July 10, 2018, https://www.burr.senate.gov/press/releases/burr-introduces-bipartisan-bill-to -improve-nations-public-health-and-medical-response-to-disasters.

12. "Pandemic and All-Hazards Preparedness Act Fact Sheet," Association of State and Territorial Health Officials, accessed July 25, 2018, http://www.astho.org /Programs/Preparedness/Public-Health-Emergency-Law/Emergency-Authority -and-Immunity-Toolkit/Pandemic-and-All-Hazards-Preparedness-Act-Fact-Sheet/.

13. "S.3678—Pandemic and All-Hazards Preparedness Act," Congress.gov, accessed July 25, 2018, https://www.congress.gov/bill/109th-congress/senate-bill/3678 /actions.

14. Jennifer Kates, Josh Michaud, Adam Wexler, and Allison Valentine, Kaiser Family Foundation, *The U.S. Response to Ebola: Status of the FY2015 Emergency Ebola Appropriation*, 2015, https://www.kff.org/global-health-policy/issue-brief/the-u-s-response -to-ebola-status-of-the-fy2015-emergency-ebola-appropriation/.

15. Kimberly Leonard, "Obama Asks GOP Congress for Ebola Funds," *US News & World Report*, November 7, 2014, https://www.usnews.com/news/articles/2014/11 /07/obama-asks-gop-congress-for-ebola-funds.

16. The Hill Staff, "List: Lawmakers Backing Travel Ban," *The Hill*, October 16, 2014, https://thehill.com/policy/transportation/220964-list-lawmakers-backing -travel-ban.

17. Kathleen Miles, "Congressional Hearing on Ebola Was 'Shameful,' Janet Napolitano Says," Huffington Post, October 19, 2014, https://www.huffingtonpost.com/2014/10 /19/congress-ebola-napolitano_n_5986754.html.

18. WHO, *Zika Strategic Response Framework & Joint Operations Plan*, 2016, https:// www.who.int/emergencies/zika-virus/strategic-response-framework.pdf?ua=1.

19. Patrícia Brasil, Jose P. Pereira, Jr., Claudia Raja Gabaglia, Luana Damasceno, Mayumi Wakimoto, Rita M. Ribeiro Nogueira, Patrícia Carvalho de Sequeira, André Machado Siqueira, et al., "Zika Virus Infection in Pregnant Women in Rio de Janeiro—Preliminary Report," *New England Journal of Medicine* (published March 4, 2016 at NEJM.org): https://www.nejm.org/doi/suppl/10.1056/NEJMoa1602412 /suppl_file/nejmoa1602412_prelim.pdf.

20. Michael A. Johansson, Luis Mier-y-Teran-Romero, Jennita Reefhuis, Suzanne M. Gilboa, and Susan L. Hills, "Zika and the Risk of Microcephaly," *New England Journal of Medicine* 375 (2016): 1–4.

21. "Sexual Transmission and Prevention," CDC, accessed July 26, 2018, https:// www.cdc.gov/zika/prevention/sexual-transmission-prevention.html.

22. Emily Crockett, "The States Zika Is Most Likely to Hit Will Be the Worst at Helping Women Deal With It," *Vox*, September 13, 2016, https://www.vox.com/2016 /9/13/12901372/zika-states-florida-texas-reproductive-health-report.

23. "Zika Travel Information," CDC, accessed July 28, 2018, https://wwwnc.cdc.gov /travel/page/zika-travel-information.

24. Julia Belluz, "The Potential Zika Virus Outbreak in Florida, Explained in Less than 600 Words," *Vox*, July 28, 2016, https://www.vox.com/2016/7/28/12248034 /florida-zika-virus-outbreak-explained.

25. Daniel Chang and Emily Cochrane, "With 10 New Zika Cases in Miami, CDC

Advises Pregnant Women to Avoid Wynwood," *Miami Herald*, August 1, 2016, https://www.miamiherald.com/news/health-care/article93057392.html.

26. "2016 Case Counts in the US," CDC, accessed July 28, 2018, https://www.cdc.gov/zika/reporting/2016-case-counts.html.

27. Kellie Mejdrich and Joseph Williams, "Obama Administration Announces Added $60 Million to Fight Zika," *Roll Call*, July 21, 2016, https://www.rollcall.com/news/policy/usda-rolls-final-rules-school-snack-foods.

28. Laurie Garrett and Gabriella Meltzer, "Don't Use Ebola Funds to Fight Zika," *US News & World Report* (blog), March 1, 2016, https://www.usnews.com/opinion/blogs/policy-dose/articles/2016-03-01/republicans-are-wrong-we-shouldnt-use-ebola-funds-to-fight-zika-virus.

29. David H. Herszenhorn, "Political Battles Color Congressional Feud Over Zika Funding," *New York Times*, May 24, 2016, https://www.nytimes.com/2016/05/25/us/politics/political-battles-color-congressional-feud-over-zika-funding.html.

30. Scott Gottlieb, "The Zika Funding Fight Isn't Over Planned Parenthood," *Forbes*, August 19, 2016, https://www.forbes.com/sites/scottgottlieb/2016/08/19/the-zika-funding-fight-isnt-over-planned-parenthood/#3b4f98decce4.

31. Editorial Board, "Hustling Dollars for Public Health," *New York Times*, June 2, 2016, https://www.nytimes.com/2016/06/02/opinion/hustling-dollars-for-public-health.html.

32. Marion E. Rice, Romeo R. Galang, Nicole M. Roth, Sascha R. Ellington, Cynthia A. Moore, Miguel Valencia-Prado, Esther M. Ellis, et al., "Vital Signs: Zika-Associated Birth Defects and Neurodevelopmental Abnormalities Possibly Associated with Congenital Zika Virus Infection—U.S. Territories and Freely Associated States, 2018," *Morbidity and Mortality Weekly Report* 67, no. 31 (2018): 858–867.

33. Emma Grey Ellis, "The Price of Zika? About $4 Million Per Child," *Wired*, August 16, 2016, https://www.wired.com/2016/08/price-zika-4-million-per-child/.

34. "HHS emPOWER Map 3.0," Office of the Assistant Secretary for Preparedness and Response, US Department of Health and Human Services, accessed July 30, 2018, https://empowermap.hhs.gov/.

35. Greg Slabodkin, "HHS Makes Medicare Data Available to Areas That Could Be Hit by Irma," *Health Data Management*, September 7, 2017, https://www.healthdatamanagement.com/news/hhs-makes-medicare-data-available-to-areas-that-could-be-hit-by-irma.

36. "Pandemic and All-Hazards Preparedness and Advancing Innovation Act of 2019," Congress.gov, accessed January 28, 2019, https://www.congress.gov/bill/116th-congress/house-bill/269?q=%7B%22search%22%3A%5B%22Pandemic+and+All-Hazards+Preparedness+and+Advancing+Innovation+Act+of+2019%22%5D%7D&s=1&r=1.

37. Tom Daschle and Judd Gregg, *Budgeting for Medical Countermeasures: An Ongoing Need for Preparedness*, Bipartisan Policy Center, 2018, https://bipartisanpolicy.org/wp-content/uploads/2018/02/BPC-Health-Budgeting-For-Medical-Countermeasures-An-Ongoing-Need-For-Preparedness.pdf.

38. Blue Ribbon Study Panel on Biodefense, *A National Blueprint for Biodefense: Leadership and Major Reform Needed to Optimize Efforts—Bipartisan Report of the Blue*

Ribbon Study Panel on Biodefense, Hudson Institute, 2015, https://www.biodefense
study.org/a-national-blueprint-for-biodefense.

39. Daschle and Gregg, *Budgeting for Medical Countermeasures*.

40. "American Perceptions of Biosecurity Preparedness," Alliance for Biosecurity, accessed July 24, 2018, https://www.allianceforbiosecurity.com/biosecurity-public -opinion-poll.

41. Ben Farmer, "Bioterrorism Could Kill More People than Nuclear War, Bill Gates to Warn World Leaders," *The Telegraph*, February 18, 2017, https://www.telegraph.co .uk/news/2017/02/17/biological-terrorism-could-kill-people-nuclear-attacks-bill/.

42. Ian Sherr, "Bill Gates Meeting Set with President Trump," *CNET*, March 15, 2018, https://www.cnet.com/news/bill-gates-foundation-microsoft-meeting-with-president -trump-white-house-foreign-aid/.

43. Lena H. Sun, "This Mock Pandemic Killed 150 Million People. Next Time It Might Not Be a Drill," *Washington Post*, May 30, 2018, https://www.washingtonpost.com /news/to-your-health/wp/2018/05/30/this-mock-pandemic-killed-150-million -people-next-time-it-might-not-be-a-drill/.

44. "The 2009 H1N1 Pandemic: Summary Highlights, April 2009–April 2010," CDC, accessed July 25, 2018, https://www.cdc.gov/h1n1flu/cdcresponse.htm.

45. "Advances in Domestic and International Vaccine Manufacturing Capacity," Office of the Assistant Secretary for Preparedness and Response, US Department of Health and Human Services, accessed July 28, 2018, https://www.phe.gov/Prepared ness/news/events/anniversary/Pages/flu-manufacturing.aspx.

46. "Seasonal Influenza Vaccination Programs Key to Pandemic Preparedness," Task Force for Global Health, accessed July 28, 2018, https://www.taskforce.org/newsroom /seasonal-influenza-vaccination-programs-key-pandemic-preparedness.

47. "Universal Flu Vaccine Could Help Strengthen Pandemic Preparedness," Task Force for Global Health, accessed July 28, 2018, https://www.taskforce.org/newsroom /universal-flu-vaccine-help-strengthen-pandemic-preparedness.

48. "Universal Influenza Vaccine Research," National Institute of Allergy and Infectious Diseases, accessed July 30, 2018, https://www.niaid.nih.gov/diseases-conditions /universal-influenza-vaccine-research.

49. Dina Fine Maron, "A New Push for a Universal Flu Vaccine," *Scientific American*, May 14, 2018, https://www.scientificamerican.com/article/a-new-push-for-a -universal-flu-vaccine/.

50. Lena H. Sun, "Bill Gates Calls on U.S. to Lead Fight against a Pandemic That Could Kill 33 Million," *Washington Post*, April 27, https://www.washingtonpost.com /news/to-your-health/wp/2018/04/27/bill-gates-calls-on-u-s-to-lead-fight-against -a-pandemic-that-could-kill-millions/?utm_term=.742d2f1820b5.

51. "Senator Markey Introduces Legislation for Enhanced Investment in Universal Flu Vaccine Development," Office of US Senator Edward Markey, accessed July 31, 2018, https://www.markey.senate.gov/news/press-releases/senator-markey -introduces-legislation-for-enhanced-investment-in-universal-flu-vaccine -development.

52. Michael T. Osterholm, "Pandemic Preparedness and Missed Opportunities," *Center for Infectious Disease Research and Policy* (blog), October 31, 2017, http://www

.cidrap.umn.edu/news-perspective/2017/10/commentary-pandemic-preparedness
-and-missed-opportunities.

53. "Executive Order—Combating Antibiotic-Resistant Bacteria," the White House, accessed July 31, 2018, https://obamawhitehouse.archives.gov/the-press-office/2014 /09/18/executive-order-combating-antibiotic-resistant-bacteria.

54. Pew Charitable Trusts, *Trends in U.S. Antibiotic Use, 2018*, 2018, https://www .pewtrusts.org/en/research-and-analysis/issue-briefs/2018/08/trends-in-us -antibiotic-use-2018.

55. "Biggest Threats and Data—Antibiotic/Antimicrobial Resistance (AR/AMR)," CDC, accessed December 1, 2018, https://www.cdc.gov/drugresistance/biggest _threats.html.

56. "What CDC Is Doing: Antibiotic Resistance (AR) Solutions Initiative—Antibiotic/ Antimicrobial Resistance (AM/AMR)," CDC, accessed December 1, 2018, https:// www.cdc.gov/drugresistance/solutions-initiative/index.html.

57. The White House, *National Strategy for Combating Antibiotic-Resistant Bacteria*, 2014, https://obamawhitehouse.archives.gov/sites/default/files/docs/carb_national _strategy.pdf.

58. "U.S. Challenges World to Intensify Global Fight against Antibiotic Resistance," CDC, accessed December 1, 2018, https://www.cdc.gov/media/releases/2018/p0925 -global-antibiotic-resistance.html.

59. Pew Charitable Trusts, *Trends in U.S. Antiobiotic Use, 2018*, https://www.pewtrusts .org/en/research-and-analysis/issue-briefs/2018/08/trends-in-us-antibiotic-use-2018.

60. Trust for America's Health, *Ready or Not? Protecting the Public's Health from Disease, Disasters and Bioterrorism*, https://www.tfah.org/report-details/ready-or -not-2017/.

Chapter 8. Is Global Health US Health?

1. Bianca DiJulio, Mira Norton, and Mollyann Brodie, "Americans' Views on the U.S. Role in Global Health," Kaiser Family Foundation, January 20, 2016, https://www.kff .org/global-health-policy/poll-finding/americans-views-on-the-u-s-role-in-global -health/.

2. Suerie Moon, Devi Sridhar, Muhammad A. Pate, Ashish K. Jha, Chelsea Clinton, Sophie Delaunay, Valnora Edwin, et al., "Will Ebola Change the Game? Ten Essential Reforms before the Next Pandemic. The Report of the Harvard-HTM Independent Panel on the Global Response to Ebola," *The Lancet* 386, no. 10009 (2015): 2204–2221.

3. "Global Preparedness Monitoring Board Convenes for the First Time in Geneva," WHO, accessed November 19, 2018, https://www.who.int/news-room/detail/10-09 -2018-global-preparedness-monitoring-board-convenes-for-the-first-time-in-geneva.

4. Moon et al., "Will Ebola Change the Game?" 2204–2221.

5. The White House, *Implementing the Global Health Security Agenda: Progress and Impact from U.S. Government Investments*, 2018, https://www.ghsagenda.org/docs /default-source/default-document-library/global-health-security-agenda-2017 -progress-and-impact-from-u-s-investments.pdf.

6. White House. *Implementing the Global Health Security Agenda*.

7. Lena H. Sun, "CDC to Cut by 80 Percent Efforts to Prevent Global Disease

Outbreak," *Washington Post*, February 1, 2018, https://www.washingtonpost.com /news/to-your-health/wp/2018/02/01/cdc-to-cut-by-80-percent-efforts-to-prevent -global-disease-outbreak/.

8. Patrick Adams and Cameron Nutt, "Trump Is Putting Us on Course for a Global Health Disaster," *Slate*, March 9, 2018, https://slate.com/technology/2018/03/trump -is-undermining-global-health-collaboration.html.

9. "About Resolve to Save Lives," Resolve to Save Lives, accessed August 8, 2018, https://www.resolvetosavelives.org/about/.

10. "Prevent Epidemics," Resolve to Save Lives, accessed August 8, 2018, https:// preventepidemics.org/.

11. "Global Partnership Launched to Prevent Epidemics with New Vaccines," Coalition for Epidemic Preparedness Innovations (CEPI), accessed August 14, 2018, https:// cepi.net/news_cepi/global-partnership-launched-to-prevent-epidemics-with-new -vaccines/.

12. "Priority Diseases," CEPI, accessed January 14, 2019, https://cepi.net/research _dev/priority-diseases/.

13. "Our Platform Technology," CEPI, accessed January 14, 2019, https://cepi.net /research_dev/technology/.

14. Gilbert Burnham, Riyadh Lafta, and Shannon Doocy, "Doctors Leaving 12 Tertiary Hospitals in Iraq, 2004–2007," *Social Science & Medicine* 69, no. 2 (2009): 172–177.

15. Tareq Amin, "U.S. Secretary of Health Says Visit to Iraq Aims at Training Doctors," *Iraqi News*, October 20, 2008, https://www.iraqinews.com/variety/u-s-secretary-of -health-says-visit-to-iraq-aims-at-training-doctors/.

16. "Iraqi Doctors Come to U.S. for Training," *Associated Press*, November 30, 2008, http://www.nbcnews.com/id/27983011/ns/world_news-mideast_n_africa/t/iraqi -doctors-come-us-training/.

17. Tom Daschle and Bill Frist, *The Case for Strategic Health Diplomacy: A Study of PEPFAR*, Bipartisan Policy Center, 2015, https://bipartisanpolicy.org/wp-content /uploads/2015/11/BPC_Strategic-Health-November-2015.pdf.

18. Daschle and Frist, *The Case for Strategic Health Diplomacy*.

19. Tom Daschle and Bill Frist, *Building Prosperity, Stability, and Security through Strategic Health Diplomacy: A Study of 15 Years of PEPFAR*, Bipartisan Policy Center, 2018, https://bipartisanpolicy.org/wp-content/uploads/2018/07/Building-Prosperity -Stability-and-Security-Through-Strategic-Health-Diplomacy-A-Study-of-15-Years -of-PEPFAR.pdf.

20. Daschle and Frist, *The Case for Strategic Health Diplomacy*.

21. Daschle and Frist, *Building Prosperity*.

22. Vin Gupta, Alexandre Mason-Sharma, Zoe M. Lyon, Endel John Orav, Ashish K. Jha, and Vanessa B. Kerry, "Has Development Assistance for Health Facilitated the Rise of More Peaceful Stories in Sub-Saharan Africa?" *Global Public Health* 13, no. 12 (2018): 1796–1806.

23. Daschle and Frist, *Building Prosperity*.

24. Daschle and Frist, *The Case for Strategic Health Diplomacy*.

25. "Noncommunicable Diseases," WHO, accessed August 14, 2018, https://www .who.int/news-room/fact-sheets/detail/noncommunicable-diseases.

26. "The U.S. Government and Global Non-Communicable Disease Efforts," Henry J. Kaiser Family Foundation, accessed August 14, 2018, https://www.kff.org/global-health-policy/fact-sheet/the-u-s-government-and-global-non-communicable-diseases/.

27. "Noncommunicable Diseases," WHO.

28. Council on Foreign Relations, *The Emerging Global Health Crisis—Noncommunicable Diseases in Low- and Middle-Income Countries*, 2014, https://www.cfr.org/report/emerging-global-health-crisis.

29. "NCD Global Monitoring Framework," WHO, accessed August 15, 2018, https://www.who.int/nmh/global_monitoring_framework/en/.

30. "UN High-Level Meetings on NCDs at a Glance," WHO, accessed January 31, 2019, https://www.who.int/ncds/governance/third-un-meeting/brochure.pdf?ua=1.

31. Council on Foreign Relations, *The Emerging Global Health Crisis*, https://www.cfr.org/report/emerging-global-health-crisis.

32. Council on Foreign Relations, *The Emerging Global Health Crisis*.

33. "Mike Bloomberg Explains Why He Has Pledged $800 Million Over Next Six Years to Fight Noncommunicable Diseases," Bloomberg Philanthropies, accessed August 15, 2018, https://www.bloomberg.org/press/releases/mike-bloomberg-explains-pledged-800-million-next-six-years-fight-noncommunicable-diseases/.

34. "Michael R. Bloomberg Becomes WHO Global Ambassador for Noncommunicable Diseases," WHO, accessed August 15, 2018, https://www.who.int/en/news-room/detail/17-08-2016-michael-r-bloomberg-becomes-who-global-ambassador-for-noncommunicable-diseases.

35. WHO and UNICEF, *Progress on Drinking Water, Sanitation and Hygiene: 2017 Update and Sustainable Development Goal Baselines*, 2017, https://www.who.int/water_sanitation_health/publications/jmp-2017/en/.

36. "Facts and Statistics," WaterAid, accessed August 25, 2018, https://www.wateraid.org/uk/facts-and-statistics.

37. Ryan Cronk and Jamie Bartram, "Environmental Conditions in Health Care Facilities in Low- and Middle-Income Countries: Coverage and Inequalities," *International Journal of Hygiene and Environmental Health* 221, no. 3 (2018), https://www.sciencedirect.com/science/article/pii/S1438463917303760.

38. WHO and United Nations' Children's Fund, *Water, Sanitation and Hygiene in Health Care Facilities—Status in Low- and Middle-Income Countries and Way Forward*, 2015, https://www.who.int/water_sanitation_health/publications/wash-health-care-facilities/en/.

39. "WASH in Health Care Facilities," WHO, accessed August 25, 2018, https://www.who.int/water_sanitation_health/facilities/healthcare/en/.

40. Julian Brookes, "Why Water Is the New Oil," *Rolling Stone*, July 7, 2011, https://www.rollingstone.com/politics/politics-news/why-water-is-the-new-oil-198747/.

41. Bill Frist, "Make Water a Top Global Priority. It's the Best, Cheapest Way to Save Lives," *USA Today*, August 15, 2018, https://www.usatoday.com/story/opinion/2018/08/15/water-top-global-priority-best-cheapest-lifesaver-bill-frist-column/934264002/.

42. United States Agency for International Development, *U.S. Government Global Water Strategy*, 2017, https://www.usaid.gov/sites/default/files/documents/1865/Global_Water_Strategy_2017_final_508v2.pdf.

43. Bill Frist and Anand Parekh, "In Fight against Extreme Poverty, Congress Must Now Protect America's Leadership," *Forbes*, July 28, 2017, https://www.forbes.com /sites/billfrist/2017/07/28/in-fight-against-extreme-poverty-congress-must-now -protect-americas-leadership/#4acc17da12ae.

44. "Summary—FY2019 State & Foreign Operations Appropriations Bill Approved by Senate Subcommittee," United States Senate Committee on Appropriations, accessed August 25, 2018, https://www.appropriations.senate.gov/news/minority/summary _--fy2019-state-and-foreign-operations-appropriations-bill-approved-by-senate -subcommittee.

45. Patricia Espinosa and Richard Horton, "Study: Climate Change Is Damaging the Health of Millions of People," *TIME*, October 31, 2017, http://time.com/4999425 /climate-change-health-2/.

46. US Global Change Research Program, *Fourth National Climate Assessment*, 2018, https://nca2018.globalchange.gov/downloads/NCA4_Ch01_Summary-Findings.pdf.

47. Laura Geggel, "Mountain of Evidence Confirms: Climate Change Is Really, Really Bad for Human Health and Well-Being," *Live Science*, December 14, 2018, https://www.livescience.com/64300-climate-change-endangers-human-health .html.

48. "Health Benefits Far Outweigh the Costs of Meeting Climate Change Goals," WHO, accessed January 31, 2019, https://www.who.int/news-room/detail/05-12 -2018-health-benefits-far-outweigh-the-costs-of-meeting-climate-change-goals.

49. Tedros Adhanom Ghebreyesus, "Air Pollution Is the New Tobacco. Time to Tackle This Epidemic," *The Guardian*, October 27, 2018, https://www.theguardian .com/commentisfree/2018/oct/27/air-pollution-is-the-new-tobacco-time-to-tackle -this-epidemic.

50. DiJulio, Norton, and Brodie, "Americans' Views."

Conclusion. Twenty-First-Century Urgent Challenges and Promising Opportunities

1. Substance Abuse and Mental Health Services Administration, *Key Substance Use and Mental Health Indicators in the United States: Results from the 2017 National Survey on Drug Use and Health*, 2018, https://www.samhsa.gov/data/sites/default/files /cbhsq-reports/NSDUHFFR2017/NSDUHFFR2017.pdf.

2. Substance Abuse and Mental Health Services Administration, *Key Substance Use*.

3. Interdepartmental Serious Mental Illness Coordinating Committee, *The Way Forward: Federal Action for a System That Works for All People Living with SMI and SED and Their Families and Caregivers*, 2017, https://store.samhsa.gov/system/files/pep17 -ismicc-rtc.pdf.

4. "Premature Death among People with Severe Mental Disorders," WHO, accessed September 4, 2018, https://www.who.int/mental_health/management/info_sheet.pdf.

5. Lenny Bernstein, "U.S. Life Expectancy Declines Again, a Dismal Trend Not Seen since World War I," *Washington Post*, November 29, 2018, https://www.washington post.com/national/health-science/us-life-expectancy-declines-again-a-dismal-trend -not-seen-since-world-war-i/2018/11/28/ae58bc8c-f28c-11e8-bc79-68604ed88993 _story.html?utm_term=.483a9d0e393a.

6. Lawrence Scholl, Puja Seth, Mbabazi Kariisa, Nana Wilson, and Grant Baldwin, "Drug and Opioid-Involved Overdose Deaths—United States, 2013–2017," *Morbidity and Mortality Weekly Report* 67, no. 5152 (2019): 1419–1427.

7. Anne Case and Angus Deaton, "Rising Morbidity and Mortality in Midlife among White Non-Hispanic Americans in the 21st Century," *PNAS* 112, no. 49 (2015): 15078–15083.

8. The US Burden of Disease Collaborators, "The State of US Health, 1990–2016—Burden of Diseases, Injuries, and Risk Factors among US States," *JAMA* 319, no. 14 (2018): 1444–1472.

9. Gery P. Guy, Jr., Kun Zhang, Michele K. Bohm, Jan Losby, Brian Lewis, Randall Young, Louise B. Murphy, et al., "Vital Signs: Changes in Opioid Prescribing in the United States, 2006–2015," *Morbidity and Mortality Weekly Report* 66, no. 26 (2017): 697–704.

10. Scholl et al., "Drug and Opioid-Involved Overdose Deaths," 1419–1427.

11. Anand K. Parekh, "A Sustainable Solution to the Evolving Opioid Crisis: Revitalizing the Office of National Drug Control Policy," testimony before the US House Committee on Oversight and Government Reform, May 17, 2018, https://bipartisan policy.org/wp-content/uploads/2018/05/BPC-Anand-Parekh-Testimony-House -Committee-Oversight-Government-Reform.pdf.

12. "Prescription Opioid Data," CDC, accessed January 31, 2019, https://www.cdc .gov/drugoverdose/data/prescribing.html.

13. Christopher M. Jones, "Heroin Use and Heroin Use Risk Behaviors among Non-medical Users of Prescription Opioid Pain Relievers—United States, 2002–2004 and 2008–2010," *Drug and Alcohol Dependence* 132, no. 1–2 (2013): 95–100.

14. "Fentanyl," Drug Enforcement Administration, accessed September 5, 2018, https://www.dea.gov/galleries/drug-images/fentanyl.

15. Customs and Border Protection, CBP Border Security Report—Fiscal Year 2017, https://www.cbp.gov/sites/default/files/assets/documents/2017-Dec/cbp-border -security-report-fy2017.pdf.

16. "S. 3057 (115th): STOP Act of 2018," *GovTrack*, accessed January 31, 2019, https:// www.govtrack.us/congress/bills/115/s3057.

17. Becky Upham, "China Commits to Greater Regulation of Fentanyl at G20 Summit," *Everyday Health*, December 6, 2018, https://www.everydayhealth.com/opioid -addiction/china-commits-greater-regulation-fentanyl-g20-summit/.

18. "The Opioid Detection Challenge," NASA Tournament Lab, https://www.opioid detectionchallenge.com, accessed April 10, 2019.

19. "Fact Sheets—Alcohol Use and Your Health," CDC, accessed September 27, 2018, https://www.cdc.gov/alcohol/fact-sheets/alcohol-use.htm.

20. "Excessive Alcohol Consumption," Community Guide, accessed September 27, 2018, https://www.thecommunityguide.org/topic/excessive-alcohol-consumption/.

21. Adam Looney, "Measuring the Loss of Life from the Senate's Tax Cuts for Alcohol Producers," Brookings Institution, https://www.brookings.edu/research/measuring -the-loss-of-life-from-the-senates-tax-cuts-for-alcohol-producers/.

22. Bridget F. Grant, S. Patricia Chou, Tulshi D. Saha, Roger P. Pickering, Bradley T. Kerridge, W. June Ruan, Boji Huang, et al., "Prevalence of 12-Month Alcohol Use, High-Risk Drinking, and *DSM-IV* Alcohol Use Disorder in the United States, 2001–

2002 to 2012–2013—Results from the National Epidemiologic Survey on Alcohol and Related Conditions," *JAMA Psychiatry* 74, no. 9 (2017): 911–923.

23. National Academies of Sciences, Engineering, and Medicine, *Getting to Zero Alcohol-Impaired Driving Fatalities: A Comprehensive Approach to a Persistent Problem*, 2018, https://doi.org/10.17226/24951.

24. Rebecca Edwards, "The Safest and Most Dangerous Roads on New Year's Eve," *SafeWise*, accessed January 31, 2019, https://www.safewise.com/blog/states-by -highest-impaired-driving-rate/.

25. "Suicide Rising across the US," CDC, accessed September 29, 2018, https://www .cdc.gov/vitalsigns/suicide/index.html.

26. "Suicide," National Institute of Mental Health, accessed September 15, 2018, https://www.nimh.nih.gov/health/statistics/suicide.shtml.

27. "Suicide Rising across the US, Vital Signs," CDC, accessed September 27, 2018, https://www.cdc.gov/vitalsigns/suicide/index.html.

28. Jacqueline Howard, "Gun Deaths in US Reach Highest Level in Nearly 40 Years, CDC Data Reveal," *CNN*, December 14, 2018, https://www.cnn.com/2018/12/13 /health/gun-deaths-highest-40-years-cdc/index.html.

29. Lindsey Tanner, "Guns Send Over 8,000 US Kids to ER Each Year, Analysis Says," *AP News*, October 28, 2018, https://apnews.com/b806812a8f0945128b4c5e 47a9f3c739.

30. Kim Soffen, "To Reduce Suicides, Look at Guns," *Washington Post*, July 13, 2016, https://www.washingtonpost.com/graphics/business/wonkblog/suicide-rates/.

31. Howard, "Gun Deaths."

32. Soffen, "To Reduce Suicides."

33. Brady Campaign to Prevent Gun Violence, *The Truth about Suicide and Guns*, 2018, http://www.bradycampaign.org/sites/default/files/SuicidePreventionReport2018.pdf.

34. Nell Greenfieldboyce, "Spending Bill Lets CDC Study Gun Violence; But Re-searchers Are Skeptical It Will Help," *NPR*, March 23, 2018, https://www.npr.org /sections/health-shots/2018/03/23/596413510/proposed-budget-allows-cdc-to -study-gun-violence-researchers-skeptical.

35. David E. Stark and Nigam H. Shah, "Funding and Publication of Research on Gun Violence and Other Leading Causes of Death," *JAMA* 317, no. 1 (2017): 84–85.

36. RAND Corporation, *The Science of Gun Policy—A Critical Synthesis of Research Evidence on the Effects of Gun Policies in the United States*, 2018, https://www.rand.org /pubs/research_reports/RR2088.html.

37. Trust for America's Health and Well Being Trust, *Pain in the Nation*, https://www .tfah.org/report-details/pain-in-the-nation/.

38. "Drugs, Brains, and Behavior: The Science of Addiction," National Institute on Drug Abuse, accessed September 7, 2018, https://www.drugabuse.gov/publications /drugs-brains-behavior-science-addiction/preventing-drug-misuse-addiction-best -strategy.

39. Ronald C. Kessler, G. Paul Amminger, Sergio Aguilar-Gaxiola, Jordi Alonso, Sing Lee, and T. Bedirhan Ustun, "Age of Onset of Mental Disorders: A Review of Recent Literature," *Current Opinion in Psychiatry* 20, no. 4 (2007): 359–364.

40. "United States Adolescent Substance Abuse Facts," US Department of Health and Human Services, accessed September 7, 2018, https://www.hhs.gov/ash/oah

/facts-and-stats/national-and-state-data-sheets/adolescents-and-substance-abuse
/united-states/index.html.

41. "United States Adolescent Mental Health Facts," US Department of Health and Human Services, accessed September 7, 2018, https://www.hhs.gov/ash/oah/facts -and-stats/national-and-state-data-sheets/adolescent-mental-health-fact-sheets /united-states/index.html.

42. Interdepartmental Serious Mental Illness Coordinating Committee, *The Way Forward*, https://store.samhsa.gov/system/files/pep17-ismicc-rtc.pdf.

43. "United States Adolescent Mental Health Facts."

44. "Adverse Childhood Experiences," Substance Abuse and Mental Health Services Administration, accessed September 7, 2018, https://www.samhsa.gov/capt /practicing-effective-prevention/prevention-behavioral-health/adverse-childhood -experiences.

45. "Practicing Effective Prevention," Substance Abuse and Mental Health Services Administration, accessed January 31, 2019, https://www.samhsa.gov/capt/practicing -effective-prevention.

46. Office of National Drug Control Policy, *Drug-Free Communities Support Program— 2012 National Evaluation Report*, 2013, https://obamawhitehouse.archives.gov/sites /default/files/dfc_2012_interim_report_annual_report_-_final.pdf.

47. "Why Prevention Matters for Teens," Addiction Center, accessed January 31, 2019, https://www.addictioncenter.com/teenage-drug-abuse/teenage-substance-abuse -prevention/.

48. "An Overview of the Human Genome Project," National Human Genome Research Institute, accessed September 15, 2018, https://www.genome.gov/12011238 /an-overview-of-the-human-genome-project/.

49. "About the *All of Us* Research Program," National Institutes of Health, accessed September 15, 2018, https://allofus.nih.gov/about/about-all-us-research-program.

50. "Genomics," HealthyPeople.gov, accessed September 15, 2018, https://www .healthypeople.gov/2020/topics-objectives/topic/genomics.

51. Huntington F. Willard, David T. Weinberg, and David H. Ledbetter, "How Geisinger Is Using Gene Screening to Prevent Disease," *Harvard Business Review*, March 14, 2018, https://hbr.org/2018/03/how-geisinger-is-using-gene-screening -to-prevent-disease.

52. "Can Genetic Risk Scores Score a Win for Precision Prevention? Time and Rigorous Studies Will Tell," CDC, accessed September 16, 2018, https://blogs.cdc .gov/genomics/2018/06/25/can-genetic-risk/.

53. "Genes Are Not Destiny—Obesity-Promoting Genes in an Obesity-Promoting World," Harvard T. H. Chan School of Public Health, accessed September 28, 2018, https://www.hsph.harvard.edu/obesity-prevention-source/obesity-causes/genes-and -obesity/.

54. "Genomics," HealthyPeople.gov, accessed September 28, 2018, https://www .healthypeople.gov/2020/topics-objectives/topic/genomics.

55. "The U.S. Surgeon General's Family History Initiative," National Human Genome Research Institute, accessed September 28, 2018, https://www.genome.gov/17516481 /the-us-surgeon-generals-family-history-initiative-family-history-initiative/.

56. Digital Therapeutics Alliance, *Digital Therapeutics: Combining Technology and*

Evidence-Based Medicine to Transform Personalized Patient Care, 2018, https://www.dtx alliance.org/wp-content/uploads/2018/09/DTA-Report_DTx-Industry-Foundations .pdf.

57. Corinna Cornejo, "Digital Therapeutics: Searching for Their Place in Healthcare," WEGO Health, May 21, 2018, https://www.wegohealth.com/2018/05/21/digital -therapeutics/.

58. "Digital Health," Food and Drug Administration, accessed January 24, 2019, https://www.fda.gov/medicaldevices/digitalhealth/.

59. "The Basics: mHealth and the FDA," National Consortium of Telehealth Resource Centers, accessed January 24, 2019, https://www.telehealthresourcecenter .org/wp-content/uploads/2018/06/mHealth-and-the-FDA.pdf.

60. Christina Farr, "The FDA Just Approved the First Mobile Device and App to Help You Quit Smoking," October 13, 2017, *CNBC*, https://www.cnbc.com/2017/10/03 /fda-approves-first-device-app-to-help-quit-smoking-carrot.html.

61. "As Part of Efforts to Combat Opioid Crisis, FDA Launches Innovation Challenge to Spur Development of Medical Devices—Including Digital Health and Diagnostics— That Target Pain, Addiction and Diversion," Food and Drug Administration, accessed September 22, 2018, https://www.fda.gov/NewsEvents/Newsroom/PressAnnounce ments/ucm609188.htm.

62. Johns Hopkins Bloomberg School of Public Health and Clinton Foundation, *The Opioid Epidemic—from Evidence to Impact*, 2017, https://www.jhsph.edu/events/2017 /americas-opioid-epidemic/report/2017-JohnsHopkins-Opioid-digital.pdf.

63. "Our Solution," Intent Solutions, accessed September 22, 2018, http://www .intentsolutions.com/solutions.

64. Jessica L. Alpert and Erin E. Sullivan, "How Digital Health Care Can Help Prevent Chronic Diseases Like Diabetes," *Harvard Business Review*, November 1, 2017, https://hbr.org/2017/11/how-digital-health-care-can-help-prevent-chronic-diseases -like-diabetes.

65. Eric Wicklund, "CMS Won't Cover Telehealth in Medicare Diabetes Prevention Program," *mHealth Intelligence*, November 3, 2017, https://mhealthintelligence.com /news/cms-wont-cover-telehealth-in-medicare-diabetes-prevention-program.

primary care (*cont.*)
nonphysician providers of, 47–48; outcomes of, 38; patient-centered medical homes and, 40–42; payment reform and, 46–47; prevention in, 35; relationship building in, 37; shortage crisis in, 38–39; spending on, 48–49; workforce policy and, 45
primary prevention, 2–3, 28
priorities for preventive services, 11–12, 157–61
process measures of quality, 25–26
Project BioShield, xi, 116, 124
public health: activities of, as invisible, 99–100; anthrax attacks and, 113–14; funding for, 107–10, 111–12, 159; gains in life expectancy due to, 99; governmental leadership in, 100–101; partnerships for, 110–12; political support for, 113; public perceptions of, 101–2, 103–4, 109–10; role of, 2; vaccination and, 105–6, 112–13; workforce for, 106–7
Public Health Leadership Forum, 109

quality, measures of, 25–28
quality-adjusted life years (QALYs), 10, 91

Raub, William, 115–16, 132
reimbursement for providers, 22–24
research on prevention, 12–15, 159–60
Resolve to Save Lives, 131–32, 133
revenue from disease prevention, 17
Rhode Island, primary care spending target in, 48
ridesharing, 75
Riley, Elise, 36–37
rural areas and transportation, 74

salt consumption, 90–91
San Antonio, A Path to Wellness program in, 66–67
Schwarz, Donald, 85
scope-of-practice laws, 47–48
Sebelius, Kathleen, 133
secondary prevention, 2, 3, 28
secondhand smoke exposure, 88

Secretary's Advisory Committee on Genetics, Health, and Society, 152
Sharfstein, Joshua, 24
shingles vaccine, 105
smoking. *See* tobacco use
SNAP (Supplemental Nutrition Assistance Program), 71–72, 91–92
Snyder, Rick, 100
social circumstances/determinants of health: community benefit requirements and, 79–80; healthcare initiatives, 76–79; housing, 67–70; influence of, 3, 4, 63–64; nutrition, 71–74; technical assistance for, 75–76; transportation, 74–75
social impact bonds, 111–12
social isolation, 66
social spending, 67
soda taxes, 92–93
State Innovation Models initiative, 77–78
STEADI (Stopping Elderly Accidents, Deaths, and injuries) Initiative, 58–59
stigma of mental illness and substance abuse, 143
strategic health diplomacy, 136–42
substance abuse: in adolescents, 150–51; opioid epidemic, 6, 145–46, 155; prevalence of, 143–44
sugar-sweetened beverages, 91–92
suicide, 6, 147–48
superutilizers, 32, 69
Supplemental Nutrition Assistance Program (SNAP), 71–72, 91–92

Tax Cuts and Jobs Act of 2017, 147
taxes on consumption, 92–93
Terry, Luther, 86
tertiary prevention, 2, 3, 29, 30–32
tobacco use: community-based interventions for, 8–9; control efforts for, 86–89, 134, 155; Medicaid expenditures and, 29; as risk factor for disease, 5
trans fats, 90
transportation, as social determinant of health, 74–75
Trump, Donald, 95, 124, 128
Trust for America's Health: "Promoting